The Making of the Civil Law

The Making of the Civil Law

Alan Watson

Harvard University Press
Cambridge, Massachusetts
and London, England
1981

Printed in the United States of America

Library of Congress Cataloging in Publication Data

Watson, Alan.
The making of the civil law.

Includes index.
1. Civil law. I. Title.
K585.W37 340.5′6 80-27591
ISBN 0-674-54310-6

for
Don and Sheila Bannister

Preface

This book is about the civil law, primarily the legal systems of western continental Europe and of Latin America. In writing it, I have not had particularly in view the aim of describing the characteristics—already well known—that make civil law systems markedly different from those of the common law world; nor have I been concerned, as have others much more learned than I, with tracing the historical development of the modern civil law systems. My main aim in this essay on comparative law has been rather to account for the existence and development of the features that are distinctive of the civil law. Thus, I have wanted to contribute to the understanding of the forces that cause law to change. It is my firm conviction that at the present time there is little knowledge of why law changes when it does, or why it changes in the direction that it does, or when and why it responds to pressure. Despite all the excellent work on the legal history of individual countries, the study of general legal development is in its infancy. As a result, though much of what appears here will be familiar to students of civil law, much, I believe, will be new even to legal scholars in Europe and Latin America. I also hope that the book will provide Anglo-American lawyers with insight into the nature of civil law systems.

The central issue can be easily stated. The legal elements, such as Roman law, Germanic customs, canon law, and feudal law, which historically have gone into the makeup of modern Western systems are everywhere the same. Yet most modern Western systems of law can be divided into civil law and common law systems, from which it follows that any civil law system is more like another than it is like any common law system. This division of legal systems, however, is not paralleled by social, economic, or political conditions in the countries in which the legal systems operate. Civil law and common law countries alike may have experienced the same extreme economic and social circumstances, such as the Industrial Revolution, that have bypassed other civil law countries. And the nature of government, whether democratic or tyrannous, does not affect the classification of the legal system.

In this context, the basic differences between civil law and common law systems are explained in terms of the legal traditions themselves; that is, the differences result from legal history rather than from social, economic, or political history. Above all, the acceptance of Justinian's *Corpus juris civilis,* in whole or in part, as authoritative or at least as directly highly persuasive determined the future nature of civil law systems and made them so distinctive. The importance of Roman law for subsequent ages is to be sought not only in the reception of legal rules and principles but even more in the approaches to law that have resulted from centuries of study, academic and practical, of the *Corpus juris.* Within the civil law tradition itself, the distinction between the Romanistic legal family and the Germanic legal family follows from the penetration of the German legal tradition by the law of reason; despite the French revolutionaries' rhetorical appeals to this law of nature, it had had little impact on the French legal tradition by the time of Napoleon's codification and thus scarcely influenced the *Code civil.*

The work on this book has necessitated the use of numerous libraries, and I should like to record my gratitude to the librarians who allowed me access to rare book rooms or otherwise gave me extraordinary service in the following institutions: the Faculty of Advocates Library and the National Library, both of Edinburgh; the British Library; the Library of Congress; the Philadelphia Bar Association Library; the law libraries of the Universities of Pennsylvania, Michigan, and California (at Berkeley), and of Harvard University; the libraries of the University of Pennsylvania and of Syracuse University. Klaus Luig of the Max-Planck Institut für europäische Rechtsgeschichte, Frankfurt, sent photocopies of European books of the sixteenth and seventeenth centuries; A. S. Hartkamp of the Dutch Ministry of Justice provided materials on the new Dutch civil code; and J. W. McKnight of Southern Methodist University supplied books relevant to Latin America. The criticisms of the typescript by John L. Barton (Oxford), Tony Carty (Glasgow), Thomas M. Green (University of Michigan), Louis B. Schwartz University of Pennsylvania), Alexander McCall Smith (Edinburgh), and Zbigniew Sobolewski (Lublin) were invaluable.

Contents

I.	The Meaning of Civil Law Systems	1
II.	The Block Effect of Roman Law	14
III.	The Formal Rationality of Civil Law	23
IV.	Case Law Before Codification	39
V.	Infiltration of Legal Ideas	53
VI.	The Institutes	62
VII.	The Law of Reason	83
VIII.	Successful Modern Codification	99
IX.	Institutes and Codes	131
X.	Divisions of the Law	144
XI.	Sources of Modern Civil Law	168
XII.	Civil Law, Society, and Legal Growth	179
	Index	193

Abbreviations

AGBG	*Das Allgemeine bürgerliche Gesetzbuch*
BGB	*Bürgerliches Gesetzbuch*
C	*Codex Justiniani*
CTh	*Codex Theodosiani*
Cappelletti et al., *Italian Legal System*	M. Cappelletti, J. H. Merryman, and J. H. Perillo, *The Italian Legal System: An Introduction* (Stanford, Stanford University Press, 1967)
Coing, *Handbuch*	H. Coing, *Handbuch der Quellen und Literatur der neueren europäischen Privatrechtsgeschichte* (Munich, Beck, 1973–)
Conrad, *Rechtsgeschichte*	H. Conrad, *Deutsche Rechtsgeschichte,* 2nd ed. (Karlsruhe, Müller, 1962), 2 vols.
D	*Digesta Justiniani*
David, *French Law*	R. David, *French Law,* trans. M. Kindred (Baton Rouge, Louisiana State University Press, 1972)
David and Brierly, *Legal Systems*	R. David and J. E. C. Brierly, *Major Legal Systems in the World Today,* 2nd ed. (London, Stevens, 1978)
General Survey	*General Survey of Events, Sources, Persons and Movements in Continental Legal History,* by various European authors (Boston, Little, Brown, 1912)
J	*Institutiones Justiniani*

Jolowicz and Nicholas, *Historical Introduction*	H. F. Jolowicz and B. Nicholas, *Historical Introduction to the Study of Roman Law,* 3rd ed. (Cambridge, Cambridge University Press, 1972)
Koschaker, *Europa*	P. Koschaker, *Europa und das römische Recht,* 3rd ed. (Munich, Beck, 1959)
Lawson, *Common Lawyer*	F. H. Lawson, *A Common Lawyer Looks at the Civil Law* (Ann Arbor, University of Michigan Law School, 1953)
L'Europa e il diritto romano	*L'Europa e il diritto romano; studi in memoria di P. Koschaker* (Milan, Giuffre, 1954)
LQR	*Law Quarterly Review*
Merryman, *Civil Law Tradition*	J. H. Merryman, *The Civil Law Tradition* (Stanford, Stanford University Press, 1969)
RHD	*Revue historique de droit français et étranger*
Tarello, *Ideologie*	G. Tarello, *Le ideologie della codificazione nel secolo xviii,* 3rd ed. (Genoa, E.C.I.G., n.d.)
Thomas, *Institutes*	J. A. C. Thomas, *The Institutes of Justinian* (Cape Town, Juta, 1975)
Thomas, *Textbook*	J. A. C. Thomas, *Textbook of Roman Law* (Amsterdam, North-Holland, 1976)
Watson, *Legal Transplants*	Alan Watson, *Legal Transplants* (Charlottesville, University Press of Virginia; Edinburgh, Scottish Academic Press, 1974)
Watson, *Nature of Law*	Alan Watson, *Nature of Law* (Edinburgh, Edinburgh University Press, 1977)
Watson, *Society and Legal Change*	Alan Watson, *Society and Legal Change* (Edinburgh, Scottish Academic Press, 1977)
Wieacker, *Privatrechtsgeschichte*	F. Wieacker, *Privatrechtsgeschichte der Neuzeit,* 2nd ed. (Göttingen, Vandenhoek & Ruprecht, 1967)
ZSS	*Zeitschrift der Savigny-Stiftung (romanistische Abteilung)*
Zweigert and Kötz, *Introduction*	K. Zweigert and H. Kötz, *Introduction to Comparative Law,* trans. T. Weir (Amsterdam, North-Holland, 1977)

I
The Meaning of Civil Law Systems

This essay in comparative law has two main interrelated aims: to illustrate and account for the features of civil law systems that distinguish them from common law systems and, in so doing, to contribute to the understanding of how law develops and is related to surrounding circumstances. A subsidiary aim is to characterize modern civil law systems for the Anglo-American student.

The Western legal tradition is basically unitary, and much the same historical legal elements have gone into the creation of the law of each nation state: Roman law, Germanic customs, canon law, feudal law, and so on. Yet the great bulk of modern Western systems are divided into common law systems that derive from English law, civil law systems that have an important historical connection—though not always easy to define—with Roman law, and mixtures of the two. This truth remains despite, on the one hand, overwhelming joint social and economic circumstances, such as the Industrial Revolution, in civil law and common law countries alike, and on the other hand, disparate political regimes, ranging from democracy to despotism, within a group of systems. As a result, the similarities between any two civil law systems are greater than between any civil law system and any common law system. The similarities between the civil law systems and their differences with common law systems are especially marked in the general structure of the systems, in the classifications and rules of what is traditionally private law, having to do with persons, property, succession, and obligations, and in the law of procedure and rules of evidence. The social, political, economic, and cultural conditions of two civil law countries, say France and Haiti, may be vastly different, whereas a civil law country and a common law country may otherwise be much alike in their societal, political, and economic circumstances. The very existence within a unitary tradition of well-recognized contrasting types of systems, civil law and common law, indicates that very influential forces are at work shaping national law, but that they are not basically inherent in each nation's general societal, political, or economic background. The aim of this book is to isolate and explain the role of the most important of these forces.

The term "civil law" has a long history with a number of technical or semitechnical meanings. Specifically in Roman law, "civil law," *ius civile,* primarily designated those parts of the law whose applicability was restricted to citizens.[1] The parts of Roman law which were also applicable to foreigners—and which in fact were among the most influential—were termed *ius gentium.* In the Middle Ages especially, "civil law" was used of Roman law and its developments as distinct from canon law. Today the term serves also to mean private law, in contrast with criminal law or military law. But the term "civil law" has a quite specific meaning for comparative lawyers; it is used to denote the systems of Western continental Europe (excluding Scandinavia) and the systems (such as those of Latin America) greatly influenced by them.

What precisely these civil law systems have in common that distinguishes them from other Western systems is not immediately obvious. It is not enough to say that these systems derive from or are heavily influenced by Roman law. They are not all derived from or influenced by Roman law to anything like the same extent. Many positive rules of Roman law were rejected by the draftsmen of the modern codes, and many differences between the substance of Roman law and that of modern codes are of a fundamental nature.[2] Moreover, some integral and important parts of the law of most civil law systems scarcely derived at all from Roman law rules. For instance, matrimonial property regimes were unknown to Roman law, but they have been for centuries and are still a prominent feature of modern civil law systems. Are we to deny these parts the status of civil law? Further, the approach both by judges and by academics to the interpretation of a modern code is necessarily different from that taken in Roman times to juristic writing or the skeletal Edict of the praetor. Again, simply to talk of "derivation" or "heavy influence" might not sufficiently distinguish these systems from, say, English law, since parts of English law too, such as the law of easements and the con-

1. See e.g. *J.*1.2.1, 2.

2. See R. B. Schlesinger, *Comparative Law: Cases—Text—Materials,* 3rd ed. (Mineola, N.Y., Foundation Press, 1970), pp. 230f.

tract of sale, at various times and to varying degrees were affected by Roman law rules and doctrines.

The claim that the main distinction between civil law systems and common law systems is that the former are codified and the latter are not is full of defects.[3] For one thing, the successful codification of the civil law systems is a modern phenomenon. For instance, the French *Code civil*—generally thought of as the earliest of contemporary style codes—came into force in 1804, and no code existed for Greece before the Second World War. Are we to say that the legal systems in these countries were not civil law systems before these dates? Surely not. Again, some German states had a national code, such as Prussia's *Allgemeines Landrecht für die preussischen Staaten* of 1794, and some Rhineland states accepted the *Code civil.* Are we to say that these territories had a civil law system, but other parts of Germany had not, before the *Bürgerliches Gesetzbuch* came into force in 1900? Again surely not. Further, some undoubted common law jurisdictions, notably California, are codified.[4]

F. H. Lawson uses the term "civil law" to designate "the group of laws which are the concern of jurists who have long been known to common lawyers as 'civilians'; that is to say, a group of laws which have been so greatly influenced by Roman law that the classical method of approaching them has been through Roman law."[5] Yet with the decline of Roman law studies in law schools within the common law jurisdictions—and in the United States, for example, Roman law studies have never at any time been very actively pursued—this classical method of approaching civil law systems is becoming less valuable as a test for distinguishing civil law from other systems.

An historical dependence on Roman law is, in fact, the common characteristic of the civil law systems, and this dependence needs to be

3. See e.g. Lawson, *Common Lawyer,* p. 47; Merryman, *Civil Law Tradition,* pp. 27ff.

4. The difficulties in determining the common nature of civil law systems emerge clearly from Von Mehren and Gordley, *The Civil Law System,* 2nd ed. (Boston, Little, Brown, 1977), p. 3: "The legal systems of the western world are, for purposes of comparison, frequently divided into two groups: the civil law system, seen in French and German law, and the common law system developed in England. Two points of difference are usually emphasized in comparing the civil and the common laws. First, in the civil law, large areas of private law are codified. Codification is not typical of the common law. Second, the civil law was strongly and variously influenced by Roman law. The Roman law influence on the common law was far less profound and in no way pervasive. These points of difference should not be allowed to obscure the extent to which the civil and the common laws share a common tradition. Both systems were developments within Western European culture; they hold many values in common. Both are products of western civilization."

5. *Common Lawyer,* p. 2.

more exactly specified. Although no magic resides in a definition, one may serve not only to identify an abstract concept and distinguish it from other phenomena, but also to provide a tool for its further analysis.[6] A working definition of a civil law system would be a system in which parts or the whole of Justinian's *Corpus juris civilis* have been in the past or are at present treated as the law of the land or, at the very least, are of direct and highly persuasive force; or else it derives from any such system.

From this definition it follows that in civil law systems the substantive law derives from Roman law in considerable measure, though the distinguishing feature is not the borrowing, direct or indirect, of particular Roman law rules, and thus the similarity or equivalence of modern rules to Roman law is not of decisive importance. It also follows that the mark of civil law systems is not codification. Again the definition provides a test for distinguishing sharply between common law systems and Scandinavian law, on the one hand, and what are commonly regarded as the civil law systems, on the other. However tempting it might be to emphasize Roman law influence in England (and it has been widely understated) or in Scandinavia, no one could claim that Justinian's *Corpus juris* was ever there treated as binding or as directly persuasive.

The working definition also excludes from the notion of a civil law system the law represented by what Ernst Levy calls "the first 'reception' of Roman Law in Germanic States."[7] Thus, though the *Codex Euricianus,* the code produced by Euric, king of the Visigoths, around 475 was apparently heavily influenced by Roman law, it was promulgated more than half a century before Justinian began to reign and owes nothing to his *Corpus juris.* As for the influence of Roman law on Germanic systems then and in the immediately succeeding centuries, great though it was, it is widely believed to have been independent of the Byzantine compilation. The necessity of excluding such systems from the notion of civil law systems is evidence of the working definition's correctness, since they are not normally regarded as civil law systems, and this attitude cannot be explained simply on the basis that they no longer represent living law. Yet it is generally conceded that Roman law influence was great.

The working definition indicates that there may be degrees of "civility." A system that "at present" regards the *Corpus juris* as authoritative is "civilian" in a deeper sense than one that "in the past" treated the *Corpus juris* as part of the law of the land. For most civil law systems the

6. For difficulties with definition in law see e.g. S. J. Shuman, "Jurisprudence and the Analysis of Fundamental Legal Terms," *Journal of Legal Education* 8 (1956): 437ff.

7. See his *Gesammelte Schriften* (Cologne, Graz, Böhlau, 1963), I, 201ff.

decisive moment for change of status is the time of codification of private law. Again, the extent to which the *Corpus juris* was ever authoritative may vary from territory to territory, as may the degree of penetration of the system by the *Corpus juris* before codification occurred.

The effects of accepting the *Corpus juris* as authoritative may not be felt all at once but may emerge and develop over a long period of time. Different systems attain a particular degree of civility at different times. Again, although the fact is not revealed by the definition, the distinguishing marks of a civil law system may be so weakened as a result of the influence of ideology or of an outside system that it seems to need reclassification. This is the case with the systems that are regarded as "mixed," partaking of elements of both common law and civil law. Modern examples of such systems are South Africa (unless it should still be considered a civil law system), Louisiana, Puerto Rico, and Scotland.[8] On the basis of the working definition, the first three of these countries were at least once civil law systems. The same can be said of Scotland. Although there the *Corpus juris* was never the law of the land, it was of highly persuasive authority. Thus in his *Institutions of the Law of Scotland,* which was first published in 1684, Sir George Mackenzie writes (1.1):

> *Civil,* or *Municipal Laws, are the particular laws, and Customes of every Nation,* or *people, who are under one Soveraign Power.*
>
> The *Romans,* having studied with great exactness, the principles of Equity, and Justice. Their Emperor Justinian, did cause digest all their laws into one body, which is now called by most polit Nations, (for its *Excellency*) the *Civil Law;* and as this Civil Law is much respected generally, so it has great influence in *Scotland,* except where Our own express Laws, or Customes, have receded from it. And by the common Law in our Acts of Parliament is meant the Civil Law.

Very much earlier, for different but equally significant purposes, Thomas Craig claimed in his *Ius feudale* (1.2.8): "But we in this kingdom are bound by the laws of the Romans insofar as they are in harmony with the laws of nature and right reason." This is not the last time that reason and the laws of nature will crop up in connection with Roman law. Craig

8. See B. Beinart, "Codification and Restatement in Uncodified Mixed Jurisdictions," *Jewish Law Annual* 2 (1979): 126ff. The legal systems of the socialist countries of Eastern Europe were also once civilian. Whether any of them should still be regarded as civil law systems, or as a new kind of mixed systems, or as a distinct family of socialist systems is in dispute.

died in 1608 and although the *Ius feudale* was not published until 1655, it was known before and circulated in manuscript among the advocates: indeed, the passage quoted here was also quoted by Sir Thomas Hope in his *Major Practicks,* in which the latest reference seems to be to the year 1633. Hope also cites various Scots statutes of the fifteenth and sixteenth centuries which he believes allowed the direct application of Roman and common law in Scotland (1.1.14). Although Hope is mistaken, it is in the highest degree significant for the influence of Roman law in Scotland that he could be in error on the point.

In its attitude to Roman law Scotland was not atypical. In most of continental Europe outside of Italy and Germany, the *Corpus juris* was of direct and highly persuasive force, but no part of it was the actual law of the land. Thus, the Dutch jurist Groenewegen in his *De legibus abrogatis,* first published in 1649, writes that Roman civil law had been received among many nations, but in some places it enjoyed greater authority, in others less:

> 2. For in France it was not received, nor is it observed except insofar as it is found to rest on reason; and therefore the judges there on taking office do not take an oath that they will observe the Civil Laws of the Emperors. 3. In the Low Countries, however, the Roman Law enjoys much greater authority; since it abounds in supreme reason and equity in all its aspects, it was formerly cited in the courts merely to exemplify justice and equity, but finally it was also received as law, and even now amongst us it as a rule carries the force and authority of law. Hence the States in making laws often make reference to the Roman law as being the common and received law: as for example in the Placaat on intestate succession of 18 December 1599, article 14. Accordingly, the judges of the courts take an oath to observe the Roman laws. 4. But above all others the Frisians adhere most strictly to the Roman law. 5. However, this rule which lays down that the Civil law of the Romans has authority of law in the Low Countries is subject to many exceptions.[9]

He goes on to list the exceptions. This passage reveals that the degree of authority of Roman law might vary not only from country to country but

9. 1. proem. 6, from B. Beinart, *Groenewegen: De legibus abrogatis (on Abrogated Laws)* (Johannesburg, Lex-Patria, 1974), I, 7f.

even inside one country, such as the United Provinces. It also shows that the acceptance of the authority of Roman law could be, as indeed it usually was, a gradual process.[10]

In France the position was immensely complicated. The country can be divided in two: the South, called the *pays de droit écrit* ("the country of written law"), where Roman law was the customary law of the land; and the North, *pays de droit coutumier,* where local customs prevailed. The *pays de droit coutumier* occupied about two-thirds of the country. At one stage every barony had its own customs, but by the mid-fifteenth century the number had been reduced to about 60 general customs and 300 special customs of very local application. As Jean Brissaud describes the situation, it "was far from being unity of law; but it was a great step in advance."[11] The multiplicity of customs means that no one statement on the role of Roman law in France can be wholly accurate, but that in general contracts, and indeed the whole field of obligations, were governed by it because the customs contained little on these matters. In other areas of law, reference was constantly made to Roman law, even when it was irrelevant.[12] The jurists of the sixteenth century disputed the authority of Roman law without ever reaching a generally acceptable conclusion. Thus, according to Guy Coquille (1523–1603),

> The Roman Civil Law is not our common law, and has not the force of law in France, but should merely be regarded as Reason. The laws made by the Romans we should call upon to help us when the constitutions and the Ordinances of our Kings or the unwritten general law of France or Customs fail us. "To help us," I say, for convenience and for its Reason, and not because of necessity. In this respect two great personages of our time, who have been successively First President of the Parliament of Paris, Maître Pierre Lizet and Maître Christophe de Thou, were of different opinions. The aforesaid Lizet held that the Roman law was our common law and as far as possible conformed our French law to it, and was reputed to be narrow in his interpretation of the law and to restrain that which was contrary to the Roman law. And the aforesaid de Thou

10. See e.g. R. Feenstra, "Zur Rezeption in den Niederlanden," *L'Europa e il diritto romano,* I, 243ff; B. H. D. Hermesdorf, *Römisches Recht in den Niederlanden,* part V.5a of *Ius Romanum medii aevi* (Milan, Giuffrè, 1968).

11. In *General Survey,* p. 261.

12. See e.g. J. Brissaud in *General Survey,* p. 208; A. Esmein, *Cours élémentaire d'histoire du droit français,* 15th ed. by R. Genestal (Paris, Sirey, 1925), p. 687.

> was of the opinion that the Customs and the law of France were our common law, and called the Roman law only written reason.[13]

The view of Coquille and others, including Charles Dumoulin, was that when a custom was not clear, reference was first made either to neighboring customs or to the Custom of Paris. If no solution was forthcoming, recourse was to be had to Roman law, but as reason, not as binding law.[14]

Since Napoleon's *Code civil,* French law has often been considered the civil law system *par excellence.* Yet before that codification the law of northern France was less of a civil law system or systems than were the laws of the *pays de droit écrit,* of the Netherlands, of Germany, and of Italy. As a result, not all of the consequences that flow from a system's being a civil law system were so pronounced there as in the other territories.[15]

The Reception in Germany is now traditionally divided into the "theoretical Reception" and the "practical Reception."[16] The theoretical Reception, which goes back to the twelfth century, had as its basis the notion that the "Roman Empire of the German Nation" was a continuation of the ancient Roman Empire. Hence Roman law was the law of the land but was subsidiary to later law, which had to take precedence. This Reception was, therefore, not of individual rules but of the *Corpus juris* as a whole.

The practical Reception, which came later and more slowly, extending over the fifteenth and sixteenth centuries, and was very much more complete than in northern France, was the acceptance of Roman rules into judicial practice. Its roots are therefore to be found in the appearance of judges and jurists who had been trained in Roman law. The creation of the Reichskammergericht, the supreme court of the Holy Roman Empire, in 1495 is usually considered a significant event in this Reception since it was enacted that half of the judges had to be *Doctores juris,* that

13. Quoted by Brissaud, *General Survey,* p. 208. See also R. Van Caenegem, *The Birth of the English Common Law* (Cambridge, Cambridge University Press, 1973), p. 13.

14. See e.g. Esmein, *Histoire,* pp. 687ff.

15. For instance, practitioners rather than academics were prominent in the drafting of the *Code civil.* J. P. Dawson, more particularly concerned with judicial decisions, calls the appropriate chapter "the French Deviation" in *The Oracles of the Law* (Ann Arbor, University of Michigan Law School, 1968), pp. 263ff.

16. See e.g. *General Survey,* pp. 336ff; Conrad, *Rechtsgeschichte,* pp. 339ff; Koschaker, *Europa,* pp. 38ff; Wieacker, *Privatrechtsgeschichte,* pp. 124ff; K. Luig, "The Institutes of National Law in the Seventeenth and Eighteenth Centuries," *Juridical Review* 17 (1972): 207ff.

is, jurists trained in Roman law. The practical Reception, therefore, related not to the *Corpus juris* as a whole but to the particular rules and institutions accepted by the courts, and these rules and institutions then became the immediate law of the land and were in no sense subsidiary. Inevitably this practical Reception contained a great deal that was not "straight" Roman law, but Roman law as interpreted and elaborated by the Glossators and other later, particularly Italian, jurists.

To a considerable extent the distinction between the theoretical and the practical Reception was less sharp than might appear—partly because the authority of the *Corpus juris* extended only to the passages that the Italian jurists had glossed, the maxim "Quidquid non agnoscit glossa, non agnoscit curia (What the *Gloss* does not recognize, the court does not recognize)" being followed here, and partly because of the acceptance of the general European concept of a "modern Roman practice," the *usus modernus pandectarum.* Moreover, with the rise of the practical Reception, the theoretical Reception lost some of its force. As Franz Wieacker observes, the creation in the sixteenth century of the "Lotharian Legend," to the effect that the Emperor Lothar of Supplinburg had expressly received Roman law by statute in 1135, is itself an indication that the acceptance of Roman law needed a new legitimation.[17] The complete defeat of the notion of a theoretical Reception is usually associated with Hermann Conring (1606–1681), through his *De origine juris Germanici* of 1643.[18] Not much later, the practical Reception was, if anything, further strengthened by the doctrine of Johann Schilter (1632–1705) that, when a protagonist relied on a glossed text of the *Corpus juris,* the presumption was that the rule was in force unless his opponent showed for the individual situation that either there was no reception or the law had been changed.[19]

Further variations in the Reception occurred in the other territories of Western Europe. The process of Romanization was accordingly gradual, incomplete, and of varying extent. Yet the acceptance of at least part of the *Corpus juris* as authoritative within a territory produced consequences wider than the mere incorporation of particular Roman law rules, and thus the impact of Roman law must be judged not primarily by the extent of surviving rules of pure Roman law, but in the emergence of a civil law system. The existence of important legal rules and notions that

17. *Privatrechtsgeschichte,* p. 145.

18. See Koschaker, *Europa,* pp. 115, 149f; Wieacker, *Privatrechtsgeschichte,* p. 206; *General Survey,* p. 428.

19. See e.g. Wieacker, *Privatrechtsgeschichte,* p. 208.

are to be found in many civil law systems but not in common law systems may, however, also be explained on the basis of the acceptance of Roman law. These consequences do not have exactly the same form everywhere because, apart from other considerations, the extent to which Roman law was authoritative varied from territory to territory. Nonetheless the consequences can be broadly characterized.

According to the working definition, some civil law systems derived from others which had accepted the *Corpus juris* or part of it as authoritative. The outstanding example is Turkey, a state that did not have a civil law system until it took over the code of a civil law country, Switzerland. In such a purely derivative civil law system there is never a time in which the *Corpus juris* or part of it is the law of the land or highly persuasive. Consequently such a system has not passed through all the typical stages of civil law development, and some features of the typical system may remain absent. Above all, the high regard for academic abstract legal education may be slow to develop. Yet there is no sharp division between derivative and other civil law systems; in fact, most derivative systems are so only in part. The most immediate influence is that of the colonial power, such as Spain or Holland, but for a time the *Corpus juris* is at least directly persuasive. This is the case for much of Latin American and for the Republic of South Africa.

The *Corpus juris,* which has had such an influence on civil law systems, dates back to the sixth century.[20] Justinian became coemperor of the Byzantine Empire with his uncle Justin in 527. Later that year, when his uncle died, he became sole emperor. Probably even while Justin had been sole ruler, Justinian was contemplating a legal codification of some kind. He issued a constitution dated February 13, 528, establishing a commission to prepare a new collection, a *Codex,* of imperial constitutions. The word "constitution" here is a general term to include all kinds of imperial enactments. The compilers were given extensive powers to collect the constitutions, to omit any, in whole or in part, that were obsolete or unnecessary, to remove contradictions and repetitions, and even to make alterations in substance. The constitutions were then to be arranged by subject matter in titles, or named sections, and within each title the constitutions were to be given in chronological order. The *Code,* which was published on April 7, 529, has not survived, but it was replaced by a second revised *Code,* which came into effect on December

20. For a standard treatment see Jolowicz and Nicholas, *Historical Introduction,* pp. 478ff. For a radical view see T. Honoré, *Tribonian* (London, Duckworth, 1978); cf. the review by A. Watson, *LQR* 94 (1978): 459ff.

29, 534. The revised *Code,* which has survived and is one of the four constituent elements of what came to be called the *Corpus juris civilis,* is divided into twelve books, subdivided into titles in which the constitutions appear chronologically. The constitutions range in date from Hadrian in the early second century to Justinian himself. A considerable proportion of the texts—2019 as against 2664—come from the time after the Empire became Christian; in fact, the bulk of the Christian rescripts is much greater.

On December 15, 530, the compilation of a collection of juristic texts, the *Digest,* was ordered, and the work came into force on December 30, 533. This massive work, twice the size of the *Code,* is in fifty books, virtually all of which are subdivided into titles. Each title consists of fragments from the writings of jurists who lived between the first century B.C. and the third century A.D. About one-third of the whole work is taken from the jurist and civil servant Ulpian, who was murdered in 223 A.D.; a further one-sixth comes from his contemporary Paul. In the opinion of some modern scholars, one jurist, Hermogenianus, was active in the fourth century, but otherwise no *Digest* text is attributable to any jurist who lived after the third century.[21] The texts of the jurists include statements of principles, discussions of rules, commentary on the scope or interpretation of edicts and statutes, qualifications of other juristic opinion, and the treatment of problem cases, real or hypothetical.

The compilers were instructed to cut out all that was superfluous or imperfect, all contradictions and repetitions, anything that was obsolete, and anything that was already in the *Code.*[22] Contrary, though, to a frequently expressed view the compilers of the *Digest* were not given power to alter the substance of the law or to bring it up to date.[23] Indeed, any such alteration as occurred would have been contrary to the spirit of the instructions. There was very little juristic writing after, say, 235, and there are very few texts from that period in the *Digest.* Changes in the law after that date were almost entirely the result of imperial constitutions. But these constitutions were collected in the *Code,* and the *Digest*

21. On the question of dating see D. Liebs, *Hermogenians iuris epitome* (Göttingen, Vandenhoek & Ruprecht, 1964).

22. *C. Deo auctore* §7, 9–10.

23. A typical exaggeration occurs in Jolowicz and Nicholas, *Historical Introduction,* p. 481: "Full power was given to cut down and alter the texts, and this extended even to the words of ancient *leges* or constitutions which were quoted by the jurists." But *C. Deo auctore* §7 gives power to change quotations from laws and constitutions only where the compilers find they are *non recte scriptum,* "incorrectly set down." It is only to be expected that the decision of the commissioners on the correct reading was to be treated as final.

commissioners were expressly instructed not to repeat in the *Digest* what was contained in the *Code.* Significantly, the commissioners were to exclude from the *Digest* what was obsolete, meaning in large measure the rules that had been replaced by imperial constitutions which were now collected in the *Code.*

This exclusion is one of the major departures of the *Digest* from the *Code.* The difference is not just that the *Digest* is a patchwork made out of juristic commentary and the *Code* a patchwork from imperial laws, or that the *Digest* is composed wholly of pagan originals and, unlike the *Code,* can be regarded as a Christian work only in a limited sense. Even more, the two works stand at different points of legal and social evolution. The *Digest* presents a picture of law and of relevant social conditions as they were in Rome at the height of the empire; insofar as the picture is inexact, this is because of excisions, not of later superimpositions, though some of the alterations of the *Digest* texts do result in the presentation of postclassical law. The *Code,* on the contrary, presents the postclassical world, where Rome was no longer the heart of empire, and early Byzantium. Because of this difference between the two works, in subsequent history the *Code* was at times more emphasized, at other times the *Digest.* The *Corpus juris* could speak with more than one voice.

The third part of the compilation is the *Institutes,* an elementary textbook for first-year students which was planned from 530 and was published on November 21, 533. It is structured on the *Institutes* of Gaius, a work written about 160 A.D., and appears in four books, though unlike Gaius' *Institutes,* the books are further subdivided into titles. The arrangement of topics—sources of law, persons, property, succession, obligations, law of actions—for which the credit should probably be given to Gaius, was the result of planning, and it differs markedly from the arrangement found in the *Digest,* which seems haphazard and is largely the unplanned result of the gradual growth of legal topics as they were rather unsystematically set out annually by the praetor in the later Roman republic and early empire. The absence of a satisfactory arrangement in the *Digest* has long been a matter for unfavorable comment. Like the other parts of the *Corpus juris,* the *Institutes* is statute law.

With the second *Code,* Justinian's work of codifying Roman law was complete. But he continued to legislate, and this subsequent legislation is now known as the *Novels.* No official collection of these constitutions was made, but there is considerable knowledge of three unofficial collections. Most of the constitutions were in Greek, some in both Greek and Latin, but translations of most of them into Latin also appeared. The bulk of the *Novels* relate to public or ecclesiastical affairs, though private law is by no means absent. Thus, *Novels* 118 and 127 reform the whole law of intestate succession, and *Novel* 22 sets out the Christian marriage law.

Justinian's *Corpus juris* is very different from a modern civil code, even though the subjects treated in modern codes are much the same as those in the *Digest* and *Institutes.* The bulk of the *Corpus juris* is many times greater than that of a modern code. The *Corpus juris* is not unitary but comprises four distinct and different parts, each of which gives a different feel to the substance and, even more, to the systematization of the law. It is in no way surprising that the various parts have had differing effects on the growth of subsequent law and have reached the heights of their prominence at different times. Indeed, the *Corpus juris* was not usually treated in later times as a unit. For instance, in the twelfth and thirteenth centuries and even later, when ordinary or basic lectures were given at universities in the morning and extraordinary ones in the afternoon, the *ordinaria* lectures usually covered what is called the *Digestum vetus,* which included books 1-24, title 2, of the *Digest* and the first nine books of the *Code.* The principal reason for this treatment may lie in the tradition that the *Corpus juris* was recovered only in stages.[24] In any event, the final three books of the *Code* are concerned with administrative law. To judge from the nature and predominance of a type of juristic book of the period, the *Summa codicis,* the *Code* may have been considered more important than the *Digest.*[25] Again, even within a particular work forming a constituent part of the *Corpus juris,* a lack of later interest may be detected by the paucity of juristic comment. For instance, the Romans treated theft primarily as a delict (tort), not a crime, and many of the early medieval manuscripts omit all discussion of theft. Sections written in Greek were ignored, and overall the *Novels* at all times played a very subordinate role.

24. See e.g. Jolowicz and Nicholas, *Historical Introduction,* p. 492.
25. See Watson, *Legal Transplants,* pp. 61ff.

II
The Block Effect of Roman Law

To know a legal system is not just to have learned its rules but to understand how the rules are put together, how the system is structured, how the rules are interpreted. Likewise, to appreciate the effect that a legal system may have on other systems, one must be aware of factors that go beyond the individual rules. Some characteristics of Roman law have long engaged the attention of legal writers of the more speculative kind. As experience has shown, its legal rules and institutions can to an extent unequaled by other major legal systems operate in societies of very different types: in economic systems based on slavery, in feudal societies, and in capitalist countries alike; in states of a variety of political or religious persuasions, including dictatorships, monarchies, oligarchies, and republics, whether pagan, Catholic, Calvinist, or Lutheran. The mobility of Roman law is geographical as well as historical: Roman-based systems are now at home in icy Quebec, tropical Panama, sunny South Africa, as well as in most of Western continental Europe—in water-filled low-lying Holland, arid, mountainous Spain, and in industrial West Germany as previously in pastoral Prussia. What has been borrowed is not always and everywhere the same; important modifications have occurred; but that serves only to emphasize the phenomenon of the "transplantability" of Roman law.

And yet, almost paradoxically, doubt has often been expressed about the quality of Roman legal rules. Not even the most enthusiastic Romanists have always claimed that the legal rules were themselves admirable. Friedrich von Savigny, who did so much to increase understanding of Roman law and its influence, himself declared that admiration of the positive law should be confined mainly to its theory of contracts; from such admiration he would exclude even the *stipulatio* and "some other superstitions."[1] Astonishingly, this admiration is for a theory of individual contracts, since the Romans never developed a general theory of contract.

One feature of Roman law that is always overlooked is nonetheless of fundamental importance not only for the spread of Roman law influence, but also for the shaping of civil law systems, their rules, systematization, and legal attitudes. Roman law, as it appears in the sources, divides naturally into self-contained and self-referential blocks. This division is found not only in the legal institutions and concepts but also in the four individual parts of Justinian's *Corpus juris civilis*. Transmission has often been of individual blocks, not of Roman law itself. The important unit for transplanting and for affecting the recipient system is the block, not the individual rule.

Although all legal institutions in any developed system can be regarded as blocks, the Roman law blocks are markedly different. To begin with, substantive law is treated in the *Corpus juris* quite separately from procedure.[2] The Roman jurists discuss whether or not an action will lie on particular facts but have no interest in what happens when the case comes to court. If it were not for the survival of book 4 of the elementary *Institutes* of both Gaius and Justinian, in each case primarily dedicated to procedure, it would not be possible to reconstruct in any measure the course of legal proceedings, whether in the archaic, classical, postclassical, or Justinianian periods. Again, the texts ignore the difficulties of proof. The jurists set out a factual situation and declare the legal decision that should flow from the facts. There is normally no indication that in practice the facts may be in dispute, and that sufficient evidence may be lacking.

To a considerable extent, this separation of legal rules from the course of the process derives from the nature of Roman law itself and

1. *Vom Beruf unsrer Zeit für Gesetzgebung und Rechtswissenschaft*, 1st ed. (Heidelberg, Mohr & Zimmer, 1814), p. 27.

2. It is commonly stated that English law and Roman law are much alike in that both are built up around forms of action; see e.g. Lawson, *Common Lawyer*, p. 102. But except in the sense that all legal rights everywhere are rights of action, this position seems wrong. The Roman forms of action themselves and technicalities of pleading were such that they provided no scope for making a significant contribution to the substantive law; see A. Watson, "The Law of Actions and the Development of Substantive Law in the Early Roman Republic," *LQR*, 1973, pp. 387ff. The surviving texts show that the Roman jurists thought above all in terms of rights and rules.

from the conditions of Roman law making. The contract of sale, for example, rested on no statutory or quasi-statutory basis. It seems to have been the creation of the praetor, the elected official or magistrate who had control over the most important civil courts. The praetor annually published an Edict setting out the circumstances in which he would grant various actions and, although no edictal clause set out that an action would lie on a sale, the Edict contained a model formula for the buyer's action and another, similar formula for the seller. That of the buyer read: "Whereas Aulus Agerius bought from Numerius Negidius a slave, the subject of this action, whatever on that account Numerius Negidius ought to give to or do for Aulus Agerius in accordance with good faith, judge condemn Numerius Negidius to Aulus Agerius in that amount; if it does not appear, absolve him." Nothing in the formula can be used to determine the essentials of sale, whether for the existence of the contract there had to be an object sold, whether the price had to be in money, what agreement was necessary; or when the action would lie although the sale was invalid; or the duties of the parties; or the moment of transfer of risk; and so on. The legal rules do not emerge from technicalities of the pleadings or process but, in fact, from juristic discussion of the scope and nature of the contract.

The lowly significance of the actual pleadings and of the action in Roman law likewise appears in many other contexts. For instance, in the *Digest* title on the acquisition of ownership, the actions relating to ownership can scarcely be said to be prominent; the reader has to wait until the twenty-eighth text of the title before one makes its appearance.[3] Again, there was a special procedure, by interdict, to protect possession. But the procedure is not mentioned at all in the main *Digest* title, 41.2., "On the Acquisition or Loss of Possession." Indeed, that title is devoted to setting out the circumstances in which a person acquires, retains, or loses possession. One would never know from it that legal protection does not always go to the present possessor; yet some interdicts protect existing possession, some are for the recovery of lost possession, and still others are to enable someone to possess although he has never had possession. In short, Roman substantive law as it appears in the *Corpus juris* is meant to be understood independently of the forms of process.

Likewise, the blocks of one institution or concept are kept rigorously separate, and even over a long period of time there is often no real movement toward integration or amalgamation. Thus, in a sense, it is entirely right that the Romans never developed a general theory of contract but

3. *D*.41.1.7.10.

only individual types of contract. The block is the individual type. There is no sign that the Romans even groped toward a general theory. It is often wrongly claimed that the introduction of the so-called "innominate contracts," perhaps beginning as early as the first century A.D., was "an enormous advance towards a general theory of contract."[4] The jurist Paul in the second or early third century stated that an action would lie on any agreement of the following four types, provided the plaintiff had fulfilled his side of the bargain. "I give that you give, I give that you do, I do that you give, I do that you do." On this basis an action will lie on any agreement that seeks to impose obligations on both parties, provided that one party has performed his side of the bargain. Although the existence of a remedy in these circumstances fills in gaps in the Roman contractual system and makes the law of contracts much more satisfactory, it is not a step toward a general view or theory of contract. Each individual type of contract, such as stipulation, loan for use, or loan for consumption, sale, hire, or mandate, remains intact with its own *sui generis* body of rules. Though contracts could be distinguished from other branches of the law and though contracts were classified according to the requirements for their formation, as verbal, literal, real, or consensual, yet for a Roman jurist it was unthinkable to write a commentary on the law of contracts or even on the law of a group of contracts, such as the consensual contracts. The same is equally true of other fields, for instance of delicts. Similarly, for the Romans there was no such topic as family law; but the various subjects which might be comprehended under that head—husband and wife, parent and child, guardianship, owner and slave—were kept quite distinct. In harmony with this approach, praedial servitudes were treated independently of land ownership.

This block effect is even to be found where a modern scholar might see only one institution. For example, the stipulation was a verbal contract, formed by oral question and answer, which existed from the mid-fifth century B.C. Its validity and the scope of each individual contract depended on the actual words used. In such circumstances implied terms were scarcely recognized in early law. For such a contract Roman law, like some other early systems, considered vital only what actually was said, not the motive for saying it. Hence, if the promisor made a stipulation as the result of fraud on him, the contract remained valid, and he could be successfully sued. Only in the first century B.C. were remedies introduced, the *actio de dolo*, "action for fraud," and the *exceptio doli*, "defense of fraud," and their original scope was apparently restricted to

4. A. Watson, *Law of the Ancient Romans* (Dallas, S.M.U. Press, 1970), p. 73.

fraud connected with stipulation or other contract of strict law.[5] Yet these remedies were treated as a separate block or blocks. A fraudulently induced stipulation continued to be valid though its effects could be negatived. Indeed, if an action on the stipulation was brought against the duped promisor, he could successfully resist only if he expressly inserted the special defense of fraud into the pleadings. This remained the law even in the time of Justinian.

With regard to these blocks of substantive law, the most significant fact is that capacity to acquire rights, especially contractual rights, is treated as something quite distinct from the rights themselves. The *Digest* titles on sale, for instance, do not indicate who can validly make the contract. Later nations could therefore "receive" the Roman contract of sale while retaining a quite different notion of capacity to contract.

A characteristic of these blocks is that to a surprising degree they are self-referential. Rarely are arguments drawn by analogy from one block to another—from, say, sale to hire, or from acquisition of possession to acquisition of ownership. Nor in general are arguments used from religion, equity, or utility. Equity and utility are at times cited by jurists, but normally to explain the past acceptance of a rule, not to win approval for a new proposition.[6] Further, for the validity or force of a legal rule, proposition, or institution, no stress is laid on the origins, whether they lie in statute, edict, or juristic doctrine. The fact that the wording of a statute, edict, or even a testament requires interpretation is a different matter. An institution, for example, is treated as existing—it is already there—and its rules and consequences are deduced from its basic nature. This characteristic has obvious advantages for future transmission. The reception of an institution or rule cannot be blocked on the ground that Roman arguments for it were drawn from now outmoded religious, moral, or political ideas, or that it depends on a statute or another institution which was not received.

Again, the Roman sources treat law quite unhistorically. The *Code* does arrange the constitutions within each title in chronological order, but there is otherwise no indication that the passage of time and new ideas have any effect on attitudes to legal rules. Roman jurists cite other jurists as authority with no apparent awareness that some authorities lived centuries earlier than others. Justinian's *Digest,* too, includes texts

5. See Cicero, *De natura deorum* 3.30.74; *D*.4.3.1.2; cf. A. Watson, "*Actio de dolo* and *actiones in factum,*" *ZSS* 78 (1961): 392ff.

6. See e.g. A. Watson, *Law Making in the Later Roman Republic* (Oxford, Clarendon Press, 1974), pp. 173ff.

by jurists of six centuries before, and their opinions are referred to in no way differently from those of their successors. The legal rules thus appear independently of time. With few exceptions, of which Gaius is the most famous, the Roman jurists were uninterested in and unmoved by history.

Whether or not this should be regarded as the almost automatic consequence of the existence of self-contained and self-referential blocks, there was considerable discussion and difference of opinion among the jurists as to the precise scope of each institution and as to the exact reach of its rules. Happily, much of this discussion is retained in Justinian's *Corpus juris,* especially in the *Digest.* A result is that later jurists felt entitled to argue as to what the Roman rules were.[7] A Roman institution might be received as a block, but some of the rules actually approved could be very different from those known at Rome of any period.

For subsequent generations the most striking blocks are the individual parts that together make up the *Corpus juris,* namely the *Digest, Code, Institutes,* and *Novels.* Finally the *Corpus juris* is in large measure devoted to private and criminal law, with public law decidedly secondary. This trait, too, corresponds to the interests of the classical jurists. For later ages the emphasis on private law was increased when, for whatever reason, it became traditional from the glossators onward to treat the last three books of the *Code* which do concern public law—separately from the first nine. Unlike the first nine, they were not expounded in the university ordinary lectures. In the early printed editions which reflect the manuscript tradition, they are not placed in the same volume as the first nine books but appear along with the neglected *Novels* and with the *Institutes.*

The Reception of these Roman blocks had several consequences for later ages. The first consequence of general importance is that, independent of the quality of the law, Roman law is the perfect vehicle of education in legal rules. The rules of an institution can be discussed, argued over, and developed quite independently of any original setting of the rules in a specific historical, political, social, and economic context. What matters is the block whose general content is clear. It is almost impossible to exaggerate the extent to which Roman juristic discussion apparently excludes nonlegal considerations. Surrounding circumstances that, in a strict black-letter law sense, are legally irrelevant are rigorously excluded.[8] Law and legal rules are seen very much as existing on their own terms, as idea, and not as morality in action, as state control of social

7. See e.g. Koschaker, *Europa,* pp. 63ff.
8. See F. Schulz, *Principles of Roman Law* (Oxford, Clarendon Press, 1936), pp. 19ff.

activity, or as a means of class domination. They are well on the way to pure legal concepts.

Second, blocks can be sensibly discussed apart from any question of their practical availability. In law schools slavery and adoption, for instance, can be—and where Roman law had authority usually were—treated as real institutions with rules and consequences even when they have no existence in actual contemporary society. Thus, the Leyden professor Johannes Voet (1647–1713) in his *Commentarius ad pandectas* gives full treatment to adoption as it was in Roman times, even though he eventually discloses that it no longer exists except in Friesland.[9] For an earlier period the Great Gloss similarly does not reveal that adoption was not then practiced. Again, the commentary first published in 1597 on the obsolete contract of stipulation by the German Johannes Goeddaeus, *Commentarius de contrahenda et committenda stipulatione,* runs to over 1000 pages of text and was not restricted to one edition. When the time becomes ripe for slavery in the West Indies and Latin America—the law of slavery had never entirely disappeared from Spain and Portugal—or for adoption in Napoleonic France, the Roman institutions can move fully formed, though with all necessary or appropriate changes, from the classroom to the plantation and the domestic and political hearth. The individual Roman law blocks can move in and out of existing later law without affecting the basic structure of the Reception or of attitudes to Roman law.

Third, the Reception of Roman law in later states can be by blocks. On the one hand, only what is considered appropriate need be taken. On the other hand, the blocks can be transferred from one field of law to another, from one state to another, and can easily be made to fit the various stages of social development, from slave states to feudalism, capitalism, and postcapitalism.

This consequence is not so paradoxical as it may seem. Part of the explanation is that some blocks are neutral in tone, others are transferable because of a permissible leeway in understanding, and virtually all of the blocks are free from any inherent religious connotation. Equally important, the block structure makes Roman law and systems based on it ideal quarries for law makers, no matter which of the three distinct Western conceptions of justice in law they hold. These three conceptions may be termed the liberal-democratic, the fascist-aristocratic, and the socialist. All three notions of justice take note of the inequalities of people but respond in a different fashion.

9. 1.7, 8.

The liberal-democratic notion of justice applied to law is that persons should be treated as formally equal, that in their standing before the law no distinction should be made between one legal *persona* and another. The conception involves great respect for the individual. As a corollary, the individual is expected to be self-reliant. Inequalities of intelligence and of financial resources, though noted, are treated by the law as irrelevant.

The fascist-aristocratic notion of justice insists that the inequalities of people should be reflected in the law, that persons should be grouped in accordance with their possession of particular attributes, and that a person's rights should depend on his inclusion in the group. Basically this notion of justice is an assertion that superior and inferior persons—however superiority and inferiority are to be determined—should be openly recognized and publicly designated as such.

The socialist notion of justice demands that all persons should in law be treated alike not just formally but in actuality. It observes that where inequalities exist and law does not take them into account, then superior talent or resources gain advantages. This notion of justice insists that these inequalities should either be eliminated—as may be possible with regard to financial resources—or countered by taking individual characteristics into account.

These three notions of justice and law—that law should treat all alike without regard to individual inequalities, that inequalities should be marked out and given support by law, and that inequalities should be eliminated by law—exist in most systems at the same time. But the prominence of the notions varies from time to time and from state to state. The Roman law block structure keeps legal institutions separate from one another and, above all keeps legal capacity and legal personality distinct from concepts such as contract and property. There can be no legal rights without the involvement of a legal person. Legal concepts or blocks change drastically in their effect if, without alteration in the concepts as they appear in laws and books, the capacity of persons, groups, or institutions to be involved in these rights is radically altered. Within the tradition itself altering group capacity for holding rights has always been easy. This separation of legal capacity from, say, contract and property remains a feature of modern civil law systems, perhaps nowhere more clearly than in the *BGB*, German civil code, and in the *Nieuw Burgerlijk Wetboek*, the new Dutch civil code, which is not yet wholly in force. In the Dutch code, for instance, capacity is dealt with in book 3, which concerns the "General Law of the Patrimony," whereas book 6 is

"General Provisions on the Law of Obligations" and book 7 is "Particular Contracts."

The fourth major consequence of the Reception is that the blocks themselves, namely concepts or institutions such as marriage, divorce, paternal power, individual contracts, ownership, possession, praedial servitudes, and testamentary succession, are highly articulated. In making the law and in deciding cases, the jurist tends to think in terms of the individual concepts and not of the overall framework.

Finally, the emphasis on blocks as distinct from one another and from nonlegal societal elements enables legal rules to be considered as existing more fully in their own right, with their own logic and *raison d'être,* independently of conditions in society. This character of Roman law is a basic factor in what Max Weber saw as the eventual "rationality" of European law, namely the ability to predict the legal outcome of a person's behavior.

III
THE FORMAL RATIONALITY OF CIVIL LAW

MAX WEBER characterized European law as having logically formal rationality, whose meaning is explained by D. M. Trubek: "Legal thought is rational to the extent that it relies on some justification that transcends the particular case, and is based on existing, unambiguous rules; formal to the extent that the criteria of decision are intrinsic to the legal system; and logical to the extent that rules or principles are consciously constructed by specialized modes of legal thought which rely on a highly logical systematization, and to the extent that decisions of specific cases are reached by processes of specialized deductive logic proceeding from previously established rules or principles." Consequently court decisions are based on rules that are general, have been previously established, and derive from autonomous legal sources.[1] This formal rationality Weber found above all displayed in German law and rather lacking in English law.

Formal rationality means that the law exists as a system in its own right, but law is not an end in itself. Legal process and legal rules are devices of society to produce effects that are strictly external to the law. This must be borne in mind when talking of the purpose of law, of what it does and what it can do. Thus, the purpose of a revenue law may be said to be to raise money for the government. So it is, but there are other devices, outside of law, which may also raise money for the government. The distinguishing feature of law is that, in the event of dispute, it gives

1. "Max Weber on Law and the Rise of Capitalism," *Wisconsin Law Review,* 1972, p. 730.

rise to the possibility of an institutionalized process which itself has the specific object of inhibiting further unregulated conflict.[2] In the case of the revenue statute, raising money is the end—though there will be other subsequent ends—and law is the means. It is easy to fall into the trap of thinking that for law the process is unimportant compared with justice, freedom, or the regulation of society, and that to emphasize the possibility of the process is to emphasize the trivial. But other means for achieving justice or freedom and for regulating society also exist. Rules count as legal rules only because they allow the possibility of a process. Thus, there is a limitation on law as a means which must always be borne in mind.

The functions of legal rules are numerous; and the ends may be general and remote, such as justice and liberty, or nearer and more particular, such as marital contentment, punishment of the supposedly wicked, and economic prosperity. It is a common phenomenon that in many individual Western law suits the ends, express or implied, that are most envisaged for the legal rules are not met, and yet usually society does not become disturbed. In part the explanation of this phenomenon is the high priority given in the West to legal rules.

The formal rationality of Western civil law systems is very much the result of treating the *Corpus juris civilis* as authoritative. Or in view of the difficulty of substantiating cause and effect, this contention should perhaps be reduced and be limited to the proposition that the form and substance of formal rationality in modern civil law systems can be plausibly explained by historically documented attitudes to the *Corpus juris*, and in this explanation societal factors need have no place.

Among the several legal consequences of making any part of the *Corpus juris* authoritative is, first, that it becomes important to learn the legal rules contained in the *Corpus juris*. Since the *Corpus juris* is composed of written books, and nothing but these, it is the books that have to be studied and the book rules that have to be explicated. The obvious place to learn these rules is in some kind of a school, where the relevant texts can be resolved, and where the shape and content of particular institutions can be analyzed. It is not appropriate to set about learning law that is apparently already contained in books by concentrating attention on what happens in individual court cases. That approach teaches techniques of advocacy and a pragmatic approach to legal problems, but cannot give a systematic training in the legal rules. Where legal rules are believed to exist, are considered important, and are thought to be con-

2. Watson, *Nature of Law*, esp. pp. 1–47.

tained in known books of manageable size, it appears unreasonable to attempt to learn this law predominantly from the haphazard appearance of suits before a court. The books themselves are the prime object of study. The learning of Roman law therefore tends to be through specific, deliberate teaching of the rules, rather than watching the performance of practitioners, and through bodies akin to "universities" rather than institutions such as "Inns of Court," although the equivalent of Inns of Court can have law schools. A barrier of some degree or kind, possibly only of approach or understanding, exists between law learned as rules and law in practice.

The three elements of the codification—the *Code, Digest* and *Institutes*—were originally intended not only to be the law but also to serve as vehicles for instruction in the law in universities. The *Institutes,* in fact, were designed as an elementary textbook. The revival of Roman law after a virtual demise of six centuries only made more important a formal study of these books for a knowledge of Roman law. The *Novels,* though part of the *Corpus juris,* were not part of the codification, and they were not intended for legal education in Byzantium. Nevertheless, with the Reception it would have been appropriate for them to be the object of university teaching, except that they were in Greek, a language little known in the West until the sixteenth century, and had relatively limited importance.

A second consequence of making the *Corpus juris* authoritative is that Roman law is learned at the feet of specifically appointed teachers and not from observing practitioners of all kinds. The teacher may be a part-time practitioner in the courts, a judge, or a consultant, but insofar as he is a teacher, his interests with regard to both status and financial reward do not coincide with those of practicing lawyers or judges. The more seriously a state takes its attachment to Roman law, the more the professors of that subject, in general, regard themselves as being teachers and scholars, increasingly remote from the practitioners. Other things being equal, the drawing power of a Roman law school derives from the scholarly reputation of the professors. One result is that the exposition of Roman law is relatively uninfluenced by the financial and status interests of the practitioners. The more famous and therefore the more influential a professor of Roman law is, the more he is a scholar, uninvolved in the practice of the law.

A third consequence is that the more distinguished a center is for Roman law studies, the more—other things being equal—it draws students from outside, since Roman law from the Middle Ages onward is inherently international in character. Illustrations come from Bologna in the thirteenth century and Leyden in the seventeenth. This outcome has a multiplying effect, especially where, as is usually the case, the professor's salary bears some relation to his reputation and number of students. Even apart from financial considerations, a professor's ability to attract "foreign" students affects his standing with his colleagues. But the more interested in attracting outside students the professor is, the less his lectures and writings reflect the particularities of his own local jurisdiction, since these particularities are only of limited interest to the "foreign" students. These foreigners usually return home, many of them to become influential in law making in their turn. The Roman law, however, that they were taught is not that which has undergone modifications for their own territory or wholly for their university's territory.

In these circumstances the local students, too, are not hearing Roman law lectures entirely adapted to their jurisdiction. Nor is the professor unaffected. He sees himself as giving lectures on a law that has no national boundaries and is perpetual in time, and he may even become impatient with the concerns of local law and local lawyers. He wishes to expound Roman law as something different both in kind and in quality from other territorial law. This attitude is summed up in the nineteenth century remark of Rudolph von Ihering on the introduction of modern codes: "The formal unity of the science (i.e. of law) as it once existed through the common possession of one and the same law book for the greater part of Europe, that working together of the jurisprudence of very different lands on the same material and the same problem has forever gone with the formal common possession of law; the science is degraded to territorial jurisprudence, the scientific frontiers come together with the political in law. A disheartening, unworthy form for a science."[3] This attitude, like the block effect of Roman law, contributed to the phenomenon of lectures being given even on quite obsolete topics without attention being called to the subject's lack of practicality. Professors of Roman law, too, were peripatetic, often knowing no national frontier. To mention a few Italians, for example, Placentinus, who died in 1192, taught at Montpellier; Azo, who died in 1232, also taught in Provence; Alciatus (1492–1550) was one of the founders of the humanist law school at Bourges; Vacarius taught in England around the middle of the twelfth century; and Alberico Gentile came to teach in Oxford in 1587. The overall effect, once again, is to separate Roman law as taught from local court practice.

3. *Geist des römischen Rechts auf den verschiedenen Stufen seiner Entwicklung*, 8th ed. (Leipzig, Breitkopf & Hartel, 1924), I, 14f.

A fourth consequence of making any part of the *Corpus juris* authoritative, at least in such conditions as prevailed all over the Western world until the advent of modern codification, is that Roman law comes to dominate university legal education, with canon law possibly its only rival. The first reason historically for this is the nature of the Roman law sources, which made them better suited for exposition than the existing sources of any other system. On the one hand, the *Institutes,* the textbook for students, showed that systematic exposition was possible both of a whole system of private law and of the individual institutions. The scheme of the *Institutes*—persons, things, and actions; or more fully sources, persons, property, succession, obligations (contracts, quasi-contracts, delicts, quasi-delicts), and actions—is generally satisfactory and indeed greatly influenced the arrangement of many of the systematic works on a local system, such as Hugo Grotius' *Inleidinge tot de hollandsche rechtsgeleertheyd,* first published in 1631, and Sir George MacKenzie's *Institutions of the Law of Scotland,* first published in 1688.[4] The *Digest* and the *Code,* badly arranged as they are both in general and within each title, provide a treasure house, second to none, of legal rules, principles, cases, and argument.[5] The student of the *Digest* is not distracted by details in the text referring to individual circumstances, to social, political, religious, or economic conditions. As the setting out of many problems in the *Magna glossa* or *Great Gloss* shows, teachers were fascinated by the method of a purely legal approach to factual situations. Students could be taught to handle problems solely on the basis of legal rules and to ignore vaguer questions of policy, an approach that is inherently satisfying. Again, for teaching, the Roman law has the inestimable advantages of being finite and easily accessible. Teacher and student alike can confine themselves to the contents of the *Corpus juris.* There is no need to hunt through multifarious writings to piece together the law, to search through bulky manuscript records for a precedent that may or may not be in point, to attempt to establish the existence of a legal custom. The legal issues can be clearly presented. Moreover, the in-

4. *J.*1.2.12.

5. On the inadequate arrangement of the *Digest* and *Code* see the Introduction to Frederick the Great's codification *Project,* §2: "it would have been very desirable, that the sovereigns who have reigned in Germany, had, from the beginning, thought of reducing those laws into the form of a system, etc." Again, Pothier, *Pandectae Justinianeae in novum ordinem digestae* (1749–1752), rearranges Justinian's texts within each title into what Pothier considered a methodical order. Antonius Faber, *Iurisprudentiae Papinianeae scientia* (dedicated in 1607, republished several times), attempts to set out all the rules of Roman law in a scientific way, i.e. following the arrangement of Justinian's *Institutes.*

ternational character of Roman law enhances its academic standing. It is inevitable that much more work is done overall on Roman law than on any territorial system, and this results in a higher standard of juristic sophistication.

Roman law intellectually pulls further and further away from its competitors, thus increasing its attractiveness for teacher and student alike. Consequently there is a neglect of local law in university teaching.[6] Customary law, fundamental though it is, was not taught in French universities until 1689 in the reign of Louis XIV.[7] In Spain, Louis XIV's grandson, Philip V of Castille, who had been educated in France, tried to uproot Roman law, declaring it to be not the law of the land.[8] But the universities continued teaching only Roman and canon law in spite of having been ordered to teach the royal law of Castille. Chairs of Spanish law were created in 1741, but the universities resisted and for some time passively failed to obey the command.[9] Even in a common law country like England, Roman law so dominated university legal education that the first lectures on English law in either Oxford or Cambridge were those of Sir William Blackstone at Oxford in 1758. Sir John Fortescue in chapter 48 of his *De laudibus legum Anglie,* written between 1467 and 1471, claims that English law was not taught in English universities because sciences were taught only in Latin, and English law was written in French, English, and Latin. Blackstone, in the first section of his introduction to the *Commentaries on the Laws of England,* prefers to put the blame for the lack on the clergy, "many of them foreigners." But since the phenomenon is international, not just English, an international explanation is required.

This academic dominance in its turn produces further consequences. Legal writing becomes concentrated on Roman law and canon law. The books may also set out rules of local law, but the treatment of these is usually regarded as of secondary importance. The significance of these works is by no means restricted to university training. They help to bridge the gap between the universities and practice, but they proceed from the university side and increase university influence. There must at times have been a reaction, even downright hostility, from practitioners

6. See e.g. David and Brierly, *Legal Systems,* p. 40.

7. See A. de Curzon, "L'Enseignement du droit français dans les universités de France aux XVIIe et XVIIIe siècles, *RHD,* 1919, pp. 208ff, 305ff.

8. Auto acordato por el Consejo en pleno, 4 de diciembre de 1713, auto 1.1.1., agregado a la Rec.; Nov. 3.2.11.

9. See e.g. F. de Castro, *Derecho civil de España,* 2nd ed. (Madrid, Instituto de estudios politicos, 1949), I, 169ff.

and laymen against the influence of this theoretical law, as lacking practical reality and so on. But newcomers to practice from a university training consciously and unconsciously see law in the way known to them. And busy practitioners, seeking the law on a point at issue, look at the works readily accessible to them, which in very many cases are books on Roman law or primarily on Roman law. The practitioner must want to win his case, for the benefit of his client and himself. Even if he disapproves of the emphasis on Roman law, he uses arguments from Roman law when they can be made to support his case.[10] Though there were disputes as to the force of Roman law in northern France in the sixteenth century, the lawyers of the time made continual reference to that system, even when it was irrelevant.[11]

One consequence is that relatively more judges than in common law jurisdictions become authors of legal books. The reason is the inevitable high prestige of legal works and of professors; judges who wish to partake of this prestige feel drawn toward writing. However, the original impetus comes from the academic not the judicial side; hence the writings even by judges tend to fit into a mold prepared by academics. In common law systems, in contrast, legal emphasis is on what the courts do rather than on systematic exposition. All eyes are on the judge, not the academic; hence a common law professor is under less pressure than his civil law colleagues to burst into print. When he does so, he may well prefer, especially in the United States, to produce a case book, a court-oriented work, rather than a systematic piece of scholarship. Textbooks—"horn books" in the derogatory phrase—may even be despised. The great exception for common law countries is constitutional law when there is a written constitution. Thus, treatises on American constitutional law abound, and professors of constitutional law have a high status, not enjoyed by their British counterpart, among their colleagues and students and even among the judges.

Books on Roman law that deal with substantive law say virtually nothing about procedure, partly because in the *Corpus juris* itself technical points of pleading scarcely appear, and partly because the books are designed to achieve a circulation outside a limited jurisdiction, whereas procedure tends to vary from place to place. Local court procedure, like

10. An analogy might be drawn from contemporary Scots law. The opinion is often expressed, even by practitioners, that English law exercises too great an influence on the development of Scots law. But the busy advocate, in the absence of obvious Scots authority or of scholarly discussion, rapidly turns to English textbooks that refer him to English case law. Much English law has come into Scots law via the Court of Session.

11. See Koschaker, *Europa,* pp. 212ff.

local substantive law, existed before the Reception, but it was not replaced by Roman, or modified-Roman, rules because these rules could not be known. What unity came to exist was mainly the result of canon law influence. The end result is in complete contrast to the intertwining of the forms of process and substantive law that are found in English common law.

This restricted interest in procedure passed into many books on local substantive law. Two examples from the seventeenth century are institutes of native law of Holland and of Scotland. Hugo de Groot's *Inleidinge tot de hollandsche rechtsgeleertheyd* was written during his imprisonment in the castle of Loevestein from June 6, 1619, to March 22, 1621; in particular, he seems to have been at work on it during the first six months of 1620. The book has the typical structure of institutes of local law: it is greatly influenced in length, in topics treated, and in order of topics, by Justinian's *Institutes.* But whereas that Byzantine work devoted more than one-half of the fourth and final book to the law of actions, Grotius' *Inleidinge* contains only three books and does not deal expressly with procedure. Even more significant, in each chapter the discussion runs almost exclusively on rules and rights. Only exceptionally is there specific mention of an available action, scarcely even of the actual procedure involved. Grotius' explains his failure to write a book in whole or in part on procedure in a letter dated January 9, 1629, to his brother William, in which he claims that he omitted procedure because this was already the object of a book by Paulus Merula.[12] The work in question is *Synopsis praxeos civilis, Maniere van procederen in dese provincien Hollandt, Zeelandt ende West-Vriesland belanghende civile zaken,* which was first published in 1592. The explanation is scarcely satisfying, partly because nowhere in the *Inleidinge* does Grotius refer to Merula, and partly because a work intended to be comprehensive within its sphere of interest should not omit important matters because they have been treated elsewhere. Brother William himself published an introduction to local procedure in 1654, *Isagoge ad Praxin Fori Batavici,* giving as his reason the fact that his brother and other writers on Dutch law, apart from Merula, omitted the subject.[13]

The other, larger book on native law is James, Lord Stair's *Institutions of the Law of Scotland.* In the version generally known, which either is or derives from the second edition of 1693 that was the last published in Stair's lifetime, the work is divided into four books, of which the

12. See H. de Groot, *Inleidinge tot de Hollandsche rechtsgeleerdheid,* ed. F. Dovring, H. F. W. D. Fischer, and E. M. Meijers (Leiden, University Press, 1952), p. 331.

13. 1.1.1.

fourth and longest is wholly devoted to actions. This version, then, belies the suggestion that local institutes omit procedure. But the first edition of 1681, which divides into two parts, is very different: neither of its parts deals with the law of actions. Appended to the two parts is a short account of actions that is described not as a third part but as a separate work.[14] More important, the *Institutions* was written without the pages on procedure. There is a dual manuscript tradition, one stem dating from around 1662, the other from around 1666.[15] Most of the manuscripts do not contain the book on actions. One that does contains the text of "The forms of process before the Lords of Counsell and Sessions, the author My Lord Stair" written at the beginning of the manuscript text of the *Institutions.*[16] And whereas the stem of this manuscript of the *Institutions* is that of around 1666, "The forms of process" contains a reference to August 30, 1672. There could be no better evidence that Stair's *Institutions* was originally written without a distinct treatment of procedure. This remains true even if other manuscripts should be found to contain "The forms of process" after the *Institutions.* The pages on procedure, when written, were intended as a separate work of very short compass. The eventual full-scale treatment was meant to make the book more directly useful for practice in the courts.[17] Thus, the earliest systematic treatise on Scots law was written without the author's feeling any necessity for a treatment of procedure. This is all the more striking in that the *Institutions* must have been written when Stair was a judge, having been appointed to the Court of Session bench under Cromwell in 1657, reappointed by King Charles II, and made president of that court in 1670. Moreover, he seems not to have received formal legal education, a surprising matter in a civilian.

This downgrading of the importance of procedure in civil law systems, which results from the central role in teaching of the *Corpus juris,*

14. Stair misleadingly claims in the Advertisement to the second edition: "In the former edition I designed the Treatise to be divided into Three parts, as being most congruous to the Subject matter of Jurisprudence." Nor is his description of the contents of the first two parts wholly in harmony with their actual contents.

15. Of the MSS in the National Library of Scotland, those belonging to the 1662 stem are Adv. Ms. 24.2.10, 25.1.8, 25.1.9, 25.1.10, 25.1.11, 25.1.14, 25.4.17, Ms. 3172, 5334, and to the 1666 stem are Adv. Ms. 25.1.5, 25.1.7, 25.1.12, 25.1.13, 25.3.2, 25.3.5, Ms. 3721, 5058, 7116.

16. MS in private collection of Dr. Nicholas Allen. It was written by Robert Baillie of Jerviswood from November 7, 1678, to June 26, 1679.

17. There is a complicated relationship between the alteration of structure for the second edition of Stair's *Institutions* and the first edition of Sir George Mackenzie's *Institutions of the Law of Scotland* published in 1684.

is apparent not just in books of local institutes and not just in point of time until the moment of codification. Procedure has a restricted place in university teaching for some time even after the introduction of a code. For example, the teaching of civil procedure and of criminal procedure was introduced into the curricula of the universities of Poland only in 1950.

There are further relevant consequences of the dominance of Roman law in university legal teaching. For one thing, writings on territorial law, and territorial law itself, come to be heavily influenced by the approach taken to Roman law. For another, the emphasis on the *Institutes* and on the rationality of law lead naturally to codification.

To sum up, when the *Corpus juris* is treated as authoritative, Roman law, regarded as being in force, is taught systematically; the rules of law, especially of substantive law, are emphasized; local variations in law are minimized; the rules are not obscured by consideration of the interest, financial or otherwise, of practitioners; and the law is set out independently of the practical problems which occur in actual cases. The students are taught to look for the decision according to known rules and legal criteria existing inside the system; Roman law methods of thinking pervade parts of the living law constructed on other lines; and procedure is kept separate from substantive law and does not affect its exposition. Even before codification, the law in civil law countries has the logically formal rationality described by Weber.

The distance between this approach to law and that found in a precedent-based system is considerable. In the latter case, procedure and substantive law tend to be intermingled, financial and status considerations of practicing lawyers have more direct effect on the shape of the law, legal rules emerge far less clearly, and legal education, even in universities, tends to emphasize practical court room issues and the legal response to particular detailed sets of facts rather than legal principle. No evidence of this educational emphasis is more telling than the long addiction of American law schools to the so-called "Socratic method" rather than to a scholarly systematic exposition of the law. Otto Kahn-Freund claims that the thought processes of the common law should be understood as the needs and habits of a legal profession organized in guilds, whereas modern continental systems were developed in the universities by legal scholars for the use of officials.[18] But the differences in approach between the two types of system can rather be primarily attributed to the

18. Introduction to K. Renner, *The Institutions of Private Law and their Social Function* (London, Routledge & Kegan Paul, 1949), p. 13.

acceptance in continental countries of Justinian's *Corpus juris* as authoritative. After the initial acceptance, everything else, including the dominant role of the universities in shaping legal thought, would follow. For this process once started, to be explicable, no reference need be made to further societal factors, including the general political structure or the organization of practicing lawyers.[19]

It is not that societal factors were unimportant, only that the overall major development can be attributed to the fact of the *Corpus juris* having been made authoritative. The course of the Reception did vary from territory to territory, both in extent and in time; and in the variations local societal factors did play a considerable role. Scotland at first sight looks aberrant, in that during the decisive period of the Reception there was no sustained university teaching of law and no books on Roman law were produced by Scottish scholars working in Scotland. But the aberration is more apparent than real. During the period in question and until the Napoleonic wars closed Europe to the Scots, it was very much the Scottish tradition to study law abroad—mainly in France before Scotland adopted Protestantism, thereafter in the Netherlands.[20] Such training was expected from intrants to the Faculty of Advocates; and by 1662 the normal procedure for admittance was by examination in the civil, that is, Roman, law.[21] Attempts were made at various times to establish university chairs in law, largely in Roman law. Their failure is for the most part attributed to shortage of funds, Scotland then being a very poor country.[22]

The case of Alexander Cunningham is instructive. He was appointed regent of humanity in the College of Edinburgh in 1679, and of philosophy in 1689. In 1698 he petitioned the parliament for a salary of £200 for six years to enable him to complete a four-volume work on the civil, or Roman, law. The first two volumes were to be a settled text of the *Digest*

19. Hence Kahn-Freund's further observation is mistaken: "It was due to political factors, to the failure of the absolute monarchy in England, to the aristocratic structure of the body politic in the 18th century, that the administration of the law remained in the hands of the lawyers' guilds. With some exaggeration one might say that it was the Revolution of 1688, not the refusal to 'receive' Roman law that, in this country, sealed the fate of systematic legal science in the continental sense."

20. See e.g. D. B. Smith, "Roman Law," in *Sources and Literature of Scots Law*, by various authors (Edinburgh, Stair Society, 1936), pp. 171ff.

21. See *Minute Books of Faculty of Advocates*, ed. J. M. Pinkerton (Edinburgh, Stair Society, 1976), I, ix f.

22. See index heading "Law" in A. Grant, *The Story of the University of Edinburgh* (London, Longman, Greens, 1884); T. B. Smith, "A Meditation on Scottish Universities and the Civil Law," *Tulane Law Review* 33 (1959): 621ff.

plus notes, volume three was to be the "Reconciliations of Opposite Laws," and volume four a "System of the Digests by way of principles and consequences." The response, apparently dictated by bureaucratic considerations, was to make him "Professor of Civil Law in this Kingdom" at an annual salary of £150. He was not expected to teach. Apparently the funds allocated to him were not available, and the work was never completed.[23]

Scotland is anomalous above all in that the university training in law, which was primarily in Roman law, was received abroad and that the Roman law textbooks used were published outside of the kingdom. Still today the Faculty of Advocates has one of the world's great collections of pre-nineteenth century Roman law books. This split between foreign legal education and home legal practice would, in its turn, have effects on the law and on legal writing. There was just no local professor of Roman law, hence no recognized expert who could be turned to for the interpretation of Roman law during the preparation for an actual law suit, and likewise no continuing living presence to reinforce the authority of Roman law among men who had been engaged in practice for years. Similarly, there was no place for the standard type of teaching book found in other jurisdictions, namely a book of Roman law which nevertheless referred to local Scottish variations. Generally, the first indication that a Roman law rule or doctrine was current in Scotland, was acceptable in whole or in part, or was unacceptable was in a decided case and not in a law book. What was lacking was a mediating force between Roman law or professorial law on the one hand and legal practice on the other. In the circumstances references in Stair's *Institutions* to cases are frequent, and precedent appears as a very important source of law: in this the *Institutions* differ markedly from institutes of local law produced for continental countries.[24] Other factors may also have been relevant for

23. See Grant, *Story,* pp. 361f.

24. This does not mean that at the time precedent was regarded more highly as a source of law in Scotland than it was in continental countries; it may indeed have been no greater than in, say, Italy or Germany. In the present state of knowledge of Scottish legal history, precision is not possible. Stair's position on the authority of precedent is not decisive, and it seems to have changed between the 1st and 2nd editions. In the second, after explaining rather tortuously that the judges of the Court of Session do in fact make law, Stair notes (1.1.16): "But there is much difference to be made betwixt a custom by frequent decisions, and a *single* decision, which hath not the like force." The remainder of that sentence in the 1st edition has been excised: "especially if it be invested with many circumstances of fact, but such are more effectual if they be in any abstract point of law"; as well as another sentence: "Their decisions are final and irrevocable, when solemnly done *in foro contradictorio,* and thereby recent custom or practice is established, both by their acts of

Stair's citation of precedent. There was the example of practicks, the older form of Scottish legal literature, which are more or less systematic arrangements of unconnected statements about Scots law, intended for the guidance of practitioners. These statements may be a brief account of a rule in a statute, of a Roman rule, of a rule deriving from a dated precedent, or even of the finding in some particular case where the names of the parties are given in addition to the date of the decision.[25] Moreover, it seems likely that English practice offered Stair another example for the citation of precedent.

Roman law as it appeared in the medieval centuries and later was naturally subject to development and therefore differed markedly in its rules from that known to the Romans. In addition, classical Roman law, what the French call "le droit romain romain," did not exhibit to anything like the same degree the logically formal rationality of modern civil law systems. Certainly classical Roman legal thought relied upon justifications that transcended the particular case; certainly the criteria of decision were intrinsic to the legal system; and certainly rules were constructed by specialized modes of legal thought. But what was missing for the Romans was precisely an authoritative body of writings such as the *Corpus juris*. The impetus toward systematic legal education was therefore lacking. Indeed, during the republic students learned their law not in law schools but in the home of a distinguished jurist by listening to him giving opinions.[26] Even in the empire it is by no means clear that the Sabinian and Proculian "schools" provided formal legal education. For H. F. Jolowicz and Barry Nicholas, it "is quite impossible to suppose that most of the men who are mentioned as heads of the Sabinian and Proculian 'schools,' many of them of consular rank and constantly engaged in public affairs, could have had either the time or the inclination to teach in such establishments." Accordingly, for them the least unsatisfactory conjecture is that the "schools" were more in the nature of aristocratic clubs formed for discussing legal matters and centering around a distinguished jurist.[27]

sederunt and decisions, &c." Thus, by the time of the 2nd edition Stair had a lower opinion of the force of a single decision. Nevertheless, in both editions he habitually cites only one or two cases, rarely more, to support a proposition of law, and these cases in the published reports do not indicate that the judgments were the culmination of a line of decisions.

25. For the last category see Hope, *Major Practicks,* under the heading in each title of "Practical Observationes."

26. See e.g. A. Watson, *Law Making in the Later Roman Republic* (Oxford, Clarendon Press, 1974), pp. 108f.

27. Jolowicz and Nicholas, *Historical Introduction,* p. 380; cf. Thomas, *Textbook,* pp. 45f.

Again, there was no fixed body of material which set out the law in a convenient form. Certainly there were statutes, magisterial edicts, and rescripts of the emperors, but the first were few in number, the second very brief and necessarily to be filled out by interpretation, the third not readily accessible. Essential to an understanding of these, as well as to the fundamental legal development by respected jurists, were the numerous and frequently massive writings of the jurists themselves: thus the commentary of Ulpian on the Edict is in eighty-three books. To find an authoritative statement on a point was not easy. It was not for nothing that the Emperors Theodosius II and Valentinian issued the "Law of Citations" in 426, enacting that the works of the jurists Papinian, Paul, Gaius, Ulpian, and Modestinus—all of them active about two centuries or more before—should be primary authorities; or that Justinian, a century later, declared the need for the *Digest,* because "we find the whole course of our statutes, such as they come down to us from the foundation of the city of Rome and from the days of Romulus, to be in a state of such confusion that they reach to an infinite length and surpass the bounds of all human capacity."[28] Moreover, the classical jurists are famous for their reluctance to lay down general legal propositions.[29]

The thought processes of the classical Roman jurists are commonly assumed to be similar to those of English lawyers.[30] One factor in this similarity is that neither set of lawyers has any authority to rely on which is akin to the *Corpus juris* or to a modern code. They have to argue from one factual situation to another, drawing what guidance they can from earlier discussions, with relatively little help even from statute either in classical Rome or in the heyday of the English judges.

In short, specific consequences flow from a territory's acceptance of the *Corpus juris* as part of the law; and in particular, logically formal rationality—to use terminology associated with Weber—can plausibly be explained as a natural consequence of this acceptance. Related to the view of Weber that logically formal rationality in the law was important for the rise of capitalism in the West is an opinion held by some Marxist scholars, notably C. S. Varga, who draws on Georg Lukács. According to this opinion, bourgeois economic activity is characterized by the desire

28. *CTh.* 1.4.3; *Con. Deo auctore,* 1.

29. See e.g. Thomas, *Textbook,* p. 49.

30. See e.g. F. Pringsheim, "The Inner Relationship Between English and Roman Law," *Gesammelte Abhandlungen* 1 (Heidelberg, Winter 1961): 76ff; W. W. Buckland and A. D. McNair, *Roman Law and Common Law,* 2nd ed. by F. H. Lawson (Cambridge, Cambridge University Press, 1952), pp. xiii ff. The similarity, however, is exaggerated and owes much to a contrast with continental jurists after the Reception.

for calculability of economic consequences, and hence economy penetrates into law to adjust the structure of law, as well as law's background ideology, to its own needs. According to Lukács, law becomes a sphere of social activity where this calculability of consequences, of profit and loss, is treated in a manner like that usual in economic life; hence positive law develops to the point where its social origin and its conditions of historical development become theoretically more and more devoid of interest compared with its purely practical usefulness. This new demand for calculation is precisely the cause of "the predominance of formally rationalized structures in law." As Varga explains it: "the new function of law directed to the certainty of foresight presupposes the 'technological' transformation of law. Hence its reestablishment in formally rationalized structures which, as mutually interrelated and organized into an in itself coherent system, are expected to serve as an optimum basis for calculation, has become a goal prevailing with ever greater purity."[31]

Varga is nevertheless mistaken. One of the problems which continually worried Weber was that England was undoubtedly a successful capitalist country yet it lacked the calculable, logically formal legal system that he thought necessary for capitalist development. Weber offered three hypotheses in explanation. One possibility was that though the English legal system offered a low degree of calculability, it nonetheless helped capitalism by denying the lower classes justice. Another was that England "achieved capitalistic supremacy among the nations not because but rather in spite of its judicial system." The third possibility was that in England "the development of the law was practically in the hands of the lawyers who, in the service of their capitalist clients, invented suitable forms for the transaction of business, and from whose midst the judges were recruited who were strictly bound to precedent, that means, to calculable schemes."[32] It remains an open question whether any of these hypotheses really serve Weber, but they point up the problem in believing that law follows the economic conditions.[33] It is not just England among modern Western nations that has a relatively low degree of logically formal rationality in its law, but also the United States, Canada, Australia, and indeed all the common law jurisdictions. The dichotomy is between

31. "The Concept of Law in Lukác's Ontology," *Rechtstheorie* 10 (1979): 321ff.

32. *On Law in Economy and Society* (New York, Bedminster, 1968), II, 814; III, 1395.

33. That belief implies that the degree of predictability would vary within a system from one field of law to another, but always in accordance with the importance of the calculability of economic consequences. But then the extent of this same formal rationality of law should show the relative need for calculability in each field from one system to another.

common law systems and civil law systems, that is, between systems of law, not between societies of different economic levels or persuasions. Hence the dichotomy between the two types of system, and therefore the growth of logically formal rationality in law itself, cannot be the result of the general economic conditions within each particular society.

It has often been suggested that the professional organization of the lawyers was what prevented the Reception of Roman law in England. However that may be, it is a long step from that proposition to the claim that the lawyers' professional organization hindered and still hinders the growth of logically formal rationality in England, and in the United States, and in Canada, and in Australia. Between England and the United States is a vast difference in professional organization, in lawyers' involvement with government, in the selection of the judiciary, and even in the kind of legal work done. Moreover, any explanation of the phenomenon along the lines of lawyers' interest and organization would have to show why logically formal rationality came to prevail in civil law systems and was not fatally hindered by lawyers' interests and professional organization, which again can differ widely from country to country.

This opinion is almost exactly opposite to Otto Kahn-Freund's in discussing the contrast between common law and civil law: "To make it articulate (which here too is the first step towards making it innocuous) is a primary task of all those concerned with European legal understanding, but to succeed in this, one must realise that it reflects half a millenium (and probably much more) of social and political history. No amount of planned or unplanned harmonisation can expunge the traces of political and social, as distinct from purely legal, history."[34] Contrary to this opinion, the main differences in common law and civil law systems, which are generally to be found in approaches to law and in structures, are primarily the result of purely legal history.[35]

34. "Common Law and Civil Law—Imaginary and Real Obstacles to Assimilation," in *New Perspectives for a Common Law of Europe*, ed. M. Cappelletti (Leyden, Sijthoff, 1978), p. 163.

35. Weber himself stresses the role of canon law in the rationalizing process, insisting that it was more capable of rationalization, thanks largely to Roman law and to university education, than other religious systems were: *On Law*, pp. 250f. But since canon law applied to England as well as to continental systems and the degree of rationality of law is much less marked in England, it might be more accurate to say that canon law was no obstacle to rationalization.

IV
Case Law Before Codification

Becoming a civil law system has consequences apart even from the acceptance of Roman-based rules. But since all systems have now developed beyond Roman law—some much further than others—elements have gone into the pattern of civil law that no longer have much direct influence, or that have influence only in some countries and no longer in others. To determine what is particular to one country and what is a more general characteristic of a stage of civil law development requires ranging over time as well as space. Indeed, as an academic discipline, comparative law is worthless without a thorough historical component. For example, understanding of a fundamental aspect of civil law systems at one stage of development, namely case law before codification, should lead to fuller understanding of deeply rooted characteristics of modern civil law. In the court room, too, the effects of a system's becoming civilian are evident; and features emerge that are generally found in uncodified civil law systems.

Legal claims are claims that give rise to the possibility of an institutionalized process which has the specific object of inhibiting further unregulated conflict, and legal rules are rules that validate decisions given in the appropriate process.[1] Hence what judges consider as the law, and the way to find the law and the appropriate authority, are basic to a legal system, whatever the standing of the judges and their decisions. Much is therefore revealed about a legal system by the reasoning of the judges, whether or not legal decisions are binding in future cases. If it makes

1. See Watson, *Nature of Law,* pp. 22ff.

sense to talk in terms of groups of systems, such as "civil law systems," then a "style" of judging must exist that is similar for the various systems in a group at a comparable stage of development. There may be differences of opinion as to what represents "a comparable stage of development," but two stages at least are sharply marked: precodification and postcodification.

Codification is an important but relatively recent feature of modern civil law systems. South Africa is the major remaining example of a primarily civil law system, though with much admixture of common law, whose private law is uncodified.[2] One volume of the South African law reports for 1977 contains four cases under the heading of fraud. The headnote of one reads:

> *Fraud*—Exceptio doli generalis.—Quaere: *Whether part of our law.*
>
> *Quaere:* The *exceptio doli generalis* was not part of Roman-Dutch law. By the time of Justinian it had already served its purpose and Roman law had no longer any need for it thereafter.
>
> The correctness of *Otto en'n Ander v Heymans,* 1971 (4) S.A. 148(T), doubted.[3]

The Roman-Dutch law referred to in the headnote is basically the law of the Province of Holland in the seventeenth century, and Justinian is, of course, the Byzantine emperor who codified Roman law in the sixth century. In his judgment, Coetzee, J. refers to the writings of three Roman law scholars of this century: Salvatore Riccobono of Italy, J. C. Van Oven from the Netherlands, and the Austrian Max Kaser, most of whose academic career has been in Germany.

In a second South African case on fraud, the question is whether it amounts to fraud if the seller deliberately conceals the fact that a pediment on immovable property has been declared a national monument.[4] In argument reference is made to the legal rules of the Roman Aediles; to Justinian's *Digest* 21.1.6, 21.1.8, and 4.3.1.2; and to the Dutch seventeenth century jurists Johannes Voet, Hugo Grotius, and Simon Van Leeuwen. In his judgment, Galgut, A. J. A. actually quotes passages from

2. Scots law is also uncodified, but the mixture there contains more common law features.

3. *Aris Enterprises (Finance) (Pty.) Ltd. v. Waterberg Koelkamers (Pty.) Ltd.* 1977(2) S.A. 436(T).

4. *Gleston House (Pty.) Ltd. v. Inag (Pty.) Ltd.* 1977(2) S.A. 846 (A D).

Voet, from the eighteenth century French writer Robert Joseph Pothier, and from J. B. Moyle's *Contract of Sale in the Civil Law,* which was published at Oxford in 1892.

What strikes the outsider above all about the references in these two cases is that they range over many centuries, are international in character, and give a place of honor to the legal scholar. In this regard, they are by no means atypical or extreme for South Africa: it requires no great effort to find cases with equal or more citation of ancient, foreign, and scholarly writings.[5] South African law accepts the doctrine of binding precedent; hence judicial citation of other types of authorities gradually diminishes. But textbooks setting out the modern law contain copious references with these three features.[6] And the three features are not independent but are different aspects of one complex phenomenon. To aid the discovery of the modern law, regard is had to an old legal rule, not necessarily of Roman origin. To establish the meaning and scope attributed to that rule, old and new scholarly writings are examined, and the scholars referred to may be from many nations. This is very different from what may occur in common law jurisdictions, as elsewhere, when the law on a point is apparently not settled and cases, or possibly writers, from other jurisdictions are cited really to indicate what might be a satisfactory approach. This is not to suggest that the South African judge cannot in practice manipulate these references to ancient law and foreign scholarship. He can, but the primary object of using them is ostensibly to discover what the modern law is, not what modern legal doctrine from elsewhere can show to be appropriate.

This approach is, at least in its intensity, unique to South Africa in the modern world. Yet it is commonly to be found in civil law countries before the introduction of civil law codes. It is, in fact, a natural consequence of attributing some degree of authority to the *Corpus juris civilis.* The supreme example from the courts is probably that of the great Italian tribunals, the rotas, which from the mid-sixteenth century gave the grounds of their decisions. In these decisions, according to G. Gorla, four

5. See e.g. *Robson v. Theron* 1978(1) *S.A.* 841 (AD); *Swadif (Pty.) Ltd. v. Dyke* 1978(1) *S.A.* 928 (AD); *Campher v. Campher* 1978 (3) *S.A.* 797 (OPD); *Wyndham-Quin v. W.-Q.* 1978(4) *S.A.* 843 (AD); *Standard Bank Financial Services Ltd. v. Taylam (Pty.) Ltd.* 1979(2) *S.A.* 353 (CPD). See also E. Kahn on the Appelate Division cases of 1965 in *Judicial Decisions and Doctrine,* ed. J. Dainow (Baton Rouge, Louisiana State University Press, 1974), p. 241.

6. See e.g. B. R. Bamford, *Law of Partnerships and Voluntary Associations in South Africa,* 2nd ed. (Cape Town, Juta, 1971); R. G. McKerron, *Law of Delict,* 7th ed. (Cape Town, Juta, 1971); *MacKeurtan's Sale of Goods in South Africa,* 4th ed. by B. O'Donovan (Cape Town, Juta, 1972).

ranks of authorities are used: Roman texts, statutes, and legal customs; judicial precedents from the supreme court of the state in question, provided the precedents formed a series demonstrating a judicial custom for the decision; judicial precedents from other states; and the legal writings of the *Doctores,* namely the *Gloss,* commentaries, and treatises, as well as the *consilia* (academics' advice on points of law submitted to them) and *allegationes* (advocates' briefs), when these had been published. Authorities (1) and (2) were treated as binding, (3) and (4) as persuasive.[7]

In Germany the first published "reports," the *Singularium observationum imperialis camerae centuriae quattuor,* in 1563, were of the supreme imperial court, the Reichskammergericht, by Joachim Mynsinger, who had been a member of the court for eight years from 1548. Mynsinger's *Observationes* are not quite law reports in the modern sense, but his aim is to record the practice of the court, as in the passage:

> 3.51.1 If it is laid down by municipal statute or on another occasion established by long custom (for such a statute or custom is valid, according to Baldus in *l. dudum C. de contrah. empt.,* Bartolus in *l.2 D. de debi. civi lib. 11,* Pope Innocent IV in *c. constitutus de rest. in inte.* Alexander Tartagna de Imola, *cons. 52 viso themate lib 1,* and Albericus de Rosate in *1 part. statu quaest. 93,* etc.; and this is observed in many places in Germany) that a relative or neighbor may not alienate unless he first gives notice to the relative or neighbor (this is called *ius prothomiseos* or *ius congrui*) and the alienation is made without the aforesaid notice, then the Interpreters disagree [2] as to the time within which the relative or neighbor may offer the price to the buyer and demand the said object if a fixed time is not laid down by custom or statute, as is the case in *l.1 dudum C. de contrah. empt.3.* [3] But when this matter arose in the Reichskammergericht, the opinion of Baldus prevailed.

7. "A Decision of the *Rota Fiorentina* of 1780 on Liability for Damages Caused by the 'Ball Game,'" *Tulane Law Review* 49 (1975): 347f. See also Gorla, "Civilian Judicial Decisions—An Historical Account of Italian Style," *Tulane Law Review* 44 (1970): 740ff; "I tribunali supremi degli stati italiani, fra i secc. XVI e XIX, quali fattori della unificazione del diritto nello stato e della sua uniformazione fra stati," *La formazione storica del diritto moderno in Europa* (Florence, Olschi, 1977), I, 447ff; "Unificazione 'legislativi' e unificazione 'giurisprudenziale.' L'esperienza del diritto commune," *Il foro italiano* 100 (1977): 1ff; "L'Origine e l'autorità delle raccolte di giurisprudenza," *Annuario di diritto comparato e di studi legislativi* 44 (1970): 1ff; "Il ricorso alla legge di un 'luogo vicino' nell' ambito del diritto comune europeo," *Il foro italiano* 96 (1973): 3ff; L. Lombardi, *Saggio sul diritto giurisprudenziale* (Milan, Giuffrè, 1967).

> He thought that for this purpose the relative or neighbor had the space of one year only, and that when this had elapsed he could not claim the said thing, or have the contract set aside even if he offered the price, as he and Cardinal Alexander said in *c.1 §. si Titius per illum text.* etc.[8]

This text is typical in the predominance of Italians cited, both civilians and canonists. Frequently the great Bartolus, who died in 1357, is the earliest jurist cited. At the other end of the time scale of jurists mentioned is the Frenchman Molinaeus, who was still alive when Mynsinger's book was first published and who died only in 1566. This text is also typical in the more general way that scholarly juristic authorities are treated with much respect and as having great authority.

Mynsinger's work may have upset the members of the court, but that of Andreas Gaill, *Practicarum observationum tam ad processum iudiciarium praesertim imperialis camerae quam causarum decisiones pertinentium, libri duo,* published fifteen years later, was highly praised by his former colleagues on the court.[9] Gaill's title indicates that the work is not what a modern reader would consider to be law reports: *Two Books of Practical Observations Relating to the Judicial Process Especially of the Imperial Chamber and to the Decisions of Cases.* Both books contain a large number of observations, each of which deals with a specific legal issue, not with the course of debate or reasoning in an individual case. There are fairly frequent references to specific cases and to lines of decision, as in "This was done in the case of *Rechle v. Baumgartner* and in many others" and "I saw this often observed in the Imperial Chamber."[10] But the primary emphasis is on the Justinianic sources, the *Gloss,* and especially on Bartolus, Baldus, and many other jurists, among whom the Italians are prominent.

A later German collection is I. H. Böhmer, *Consultationum et decisionum iuris libri* (Halle, 1734). Volume two is devoted to civil and criminal law and, though written in German, follows the order of Justinian's *Digest.* Each *responsum* (reply) has *themata* (topics), then *summaria* (summaries) in which are set out the appropriate legal propositions. Then the large legal problem is broken down into individual questions, for each of which are given first the reasons for doubt (*rationes dubitandi*),

8. See also 4.5; J. P. Dawson, *Oracles of the Law* (Ann Arbor, University of Michigan Law School, 1968), pp. 218ff.

9. The *Observationes* of Gaill and Mynsinger came to be published together.

10. 1.43.18, 1.48.4.

then the reasons for the decision (*rationes decidendi*). Both sets of *rationes* give numerous references to the *Digest* and *Code* and to recent writers, such as Davidus Mevius, Sam Stryk, and Benedictus Carpzovius.

Likewise in France, when the decisions of the parlements came to be revealed, a similar picture emerges of the citation of Roman texts, of foreign and domestic authors of various ages on the meaning of the texts, and of respect for scholarly opinion. The use made of these sources of law, and of local sources, varied considerably from one country to another, and even within one country, as in France itself.[11] For instance, reports from northern France give fewer references to Roman law than do those from the south. Collections of decisions are particularly numerous for France. For northern France examples are G. Lovet, *Recueil d'aucuns notables arrests donnez en la cour de Parlement de Paris* (a second edition dates from 1610), which nevertheless has many Roman references; M. F. Des-Maisons, *Nouveau recueil d'arrests et reglemens du Parlement de Paris* (1667); and P. Bardet, *Recueil d'arrests du Parlement de Paris* (1690). Examples from the south are A. de Lestang, *Arrests de la cour de Parlement de Tolose* (1612), which reports the cases at length but is not provided with a reasonable index, and J. de Cambolas, *Decisions notables sur diverses questions de droit* (1659), also for Toulouse. Despite differences in approach, if a later state wishes to attribute practical legal significance to Roman law, in any sophisticated system, this entails, at least in part, an approach transcending ages of time and geographical boundaries and giving some prominence to legal scholarship.

Likewise in the Low Countries there were local variations in the extent to which Roman law was cited. The Frisians gave particular importance to Roman law, and one collection of decisions of the seventeenth century is Johannes à Sande, *Decisiones Frisicae*. For what is in effect modern Belgium, a collection is Paulus Christinaeus of Mechelen (1553–1631), *Practicarum questionum rerumque in supremis Belgarum curiis decisiones*. This work, which was published at Antwerp several times in the seventeenth century, is in six volumes. Volume one contains cases arranged "promiscuously, as they arise in court." Volumes two to five contain decisions following the order of Justinian's *Code*. Volume six sets out cases dealing with the *constitutiones feudorum*.

The practice of ancient and foreign juristic citation is not confined to private law. For instance, in the Scottish trial of James Hairt (or Heart) for murder in March 1637, the *Digest* is cited, so is Justinian's *Code*, the *Gloss* on the *Code*, the opinion of the doctors agreeing among them-

11. See Dawson, *Oracles*, pp. 314ff.

selves, the sixteenth century Italians Iulius Clarus and Farinacius, and the Spaniard Gomesius, as well as less well-known jurists.[12]

Again, to revert to contemporary South Africa, in a recent case on theft (or theft of use) the following passage occurs after a citation of Roman sources:

> The reference to *usus* in the definition of theft given above is with some isolated exceptions generally accepted by Roman and Roman-Dutch Law jurists as the foundation of their comments on the subject and, among the authors I have consulted, the following may be mentioned in that regard: Cujacius, *In instit. d. Justiniani* (*lib.* IV, vol. 8, *cap.* 1, sec. 1, p. 1194); Mommsen, *Römisches Strafrecht* (part 8, p. 736, note 3); Huber, *Hedend. rechtsg.* (6.5.12 and 16); v. Leeuwen, *Cens. forensis* (5.29.1); Gluck, *Commentar.* (vol. 13, bk. 13, tit. 1, sec. 839, p. 230); *Sohm* (Ledlie's translation, 3rd ed., sec. 85, p. 418); Puchta, *Pandecten* (sec. f 75, p. 547, note (d)); van Hasselt, *Over de misdaden* (1770 ed., bk. 3, ch. 3, sec. 2, p. 312); Moyle, *Inst.* (3rd ed., note to b. IV, tit. 1, p. 519); Muhlenbruch, *Doctrina pandectarum* (vol. II *pars spec. lib.* 3, ch. 11, sec. 445); Damhouder, *De practyke of gebruyk zoo van civiele als criminele zaken* (1656 ed., ch. 103); Voet (47-2-1 and 5); Brunneman, *Commentar. in pandect.* (47-2-3 *ad. Leg.* 1); Pothier, *Pandectes de Justinien* (1823 ed., vol. 19, bk. 47, tit. II, p. 442, sec. 2); and U. Huber, *Praelectionum juris civilis* (*Tom. III* bk. 4, tit. 1, pp. 356–7).[13]

This passage highlights a further striking feature of precodified civilian decisions, that though the authorities referred to come from several different centuries, the judicial approach is basically ahistorical. This is also usually true of juristic discussion. No distinction is made anywhere in the citation between French or Netherlandish jurists of the sixteenth century, like Jacques Cujas and Joost van Damhouder, and German or English jurists of the 19th century, like Theodor Mommsen or Rudolph Sohm and J. B. Moyle (who actually worked well into this century). Nor need a distinction always be drawn between a book that tries to establish what the Roman law was, like that of Mommsen, and one that rather concen-

12. See *Selected Justiciary Cases 1624–1650*, ed. J. Irvine Smith (Edinburgh, Stair Society, 1972), II, 333.

13. *R. v. Mtaung* 1948(4) SA 120 (OPD). For the same style of approach in a modern textbook on criminal law see P. M. S. Hunt, *South African Criminal Law and Procedure* (Cape Town, Juta, 1970), vol. 2.

trates on practical adaptations, like those of Ulrich Huber, Simon van Leeuwen, and Damhouder.

The practice of citation of Roman texts and of foreign and domestic authorities and respect for scholarly opinion is not confined in precodified civilian systems to branches of law that are regarded as Roman law derivations. The same is to be found in the law most antithetical to that of Rome, namely feudal law. The reliance on early law as understood by scholars even of other lands is well evidenced in the books on feudal law, of which the Scotsman Thomas Craig's *Ius feudale,* first published in 1655—though Craig had died in 1608—serves as an example.[14] For instance, on the question of the rights of the crown to fisheries and the profits therefrom, Craig cites D.41.1.1, François Hotman, Cujas, and the *Speculum Saxonicum.*[15] On the right to property where the deceased left no heir, he cites C.4.10.1, D.34.9, C.8.6.34, C.5.5.6, Nov. 12.1, C.9.49.10, Nov. 134.13, Decretals 5.7.10, D.48.21.3.1,4, C.9.50.1,2, and D.48.38.12.[16] And on a textual difficulty in the *Books of the Feus* on the distinction between new grants of ancient feus and the grants of new feus, he cites Silemanus, Hostiensis, Cujas, Alvarottus, Zasius, the *Gloss,* Baldus, and Hotman.[17] The explanation of this approach in feudal and other law is partly the dominant influence of Roman law, partly the ill-founded belief that these laws were themselves of Roman extraction. As Craig puts it:

> In strict order I should pass next to consider the Feudal Law; for, when the Civil Law was swept away, the Feudal Law came in its place—the Canon Law being later in date. Indeed, some of the most learned will have it that feus are part of the Civil Law, and of the Authentical Constitutions in particular. It is true that the Feudal Law is almost entirely made up of imperial constitutions, and the above-mentioned Hugolinus made a collection of them which some reckon as the tenth book of the Authenticae, there being nine books of the Authenticae Constitutiones of Justinian.[18]

14. Craig, *The Jus Feudale,* trans. J. A. Clyde (Edinburgh & London, Hodge, 1934), 2 vols.

15. 1.16.38 (in L. Mencken's Leipzig edition of 1716 it appears as 1.16.24).

16. 1.16.30, 31 (1.16.20 in Mencken's edition).

17. 1.13.17 (1.13.13 in Mencken's edition).

18. Clyde's translation, p. 29. The passage appears as 1.2.15 in T. Ruddiman's edition (Edinburgh, 1732); as 1.2.9 in Mencken's edition. Craig, who had a sharp historical awareness, knew that this view was wrong: 1.5.

This approach to legal authority has been considered mainly from the angle of judicial decision making, but it is equally to be found in the numerous legal commentaries and treatises.

Uncodified civilian reported cases—or perhaps better, collections of decisions—have three other features that contrast with common law reports. First, the facts of the case are set out in far less detail than is found in the common law.[19] They give the strong impression that the reporter believes that only the few legally relevant facts need be stated, either because minor differences of fact between one case and another should not be the basis of varying decisions, or because the legal rules or principles, which make the case legally interesting, are dependent on a few basic facts. In any event, the outcome is that the reports are much more rule oriented and far less fact oriented than are common law reports. Roman juristic texts that relate to individual legal problems are basically similar, though the facts are set out even more briefly. Second, the decision appears to have been arrived at after far-reaching consideration of juristic doctrine and other reported cases, which serves to set this decision into a theoretical and systematic framework. In other words, what the court seems to be doing is not just finding a legal answer that corresponds to a particular set of facts, but considering the particular practical issue along with a range of hypothetical issues in order to come up with a properly coherent set of legal rules. This approach, so different from that of the common law, is all the more important if one believes that the life of the law is or ought to be "not logic but experience." By sticking much more rigidly to the facts of the instant case, common law judges also restrict their legal experience. Third, the main concern of the reporter seems to be to set out the legal rules and principles that are illustrated by the decision. The emphasis is all on the generality, not the particularity of law.

These three features, which have already emerged to some extent in the quotation from Mynsinger, appear more clearly still in a typical decision by the rota of the Republic of Genoa in the early seventeenth century, whose author or reporter is Flaminius Chartarius.[20] Each decision, as is usual in Italian collections of cases, is set out in three parts. First is the *argumentum,* that is, the legal question or questions to be answered.

19. South Africa is a partial exception, since it has been much exposed to English influence, and its legal system is now usually classed as "mixed."

20. *Decisiones rotae causarum executivarum reipub. genuensis* (Venice, 1626). See also J. Accarisius, *Decisiones rotae florentinae* (1713), which relates to Florentine cases decided in the 1640s, and whose publication testifies to the continuing value that case law was thought to have.

Second comes the *summarium,* that is, the legal propositions which correspond to the decision. The setting out of these propositions involves an extra skill because the index is composed of all the propositions from all the cases collected together and arranged in alphabetical order; hence the proposition must begin with the most legally important word. Third is the *decisio* itself, which sets out the facts of the case and the legal reasonings:

Argumentum

Can a woman whose husband is verging on destitution bring an action against her father who promised a dowry or against his heir for the dowry which is not yet exacted; and next can she prevent execution being made against the paternal property at the instance of creditors, so that the dowry may be preserved for her, because her father was insolvent?

Summarium

1. Wife, can she, when her husband is verging on destitution bring an action against her father who promised a dowry and thus inhibit execution at the instance of the creditors against the paternal property which is not sufficient for everyone?

2. Wife has no action on the promise of a dowry made on account of her to her husband by her father.

This proposition fails on the ground of equity when the husband is dead—paragraph 3.

Contra—paragraph 5.

Likewise it fails when the husband is verging on destitution—paragraph 4.

Likewise when the promise is sworn by oath—paragraph 8.

6. Guarantee clause that a wife can sue on a promise of dowry made to the husband in her name.

7. Oath brings it about that an action is acquired for an absent person in that case where, without an oath, it is acquired by means of cession. Provided the promise was made to someone who is present who accepts for someone who is absent—paragraph 10.

9. Action is acquired by a wife without cession on the promise of dowry made by a father with an oath to a husband taking the promise on behalf of the wife.

Decisio XLIII

1. A father had promised a dowry for his daughter to her husband, and she then, when her husband was verging on destitution

and the dowry had not been exacted and execution had been made against the paternal property at the instance of creditors, raised objection in order to inhibit the said execution and thus acquire the dowry promised for her, lest otherwise it would happen that she remain undowered: for her father's property was not enough for her and the creditors. The question was raised whether she could lawfully so act? And the Rota held that the said woman could not so act, (2) because on the promise of a dowry made to the husband by the father the woman on account of whom the promise was made has no action.

Sources: *in l. si pro te. C. de dot. promiss.;* Johannes Franciscus de Ripa in *l. 1. nu. 53. D. sol. matri.;* Massuerus in *prac. tit. de dote, versic. item maritus et non uxor;* Guido Papa, *decis. 375;* Petrus Boherius, *dec. 328 nu. 2;* Antonius Gabrielius, *lib. 3 com. concl. tit. de iure dot. conclus. 3. nu. 1;* Aymo Cravetta, *cons. 304. in fi. lib. 2;* Hieronymus Gabrielius, *cons. 165. no. 8 lib. 1;* Doctores (of Bologna) in *l. socer § Lucius, D. sol. matrim.*

3. It is true that Guido Papa in the said decis. 375 declared that when a husband is dead, a daughter can in equity bring an action of a promise of dowry made to her husband against her father's heirs, and he added that it had been so held in parliament.[21] (4) and the same is true when the husband is verging on destitution, Boherius, said *decis. 328 n. 2.* But Baldus in said *l. si pro te* holds the opposite on the ground that not even when the husband is dead can a woman bring an action against her father and his heirs; and Johannes Corasius[22] holds the same, *cons. 1 vers. pro residuo autem dotis, lib. 2 & cons. 318 vers. his tamen non obstantibus, vol. 3,* to which Antonius Gabrielius himself seems to subscribe, said *conclus. 3 nu 6, vers.* Differently, however, (5) Baldus—and moreover when the husband is alive this equity does not appear, for which per Guido Papa in said *decis. 375,* because the husband will be able to sue for the exaction of the dowry or to cede his action to his wife who thus will then be able to sue, as by all the above-mentioned Doctors in the said places, which cannot be done when the husband is dead and (6) therefore Guido Papa added in the same place that he, when he was in practice, advised that a cession of this kind be made so that the wife could sue.

21. See A. Marongiu, *Medieval Parliaments* (London, Eyre & Spottiswoode, 1968).

22. It is not certain that the abbreviation used here stands for Corasius, although the exact jurist referred to is immaterial.

7. Nor can the stipulation, to which the witnesses testified, made by the husband for her, benefit the said woman because the oath was lacking whose force is that without cession an action is acquired for an absent person for whom someone takes a stipulation in that case in which the action is acquired without an oath but by cession, as is in the *Glossa ordinaria* in *cap. quoties cordi l.g.7.8* note in *l. stipulatio ista § alteri D. de verb. oblig.* on which Alexander Tartagna de Imola, *n. 9,* Jason de Maino, *col. 3, limit. 4.* Others cited by Seraphinus de Seraphi in *tract. de privileg. iuramenti, privileg. 25 num 2,* and specifically on promised dowry Alexander gave an opinion, *cons. 207,* and *cons. 208 lib. 7.* Cravetta in said *cons. 304,* and Hieronymus Gabrielius said *consil. 165 nu. 9, lib. 1,* and Antonius Gabrielius said *conclus. 3.* And (8) if there had been an oath the woman could have sued and inhibited that execution so that the dowry would be safe because (9) without any cession that action would have been acquired for her because the dowry had been promised on behalf of the woman with the husband taking the stipulation as is said by the above-mentioned Doctors in the said places and especially by Hieronymus Gabrielius in the said *cons. 165 nu. 9,* who specifically observes that (10) in order that the oath come into operation it is necessary that the promise be made to someone present who accepts for someone who is absent, as he wrote there following Paris de Puteo, Hieronymus Gratus and Alexander Tartagna de Imola. Thus it was decided by the common vote.

So runs the case. No one case can ever be typical in all respects. Most other cases give the names of the parties, and most others refer to perhaps one or two reported decisions. But this case is like the others in the very limited facts that are recorded, in the all-around discussion, not restricted to the immediate question, in the citation of authorities on both sides, and above all in the heavy citation of scholarly doctrine and of jurists' printed opinions. The decision seems to turn on the arguments in paragraph 5, which is relatively unstressed.[23]

One remaining feature of precodification civilian case law is the great emphasis that the decisions place on juristic authority which is often centuries old and foreign as well. Frequently, generations pass be-

23. Cf. O. Marta, *Digesta novissima totius iuris controversi* (1622), 6 vols., which attempts to collect from the printed sources reports from everywhere on civil judgments, criminal judgments, contracts, feudal law, last wills, and spiritual matters.

fore an opinion expressed by a great jurist becomes authoritative. But this phenomenon casts doubt on the close relationship that is often said to exist between legal rules on the one hand and political, social, and economic conditions on the other in the territory in which the rules operate. Suppose that political, social, and economic conditions have remained static in the home territory and other accepting states since the expression of the opinion. Then one would have to say that either it has taken a long time for judges to bring the law into line with these conditions, or there is no direct connection between the legal rules and these conditions. On a different hypothesis, suppose that political, social, and economic conditions have changed. Then one would have to say that either the juristic opinion foreshadowed the changes at home and abroad in political, social, or economic conditions, or there is no direct connection between the legal rules and these conditions. It might be suggested that, since the courts and jurists can be selective as to the older opinions that they adopt, they take over only those rules that are in line with current political, social, and economic conditions. Although such a suggestion contains much truth, it meets with two difficulties. First, some earlier jurists, notably the *Doctores* of Bologna and Bartolus, are more consistently authoritative than others. One cannot suppose that the true explanation of the old and perennial saying "Nemo jurista, nisi Bartolista (No one is a jurist who is not a Bartolist)" is that Bartolus was great because he more than any other had the gift of foretelling changes in political, social, and economic conditions. Second, the tendency was very strong for the same jurists to be accepted everywhere. This does not imply that when the changes occurred, they were similar everywhere.

One point seems undeniable.[24] Because of her connection with the civil law tradition, Scotland accepted a modern system of contract in the seventeenth century, during a period noted for its economic stagnation. By contrast, England, which stood outside of the civil law tradition, did not achieve a similar modern system or any system approaching that in clarity or efficaciousness until the nineteenth century, and yet she had behind her more than a century of proud economic progress and trade.[25] The change in Scotland's contract law can be put between the years 1633 and 1665. This episode, viewed in isolation, appears to indicate that a strong shared legal tradition may induce a participating system to "mod-

24. See A. Watson, "Comparative Law and Legal Change," *Cambridge Law Journal* 37 (1978): 334.

25. See A. W. B. Simpson, "Innovation in Nineteenth Century Contract Law," *LQR* 91 (1975): 251.

ernize" more than is necessary, provided no great social or economic harm results. But the fragility of this idea is revealed by the corresponding situation in England. Although the intellectual quality of the universities of Oxford and Cambridge varied from time to time, civil law was taught there, and many of these university graduates practiced at the English bar after further training at the Inns of Court. It is inconceivable that civilian notions of contract were unknown to English lawyers long before the English law was systematized, with much assistance from the civil law, and at a time when the change could have been economically beneficial.

Changed circumstances may alter law and legal attitudes, and in this instance codification of the civil law type imposes its own approach to legal authority. However, the centuries of direct influence of Roman law have left their mark, accounting for some of the most striking differences of attitude between the lawyers of the common law and those of the civil law systems. Thus, modern civilian law reports retain many elements from their precodification ancestors.

It is a commonplace of comparative law that comparison is fruitless unless the systems to be compared are each examined at the most appropriate time. Yet the appropriate time may vary from one system to another and may not occur at the same point of historiy. For the issue of style of judicial decision, South Africa can be put into perspective only when comparison is made with civil law systems as they were before codification.

V
INFILTRATION OF LEGAL IDEAS

ROMAN LAW had the capacity to affect local or other law even in fields where non-Roman law continued to survive or even predominate. The process of the infiltration of Roman law or Roman influenced thinking into these areas can be shown by three books written during the Reception, each of a different nature, each typical in its way, none epoch-making or written by a jurist of the first rank, but all influential. Almost any book, however, that treated of the local law could serve as an example, for once the *Corpus juris civilis* has received any position of authority in a country's law, is taught in universities, and is, if only in part, considered directly relevant in resolving disputes in court, then it will, as a natural consequence, extend its influence through the medium of law books of various types that are not ostensibly directed at the expounding of Roman law or at extolling its glories.

The first and earliest of the three books was published under a variety of titles, such as *Loci argumentorum legales* and *Topicorum seu de locis legalibus liber,* and first appeared at Louvain in 1516. It was the work of Nicolas Everardi (Everts), who was born in Zeeland in 1462 and died in 1532. He studied at Louvain University, graduating as doctor of civil law and canon law in 1493. He became professor of law there and later, in 1504 *rector magnificus.* In 1498 he was appointed "official," or ecclesiastical judge, representing the bishop of Cambrai, at Brussels, and from 1509 to 1527 he was president of the Court of Holland. In the latter year he became president of the Supreme Court of Holland, Zeeland, and Friesland at Mechelen. This type of career, a combination of professor and judge, of public servant and ecclesiastical officer, is not unusual for the period.

The *Loci argumentorum legales* is an innovation in legal literature in that, although interest in legal argument was not new, the author for the first time sets out fully and systematically the various kinds of argument which can be used in legal matters.[1] Of concern here are not the general *loci* (points for discussion) on drawing arguments from etymology, from the genus to the species, and from the whole to the part, but quite a number of *loci,* all based on argument by analogy and all dealing with individual legal subjects, whose arguments are drawn from Roman law to non-Roman law: thus, from slave to monk (*locus* 24); from freedman to vassal (*locus* 25); from "miles armatae militiae (soldier of armed warfare)" to "miles caelestis militiae (soldier of heavenly warfare)" that is, from the rights and duties of a Roman soldier to those of a Christian cleric, priest, or bishop (*locus* 56); from soldier to church or *pia causa* (*locus* 57); from liberty (basically presumption or interpretation in favor of liberty) to *pia causa* (*locus* 58); from fisc to church or *pia causa* (*locus* 61); and from minors to church or *pia causa* (*locus* 74). *Locus* 29, though entitled "from feu to emphyteusis" (Roman long lease of imperial land or of private land for a rent in kind), also deals with arguments from either one to the other.

In all of these the non-Roman element is in effect being delineated in terms of the Roman law. Roman law is regarded as providing a good analogy, and since it is fuller and more developed, gaps or presumed gaps in the other law can be filled. In the process, the non-Roman area of law receives rules of Roman law, and to an extent, the non-Roman element is seen in Roman law terms. More significantly, the system of Roman law is being extended to incorporate the later non-Roman elements. Roman law is being treated as living and developing law. It is appropriate that Everardi continually points out that the analogy is not complete—that, for instance, not on all points is the legal position of a monk identical with that of a slave. Everardi is by no means the initiator of the process, and among the many jurists he cites, the most frequent references are to the *Gloss,* Baldus, and Bartolus.[2] Everardi's main role is that of systematizer.

What is above all striking is the detail of the analogy. For example, the *locus* from slave to monk reports that just as there can be no successor on death to a slave, so there can be none to a monk; a monk can hold property, as if it is his own, with the consent of his superior; there can be

1. See e.g. R. Dekkers, *Het humanisme en de rechtswetenschap in de Nederlanden* (Antwerp, Vlaamsche rechtskundige bibliotheek, 1938), pp. 8ff.

2. See e.g. Dekkers, *Het humanisme,* pp. 14ff.

no valid transaction between monk and superior, though this is slightly qualified; as a slave acquires for his owner, so the monk acquires for the monastery; an action, when a monk has control of something, should be brought not against him but against the abbot or prelate; the monk cannot be a party to an action; monks cannot be witnesses to a will; and the superior must not cruelly punish the monk.

The second book is Johann Joachim Schoepffer's *Synopsis juris privati Romani et forensis,* first published in 1692, which was still being republished as late as 1870. Schoepffer was born in 1661, studied at the universities of Leipzig, Jena, and Frankfurt-am-Oder, at the last of which he became Privatdozent in 1683, professor extraordinarius in 1687, and a doctor of both civil and canon law in 1688. In 1693 he became full professor and assistant consistorial judge (*consistorialassessor*) at Rostock. In 1707 he became a council member and vice-director of the ducal chancery in Rostock, and in 1715 director of the consistory. He became more and more involved in local politics, using his legal talent arbitrarily on the side of ducal despotism. When in 1717 an imperial commission, insofar as it could, took from the duke his powers of governing, Schoeppfer was removed from all his offices. He died in the same year.

As the title signifies, the book sets out in short compass, rather less than nine-hundred smallish pages, both the basics of Roman law and the variations accepted by the jurists and courts of Schoeppfer's time, primarily in Saxony. The primacy of Roman law is shown by the arrangement, which is that of the books and titles of Justinian's *Digest.* Given that normally the arrangement of the *Digest* was properly regarded with a lack of enthusiasm, the fact that both Schoeppfer and others follow it makes sense only on one of two hypotheses, which may be interrelated.[3] Either such a book is to be treated as an auxiliary to lectures on the *Digest,* or the order of the *Digest* is to be regarded as so well-known that the reader's convenience is thought best served if a law book keeps to it. From either hypothesis three consequences ensue. First, the classification of legal elements, and the boundaries of legal concepts, are forced into those of Roman law or remain identical to those of Roman law. Second, local law is seen as a qualification of or even a postscript to Roman law.

3. See e.g. J. Voet, *Commentarius ad pandectas* (1698–1704); P. Busius, *Commentarius in universas pandectas domini Iustiniani* (1656); who expressly spells out in the title page that he will set out the differences of the common customs of Germany, France and Belgium, and of canon law; C. R. ab Oosterga, *Censura belgica in priores 25 libros pandectarum* (1651), follows the *Digest* order, giving modern law, especially of '*Belgium*'; J.-V. Bechmann, *Commentarius pandectarum theoretico-practicus* (1658), gives modern law, for Saxony and the *ius commune.*

Third, the subject matter of every *Digest* title appears to be of continuing importance, and contemporary law which does not fit that mold is omitted, hence downgraded. The result is seen in the discussion of book 9, chapter 2, on the *lex Aquilia,* the Roman statute that deals with damage to property. Although later law did not exhibit the peculiarities of the Roman action, Schoeppfer's discussion, like that of other jurists, proceeds on the Roman basis, even though he points out the differences. To this type of treatment should be attributed much of the detail of the law in Schoeppfer's time, such as the doubling of damages when the defendant denies liability, and the prominence of a rule—fundamental in Roman law, but not so later until the Reception, and now again seriously under challenge—that the availability of a remedy depends upon fault that can be attributed to the injuring party.[4]

The general arrangement with its consequences is of possible benefit to the author, who will seem to be in the international tradition and hence will sell more copies of his book abroad and will even be more likely to be offered chairs abroad. As an indication of this internationalism, my copy of the 1702 edition of Schoepffer was owned by a Scottish advocate, John Rutherford of Edgerston, in the early eighteenth century. The marginal notes are not numerous, and most of them indicate where the text disagrees with the Dutchman Cornelis van Eck, whose book *Principia juris civilis* was used as the basic textbook by the first professor of civil law at the University of Edinburgh, James Craig, who was appointed in 1710.

The third book is Sir Thomas Craig's *Jus feudale* ("Feudal Law"). Craig, the great-great-grandfather of James Craig, was born in Scotland in 1538, was educated in arts at the University of St. Andrews, and studied law in France, probably mainly in Paris, where he remained for seven years from 1555.[5] He became an advocate in 1563 and, partly from lack of ambition, never reached the heights of his profession. He was a strong supporter of the union of the crowns of Scotland and England and was one of the union commissioners. It was this union that induced him to write the *Jus feudale* after 1603. He died in 1608, and although his manuscript circulated among the advocates, the book was not published until 1655.

The book relates to that branch of Western private law which, with the possible exception of matrimonial property regimes, owes least to

4. An early important inroad is found in §829 of the German *BGB.*

5. See D. B. Smith, "Sir Thomas Craig, Feudalist," *Scottish Historical Review* 12 (1915): pp. 272ff.

Roman law. Craig's *Jus feudale* is the first systematic treatise on any branch of Scots law, but its worth has often been suspect, partly because of a political purpose disclosed by a statement in the *epistula nuncupatoria,* or announcement, that the same fundamentals of law can be observed in both Scotland and England, whose laws have very great affinity.[6] But this belief of Craig makes the work the more important, since Roman law was not authoritative in England and thus the work should *a fortiori* display little influence from that system. But this is far from being the case. Craig was a humanist by inclination as well as by training, and the prevailing impression gained from his book is of his historical awareness and his internationality of outlook. The first quality leads him to assert very properly that feudal law is not part of Roman law.[7] The second leads him to make use of international scholarship, whether of canon or civil law or of works specifically on feudal law.[8] Classical allusions are frequent, and he uses Roman law in various ways—to point an analogy, to support an accepted proposition, to indicate that a detail of feudal law rests on a general principle of Roman law, or to suggest a reform in the law of Scotland. This last usage is perhaps the most interesting. He argues, for instance, particularly from Roman but also from general feudal law, that prescription should be more accepted as a mode of constituting a feu in Scotland, and in the course of argument he cites C.7.39.2, 7.39.7.6, D.41.3.9, 48.11.8, and C.7.39.3 and 4.[9]

The influence on Craig of Roman law thinking with its stress on internationality is best seen in his treatment of feudal law as international in character though subject to local variation. It is in no way surprising that the second edition of the *Jus feudale* was published, in 1716, at Leipzig. The internationality of feudal law is to be traced to the *Libri feudorum, the Books of the Feus,* and they could have had little authority outside the empire had they not long been regarded as part of or a continuation of Roman law, habitually published with the other parts of the *Corpus juris.* Many of the most important writers on feudal law, such as Baldus, Bartolus, Duarenus, Hotman, Cujas, Zasius, and Paulus de Castro, are now best remembered for their Roman law studies.

The dominance of Roman law on minds such as Craig's is shown in his general account of English law:

6. See e.g. H. McKechnie, in *Sources and Literature of Scots Law,* by various authors (Edinburgh, Stair Society, 1936), p. 33.

7. 1.5.

8. For the numerous writers on feudal law cited by Craig see Smith, "Craig," p. 294n1. For a modern list of such works see Coing, *Handbuch* 2.1, pp. 395f.

9. T. Craig, *Jus feudale,* 2.1.8–10 in Ruddiman's edition; 2.1.4,5 in Mencken's.

> The Civil Law is but little followed in England; and, although that country abounds with distinguished men in every department of learning, most of them are content with a bowing acquaintance with it. The reason why the Civil Law attracts so few students in England is that the law of that country is so thickly overgrown with native customs and venerable institutions. Hence the saying that the English observe a municipal law of their own while the Scots are under the rule of the Civil Law. But in truth, so little has the Law of England been able to make itself independent of the Civil Law that every part of it is illuminated by principles and precedents derived from that system upon which indeed the solution of its most controversial topics depends. The English are fond of attributing those principles and precedents to the genius of English jurisprudence and are unwilling to admit how much they owe to the jurisconsults of ancient Rome. But how powerfully the Civil Law influences the discussion of legal problems in England is patent to anyone, possessed of a sound knowledge of it, who takes the trouble to examine the more important cases which occupy the attention of the English courts. It will be found that the key to the solution of the difficulties presented in them often lies in the "responsa" of the Roma emperors and jurisconsults which form the sources of the Civil Law. Many instances of this occur in the reports of Plowden and Dyer.[10]

These three books—none devoted exclusively to Roman law, and only one, Schoeppfer's, about Roman law in the main—all reflect and increase the fundamental role of Roman law in their day. Roman law has undoubtedly meant different things at different times, and attitudes to it are part of more general cultural trends. Each book therefore bears considerable traces of its own society and age, and Roman law was seen by each author in a way appropriate to his time and country. Yet when the *Corpus juris* is directly authoritative, there is an inevitable tendency, expressed in law books of various kinds, to increase the sphere of Roman law rules and of modes of thinking influenced by the study of Roman law. Each of the three books, though situated in a particular time and place, nonetheless had a long and international usefulness. Thus, the book of Everardi, first published at Louvain in 1516, was republished in Italy, Switzerland, France, and Germany, and appeared as late as 1648. Craig's work, written in Scotland in the first decade of the seventeenth

10. Craig, *The Jus feudale,* trans. J. A. Clyde (Edinburgh & London, Hodge, 1934), I, 95f; 1.7.22 in Ruddiman's edition; 1.7.11 in Mencken's.

century, was republished in 1716 in Leipzig and again in Edinburgh in 1732. Moreover, these authors are by no means among the most popular.[11] The phenomenon of the continued long use of their books occurred along with the citation in court of very old and foreign authorities. These are complementary aspects of the civil law tradition before codification.

The infiltration of Roman law into local law also occurred through the medium of works specifically on Roman law. That infiltration could in a sense be controlled, since the nature of the books was obvious. Yet one type of book specifically on Roman law is particularly important. The very last title of Justinian's *Digest,* book 50, title 17, is entitled *De diversis regulis juris antiqui,* "On various rules of old law," and 211 texts set out established rules or maxims that still had validity in Justinian's time, such as *h.t.* 3, "Whoever has the power to consent has the power to refuse"; *h.t.* 10, "It is in accordance with nature that the benefits of anything go to that person who receives the disadvantages"; *h.t.* 12, "In wills, the intention of the testator is to be interpreted more fully"; and *h.t.* 56, "In cases of doubt, the more benevolent intention is to be preferred." This title became the object of a very large number of commentaries.

An early but detailed example is the work *In tit. ff De regulis iuris* of Philippus Decius (1454–1535), which was republished more than once with the notes of Molinaeus. Another is the *Commentaria in titulum de verborum significatione et diversis regulis* of Julius van Beyma (circa 1539–1598), who was successively professor at Wittenberg, Leiden, and Franeker. This work is typical in that it also contains a commentary on D. 50.16, "On the Meaning of Words," as does also D. Magirus, *Praelectiones ad postremos duos digestorum titulos* (1628). Again there is the commentary on D. 50.17 of the Livonian jurist, Christophorus Sturcius, written in Rostock in 1590 and dedicated to King Sigismund III of Poland. Another elegant version is that by Everardus Bronchorst, first published in 1607. There was even a "Notes and Strictures" on Bronchorst, A. M. Holtermann's *Notae et stricturae in Bronchorstii commentarium ad tit. pandectarum de regulis iuris antiqui,* published posthumously in 1680. G. Dyemenus (1508–1583), a Dutch judge and practitioner, was the author of another commentary, as was J. Neldelius, a professor in Leipzig, whose work was first published in 1614. The commentary of the Saxon C. Güntzelius went into several editions in the seventeenth cen-

11. For the works of the three Leiden professors—Bronchorst, Vinnius, and J. Voet—published outside the Netherlands see R. Feenstra and C. J. D. Waal, *Seventeenth Century Leyden Law Professors* (Amsterdam, Oxford, North-Holland, 1975), pp. 111ff.

tury. A French example is the work of Petrus Faber (1540 or 1541–1600) of Toulouse.

The very subject matter of the title meant that the use of Roman law for expressing legal maxims gave that system considerable scope for infiltration, but in addition the title played an important role in legal education. Hence a teaching edition of Justinian's *Institutes* would often contain this *Digest* title at the end. A striking example for teaching is the Elzevier edition of the *Institutes,* published for instance in 1654. This prints in red the words, phrases, and sentences of the *Institutes* that are considered particularly valuable for students, and it contains in addition both D. 50.16 and D. 50.17. So popular was the use of *regulae* (rules or maxims) that jurists came to compose books of canon law *regulae.* A curious variation on the theme is appended by Samuel Strykius to his edition of the *Institutes* at the end of the seventeenth century: the *regulae* of both civil and canon law are set out in terms of the first letter of their first word to form the name LEOPOLDUS IGNATIUS, who was then king of Hungary and Bohemia.

The *Libri feudorum* provide a striking illustration of the infiltration of Roman law. The *Libri feudorum* appear to have been composed primarily in Milan in the first half of the twelfth century, and a second version contained the constitutions of 1154 and 1158 of the Emperor Frederick I. A third version was completed by the Bolognese jurist Hugolinus in 1233 and inserted into what is called the *volumen parvum,* which contains the *Institutes* and the *Authenticum* (a version of the *Novels*) of the *Corpus juris.* It was treated as an appendix to the nine *collationes* of the *Authenticum* and hence was even called the tenth, *decem collatio.* The *Libri feudorum,* now part of the medieval *Corpus juris,* though that name comes later, were provided with a gloss which was accepted by Accursius with his additions as the *Glossa ordinaria.* The fortune of the *Libri feudorum* was thus linked to that of the *Corpus juris,* and from an early date the *Libri feudorum* formed part of the ordinary teaching of the Italian universities. They were taught by the same teachers who were responsible for the revival of Roman law.

Just as the teaching of Justinian's codification was to lead to a Roman *ius commune* (common law), so the teaching of the *Libri feudorum* was to lead to a feudal *ius commune.* Just as there was a belief in a body of universal civil law in which the prospective lawyer should be trained, though local law permitted deviations to a greater or lesser extent, so there was a belief in a universal and supranational feudal law from which the feudal laws of particular countries were deviations. To this belief is finally owed the feudal system—a phrase which implies not only that it is a system but also that only one such system exists. If practical utility had been the sole or even primary consideration, Cujas, for instance, would not have commented on the *Libri feudorum,* because in France the local feudal customs tended to deviate radically from "the common law of feus," especially on such important topics as alienability and inheritance. Cujas commented on the *Libri feudorum* because they were a standard academic text, important in the same way, if not quite to the same extent, as the *Corpus juris.* The *Libri feudorum,* that is, provided a model of the nature of the feudal relationship and might serve as a basis for decision, especially when the local law failed. Likewise it was worth reprinting Craig's *Jus feudale* in Germany, for the basis of common principle was sufficiently extensive for it to be read by a German who had no interest in rules that were specifically Scottish.

VI
The Institutes

Inevitably, sooner or later—and probably sooner rather than later—any society that regards part of the *Corpus juris civilis* as the law of the land or directly of importance in discovering the law gives a place of particular honor to Justinian's *Institutes*. The reason is not that the law in the *Institutes* is more satisfactory for practice or more satisfying to the intellect than that contained in the other parts of the *Corpus juris;* it is purely educational. In territories that adopt the *Corpus juris,* Roman law studies dominate legal education; and in the process, great stress is placed on the *Institutes*. One explanation is that, on the one hand, the *Institutes,* like all of the *Corpus juris,* were issued as statute and, on the other, they were intended as a student's elementary textbook. Moreover, as Justinian well knew, the *Digest* and *Code* make extremely difficult reading for the beginner. It is only to be expected that, with the resurgence of Roman law studies, the *Institutes* take over their old role of the student's first law book.

Numerous introductions to the *Institutes* are known to have been written by the earliest glossators in the twelfth century, and among the vast amount of surviving material there is an introduction that Hermann Kantorowicz plausibly ascribes to Irnerius (1055?–1130?), with whom Roman law teaching at Bologna traditionally begins.[1] The content and structure of these introductions differ greatly from another popular type of work, introductions to the *Code,* because even by this date introduc-

1. *Glossators of the Roman Law* (Cambridge, Cambridge University Press, 1938), p. 64.

tions to the *Institutes* were intended for beginners and served as an introduction to all law books, not just to the *Institutes*.[2] A manuscript survives of lectures on the *Institutes* by Vacarius, who came to England around 1143 and established the civil law tradition there.[3] In many libraries manuscripts exist of the *Institutes* as a separate work, usually glossed; and the first printed edition of the *Institutes* was published in 1468 at Mainz by Peter Schoeffer, earlier than either the *Digest*, the *Code*, or the entire *Corpus juris*. Much later, Justinian's *Institutes* had become the teaching book par excellence to such an extent that "examinations" of the *Institutes* were published, that is, books setting out questions on the *Institutes* that might be put to students at examination time, with the appropriate answers. Two Dutch examples of such books are Johannes Arnaldus Corvinus, *Elementa juris civilis* (1645), and T. Trigland, *Paedia juris* or *Examen institutionum juris* (1671, republished at Oxford in 1710). One by a Spanish Jesuit is Antonio Perez, *Institutiones imperiales erotematibus distinctae*, which appeared in many editions between 1646 and 1719. At least one existing Roman law teaching book, also follows the arrangement of the *Digest*, namely Bernardus Schotanus, *Examen juridicum*, which was popular enough to be republished several times in Holland in the seventeenth century.

In keeping with the book's nature, the *Institutes* are dedicated to "the young desirous of legal knowledge." The prooemium, §4, relates that Justinian gave a special charge to Tribonian, Theophilus, and Dorotheus:

> They were, by our authority and with our encouragement, to compose Institutes so that you might acquire your first rudiments of law not from ancient stories but through the splendour of the Emperor and that both your ears and your minds might receive the truth in these matters without that which is unnecessary or erroneous. And whereas previously at least four years would elapse before you came to read imperial constitutions, begin now at the outset with this work, meriting such honour and rejoicing in the fact that now

2. See Kantorowicz, *Glossators*, p. 56.

3. The manuscript, to be published by P. Stein, was discovered in the British Museum by F. de Zulueta: *British Museum Royal MS. 4 B IV, item 9*. See also P. Stein, "Vacarius and the Civil Law," in *Church and Government in the Middle Ages*, ed. C. N. L. Brooke et al. (Cambridge, Cambridge University Press, 1976), pp. 119ff; R. W. Southern, "Master Vacarius and the Beginning of an English Academic Tradition," in *Medieval Learning and Literature: Essays Presented to R. W. Hunt*, ed. J. J. G. Alexander et al. (Oxford, Clarendon Press, 1976), p. 257ff.

> both the commencement and the completion of your legal education proceed from the mouth of the Emperor."[4]

The prooemium also remarks that the *Institutes* were compiled especially on the model of Gaius' *Institutes* and *Res cottidianae*. The reference to Gaius' work as the main source is of particular importance, since that jurist's *Institutes* provided the general layout. Both works not only have the same pattern of treatment, but both are of approximately the same length and are divided into four books. The book length and division are significant for conservatism, because in Gaius' time the length of a book was largely predetermined: a book was set out on a roll and could be only as long as could be conveniently held. This lack of flexibility could entail inelegancies of arrangement. But by the time of Justinian, books (*codices*) had very much their modern form, and the length of a book was by no means so predetermined but depended more on contents.

In the end, the Justinianic division into books was taken over into modern civil codes. But the particular Justinianic division was so far from satisfactory that the attempts to divide the books differently have been numerous. The absence of a satisfactory model in Justinian has led to a diversity of divisions in the codes, which contrasts with the fact that the subjects thought proper to include in a civil code are much the same everywhere.

Book 1 of Gaius' *Institutes* is divided by modern scholars into two-hundred sections. All except the first eight sections concern the law of persons. The first distinguishes between *ius civile* and *ius gentium*, sections two to seven discuss the sources of Roman law, and section eight presents the division of the subject. Quite naturally for the time, these introductory matters do not form a separate book. Justinian unnecessarily follows the same pattern. In his book 1, the first title is "On Natural Law, the Law of Nations, and the Civil Law;" the remaining twenty-four titles are all on the law of persons. And so it continues, the beginning and end of a book of Gaius not necessarily corresponding to the most appropriate places for divisions. Book 2 is things, acquistion of property, and testate succession; book 3 is intestate succession and obligations; book 4 is actions. The pattern is projected into Justinian's *Institutes:* book 2 corresponds to that of Gaius; book 3 is intestate succession, contracts, and quasi-contracts; book 4 is delict, quasi-delict, and actions.

A direct line runs between the acceptance of the *Corpus juris* as authoritative or persuasive, the dominance of Roman law in legal educa-

4. *Institutes of Justinian,* trans. J. A. C. Thomas (Cape Town, Juta, 1975), p. 1.

tion, the role of Justinian's *Institutes* as the first book of law, and—one of the characteristic products of the civil law systems in the seventeenth and eighteenth centuries—the institutes of national law.[5] These institutes are the direct descendants of Justinian's *Institutes*. The inspiration of Justinian is almost always immediately apparent in their overall form and structure, and in their intention of setting out in a clear, concise, simple, and systematic manner the basic principles of the law. This remains true even though the substance of the law in local institutes may differ greatly from that in Justinian. There are three contrasts, however, between the new and the old institutes. First, frequently it was not the author's intention that his local institutes be used in formal legal education. Rather they were meant to provide material to fill a gap that existed and would continue to exist in legal education.[6] Second, the local institutes were intended to describe the law; they were in no sense authoritative themselves. Any influence they came to possess was due to their own inherent qualities and to the absence of plausible rivals. Third, the local institutes do not form part of a complex whole akin to the *Corpus juris*. Indeed in most cases—the prime exception being France—the institutes are not supported by existing comprehensive treatises from which one can easily learn the details of the local law.

Too sharp a division should not be drawn between these local institutes of the seventeenth century and earlier writings. It would be possible to claim, for instance, that Scotland's *Regiam majestatem* of the fourteenth century is an early example of local institutes and shows typical features, including the influence of Justinian's *Institutes*. But there was a sudden flowering of such works in the early seventeenth century, as in France, where the early local *Institution* of Guy Coquille was published in 1607, even though the extent to which there was not a Reception in northern France is exceptional for Western continental Europe.[7] The main practical impetus there to something akin to an institutional work lay in the multitudinous customs which prevailed each in its own district,

5. See K. Luig, "The Institutes of National Law in the Seventeenth and Eighteenth Centuries," *Juridical Review* 17 (1972): 193ff.

6. Thus Guy Coquille, *Institution au droit françois*, was written before French law was taught in universities; Stair, *Institutions of the Law of Scotland*, and Mackenzie, *Institutions of the Law of Scotland*, were published when no formal legal education existed in Scotland, and Grotius, *Inleidinge tot de Hollandsche rechtsgeleertheyd*, was intended for his sons (see Address to the Reader, by Grotius' brother?).

7. See also Jean Imbert, *Enchiridion iuris scripti Galliae moribus et consuetudine frequentiore usitati* (Lyon, 1556), where the contents are arranged according to the alphabet; thus the first topic is *Abusus*, then *Absens*, *Abbates*, etc.

great or small. By the time of Coquille the work of codifying these local customs was well under way, and he, in fact, published the Custom of Nevers.[8] Charles Dumoulin, or Molinaeus (1500–1566), had already expressed the ideal that Coquille aimed for: "Moreover, nothing is more worthy of praise, nothing more useful or desirable in the whole state than the reduction into a short, very clear and just, harmonious, whole of all the very diffuse and often stupidly varying customs of this Kingdom."[9]

Coquille's *Institution* shows few signs of the direct influence of Justinian's *Institutes.* It is written in French, is not divided into books, contains no treatment of the nature of law at the beginning, and varies considerably from the Roman *Institutes* in its arrangement of topics. Moreover, within the subjects treated, the law set out is not comprehensive but is only that of the customs and royal legislation. The Roman law rules accepted in France are not set out, even when, as with contract, they are dominant. Not that Roman law could be excluded; references to it are frequent, as in the works of Everardi, Schoepffer, and Craig that show infiltration. Roman law is cited in various ways—as a standard of reason, as support for a proposition, as explanation for the development of a customary rule, or even as an aberration—but it is never treated as irrelevant. For example, in discussing family community property, which did not exist in developed Roman law, Coquille observes that in matters of succession the Custom of Nevers—his own special field—differs from all others in that when one parent dies, the male children of fourteen or over and the female of twelve or over acquire shares *per caput* equally with the surviving parent. Coquille prefers the common view of the other customs that, until the children reach eighteen, they should be counted not *per caput* but as a single unit. He explains the exception of Nevers as the result of following the Roman rules on the age of attaining puberty, though in his opinion, it would have been better to take the Roman "full puberty" at eighteen as the test.[10] Thus, in this instance he claims, rightly or wrongly, that Roman law influenced the Custom. He then suggests that the foreign, or Roman, origin may be a reason for rejecting the law in the Custom of Nevers, although he also argues for the adoption of the generally accepted rule of the Customs on the basis that is harmonizes

8. See e.g. J. P. Dawson, "The Codification of the French Customs," *Michigan Law Review* 38 (1940): 765ff.

9. *Oratio de concordia et unione consuetudinum Franciae,* in his *Omnia quae extant opera* (Paris, 1681), II, 690ff. See also Luig, "Institutes," p. 203: "Only the Code Civil was the fulfilment of Dumoulin's desire for the *brevissimus, candidissimus, expeditissimus et absolutissimus libellus* of French law."

10. Coquille, *Oeuvres* (Bordeaux, 1703), II, 58.

with another, rather dubious proposition of Roman law.[11] The tension between customary and Roman law is patent, but so is the importance of Roman law for French legal thinking.

This considerable autonomy of French institutes from Justinian's *Institutes* was not to last. Students introduced to law through Justinian's *Institutes* would find that an approach to local law was much easier if that particular format was used. Again, a particular factor that might be adduced for France is that in the south, in the "pays de droit écrit," Roman law was the custom, and writings on French law written in that area tended to follow Justinian's arrangement.[12] Authors of these institutes might equally be a royal professor of French law appointed under Louis XIV's reform of 1689 or a practicing advocate.

Thus, Jerôme Mercier, an advocate at the Parlement of Paris, published in that city in 1665 his *Remarques nouvelles de droit François sur les institutes de l'empereur Justinien.* Despite the claim in the "Notice to the Reader" that the work "is a faithful translation of Justinian's *Institutes,*" it does not contain a translation. Again, despite the "Notice," the work does not contain everything most useful and necessary for an understanding of Roman law. But it is a commentary on the law of France, with citation of customs and decisions, all seen from the angle of Justinian's *Institutes.* The order is entirely that of Justinian, and thus there are titles on "Justice and Law" and on "Natural Law, Law of Nations, and Civil Law" at the beginning of the work. Not every title of Justinian receives its individual treatment, but many particular paragraphs do. This method of proceeding means that parts of French law that had no analogue at Rome, such as marital property regimes, are neglected.

Of more interest are the works that break away from the strict order of Justinian. Pride of place should be given to the two-volume *Institution au droit François* of Gabriel Argou, another advocate before the Parlement of Paris. It was first published in Paris in 1692, and the last edition, the eleventh, appeared two years before the Revolution. The posthumous editions contain in the "Notice" a flattering comparison between this institutes and previous ones, maintaining that those of Coquille and Antoyne Loysel contain only customary law, whereas the present work treats both the customary and the written Roman law.

11. See G. Beyer, *Delineatio iuris Germanici,* (1718) 3.4.15.

12. See e.g. F. de Boutaric, *Les institutes de l'empereur Justinien conférées avec le droit françois,* published posthumously in 1738 at Toulouse, where the author had been professor of French law; and Claude Serres, *Les institutions du droit françois suivant l'ordre de celles de Justinien* (Paris, 1753), whose author had been professor of French law at the University of Montpellier.

The work is divided into four books, with a preliminary title explaining that French law has two parts, public law and the law of individuals, only the second of which shall be covered. The first book is on the civil condition of persons, and full weight is given to topics that had no exact parallel in Roman law. Thus, the first chapter deals with the serfs de main-morte, and the second is "De la noblesse." Book 2 concerns things, hereditary rights, gifts, wills, and intestate succession. Book 3 is obligations; after a first chapter on obligations in general come marriage, the marriage contract, community of property (in several chapters), dowry, the individual contracts, crimes, and penalties. But since this is a work on private law, the chapters on crimes and penalties are concerned with the obligations between individuals, not the public offense: dealt with above all are adultery, fraudulent bankruptcy, and the production of false evidence in a civil suit. Book 4 is accessory obligations and the consequences of obligations. The four books are not of the same size, book 2 being fully four times the length of book 1. And there is no preliminary treatment of justice and law, or of the distinction between natural law, law of nations, and civil law.

The *Institution* of Argou is similar in arrangement to Napoleon's *Code civil.* Scholars frequently claim that the codes of the eighteenth century are a product of the spirit of rationalism influenced by doctrines of natural law. In at least one sense the claim is accurate, but in view of the absence from Napoleon's *Code civil*—and from Argou's *Institution*—of a specific treatment of justice and of natural law, and in view of the similarity between the arrangement of the *Code* and of institutional writings, the onus of proof should be on those who maintain that natural law ideas had a predominant influence. It is not enough to claim that the idea of a short, systematic, authoritative account of the law itself derives from natural law. The impetus for that derives directly from the study of Justinian's *Institutes.*[13]

Outside France, indeed in Holland, one of the earliest such institutes, and one that greatly derives from Justinian, is also the most famous. Grotius' *Inleidinge tot de Hollandsche rechtsgeleerdheid,* though first published in 1631, was written while the author was imprisoned in the castle of Loevestein between 1619 and 1621. The work excludes a specific treatment of procedure, but otherwise the dependence on Justinian is marked. There are differences of arrangement, most of which may count as improvements. There are three books, but book 1 is only about

13. In addition to institutes there were treatises on French law, of which the best remembered are those of Pothier.

one-fourth of the length of the other two. The books are divided into chapters. Book 1 has fifteen chapters, of which the first is "Of Jurisprudence and Justice," the second "Of Different Kinds of Laws and their Working," and the rest deal with the law of persons. Book 2 is real rights: things, acquisition of ownership, testate and intestate succession, and real rights. Book 3 is personal rights: obligations in general, donation, the individual contracts, delicts, the extinction of obligation. By and large, the amount of detail corresponds to that of Justinian's *Institutes.* In distinction to Justinian's *Institutes,* however, the *Inleidinge* contains topics that are conventionally regarded as part of commercial law in civil law countries. Other Dutch works follow the model of Grotius, though the treatment of such topics is briefer than of others.

Grotius' impetus to the work was not quite that which drove Coquille. Although the Netherlands, like France, had different legal systems operating in different places, Grotius is concerned only with the law of the province of Holland with West Friesland. No attempt is made to harmonize or even describe the law of all the provinces, though there are frequent references to natural law, Roman law, and Germanic law.

Subsequent Dutch works of a similar character are Simon van Leeuwen, *Paratitula juris novissimi, dat is, een kort begrip van het Rooms-Hollandts-reght* (1652), and his more important *Het Roomsch Hollandsch recht* (1664); Ulric Huber, *Heedendaegse rechtsgeleertheyt* (1686); and Johannes van der Linden, *Rechtsgeleerd practicaal en koopmans handbook, ten dienste van regters, praktizijns, kooplieden, en allen die een algemeen overzich van rechtskennis verlangen* (1806).

Van Leeuwen, *Het Roomsch Hollandsch recht,* is in five books. Book 1, after introducing material on law in general and on the Reception and the constitution of Holland, deals with persons; book 2 is on property; book 3 on succession, testate, and intestate; book 4 on obligations, including crimes that appear in the position reserved for delict in Justinian, followed by "Obligations from Causes Similar to Crime," and then by a chapter on the extinction of obligations; and book 5 is procedure. The arrangement is thus particularly close to Justinian.

The work of Huber is in six books, of which the first three closely follow Justinian's *Institutes,* apart from actions and crimes. Book 4 is "Of the State and the Officers of Justice," book 5 is on procedure, and book 6 is on crimes. The rational position for the first half of book 4 would be at the beginning of the entire work; its absence from there can be attributed only to the power of the established institutional tradition.

Van der Linden's work is in three books, of which the second, on crime, and the third, on actions, are very short. This treatise is of particular importance because by the first appendix to the Grondwet, the "Constitution" of September 19, 1859, it was given the status of official law book of the South African Republic. When a matter was not dealt with, or only with insufficient clarity, recourse was to be had to Van Leeuwen, *Het Roomsch Hollandsch recht,* or Grotius, *Inleidinge,* as subsidiary authorities.

The first major, reasonably systematic account of Austrian law is in the series of tractates by Bernhard Walther (1516–1584), which are together known as the *Aurei iuris austriaci tractatus.*[14] These have not the institutional form and do not comprehend the whole of private law but concentrate on those parts that are most based on custom. More to the purpose is Johann Weingärtler, *Con- et discordantia iuris consuetudinarii Austriaci supra Anasum cum iure communi, in quattuor institutionum libris remonstrata,* first published in 1674.[15]

The fashion for institutes of local law spread through Europe, even into countries that even now, cannot boast of a modern codification, such as Scotland and Scandinavia.[16] Thus, the earliest example from Scotland is Lord Stair's *Institutions of the Law of Scotland,* written in the early 1660s and first published, considerably revised, in 1681, and then again with substantial modifications in 1693. The very short *Institutions of the Law of Scotland* of Sir George Mackenzie of 1684, closer in structure to Justinian's *Institutes,* determined the form of the main work of the following century, John Erskine's *Institute of the Law of Scotland,* (1773).

Jurists in the Italian States also produced institutes of local law, but none of outstanding significance or merit. Possibly this is not surprising, since the *Corpus juris* was regarded here more than anywhere else as very much the law of the land. Of such institutes, one example is Josephus Basta, *Institutiones iuris privati Neapolitani,* whose third edition was published in 1803. The work is in four books. Book 1 contains a little on sources of law but mainly concerns the law of persons; book 2 is things or rights *in re* and includes succession; book 3 is rights *in personam* or

14. Although well known to jurists, these tractates were first published in 1716 as an appendix to J. B. Suttinger, *Consuetudines austriacae.* See also *Bernhard Walther: Privatrechtliche Traktate aus dem 16. Jahrhundert,* ed. M. Rintelen (Leipzig, Hirzel, 1937).

15. J. G. Kees, *Commentarius ad Justiniani institutionum imperialium quattuor libros* (1726), is a commentary on Justinian with reference to Austrian practice, but the jurists cited in support are by no means only Austrian; German and Dutch writers are prominent. In much the same vein but proceeding from the Archibishopric of Salzburg is the slightly earlier J. B. Franz, *Jurisprudentia elementaris, seu prima elementa totius legitimae scientiae juxta ordinem institutionum imperialium* (1718).

16. See Luig, "Institutes."

obligations; and book 4 is actions. Although procedure is thus dealt with, criminal law is not. Basta does not restrict his citation of post-Roman jurists to those of Naples or of his own time, as indeed there seems to have been little law that was distinctively Neapolitan, and he ranges widely. Thus, in title 25 of book 3, on wrongful damage, he refers to the Dutchmen Gerhardus Noodt, Arnold Vinnius, Grotius, and Cornelis van Bynkenshoek; to François Hotman, Dionysius Gothofredus, and Jacobus Cuiacius of France; to the German Johann G. Heineccius; as well as to Chilffetius and Iacobus Constantinaeus. Basta is also interested in legal history, as in his discussion of the origins of letters of change in fourteenth century Lombardy, and has a number of references to the Normans in Southern Italy.

To a modern civilian, one of the most striking features of these local institutes is that they appear so thoroughly modern—in structure, in the subjects treated, and in general legal reasoning and argument. This is in sharp contrast to books such as Nicholas Everardi, *Loci argumentorum legales,* to the books of practicks written in Scotland in the days before Stair, and even to works such as Grotius, *De jure belli ac pacis.*

The majority of the local institutes vary among themselves and from Justinian's *Institutes* only slightly both in form and in contents. There are two main differences. First, there was a realization that Justinian's arrangement was not perfect, and many were the attempts at improvement. No one arrangement, however, prevailed, and in virtually all the influence of Justinian is paramount. Second, although Justinian's *Institutes* determined the outer limits of the contents, such as no mercantile law, no guild or similar rules, no administrative law, and no law of evidence, the Roman division of law into private or public was often observed more stringently than by Justinian, and what little of the latter is to be found in the Byzantine *Institutes* often has no counterpart in later local institutes.[17] Thus, public, that is criminal, actions, to which the last title in Justinian was devoted, are frequently omitted: or as in Argou's *Institution au droit françois,* the treatment of crimes is concerned with the obligations between individuals. Likewise, procedure is often left out of the work.

In the case of books so pregnant with consequences as are these local institutes, it is not enough to show that they are the direct descendants of Justinian's *Institutes.* One must also explain why they flourished when and where they did. They have points in common with the natural law movement of the seventeenth and eighteenth centuries. They are, to begin

17. *J.*1.1.4.

with, largely contemporaneous. Second, the same jurists are sometimes leaders both in promoting local law and in developing doctrines of natural law. The great Grotius, for instance, is usually regarded as one of the founders of natural law. One of the most famous of all natural lawyers, Christianus Thomasius (1655–1728), also wrote a short history of Roman and German law which was widely appreciated.[18] Natural law ideas inform much of the arrangement of Stair's *Institutes;* although he seems never to have received formal legal training, he had been a regent in the University of Glasgow, where he taught logic, morals, politics, and mathematics. Third, few local institutes are free from references to natural law, in which they often are doing no more than echoing Justinian's *Institutes.*

Nonetheless, by no means can natural law be regarded as the intellectual spring of works on local law. This is shown most evidently by the difference in structure between books on natural law and local institutes, coupled with the relationship between the latter and Justinian's *Institutes.* More important, the basic notion of seventeenth century natural law is out of harmony with the very emphasis inherent in works of local law. For the natural lawyer, law should derive from reason; the basic rules once thus established should lead to a working out of much of the detail, though it is accepted that at times more than one rule may be equally satisfactory. In contrast, local institutes, however much they declare that justice and the basic principles of law are everywhere the same, nonetheless emphasize the particularity of the rules found within a specific territory, many of them even containing praise for the high quality of the law with which they deal. Thus, in the dedication to the first edition, Stair writes: "And as everywhere the most pregnant and active spirits apply themselves to the study and practice of law, so those that applied themselves to that profession amongst us, have given great evidence of sharp and piercing spirits, with much readiness of conception and dexterity of expression; which are necessary qualifications both of the bench and bar, whereby the law of this kingdom hath attained to so great perfection, that it may, without arrogance, be compared with the laws of any of our neighbouring nations."

Surprisingly perhaps, the immediate intellectual *causa causans* of local institutes is legal humanism. The main aim of legal humanism is fundamentally the same as that of humanism in general: to understand the classical world as well as possible. To this end, satisfactory editions of

18. *Delineatio historiae juris Romani et Germanici,* published at Leipzig in 1704 along with François Hotman's *Antitribonianus.*

the texts had to be prepared, faulty emendations discarded, and subsequent barbarous interpretations recognized and rejected. Naturally in the case of law, attention centered on Rome, not on Greece. The first task, apart from establishing the text, was to free the Roman sources from the interpretation, whether for practice or not, of the glossators and postglossators. Among the humanists, Bartolus and his followers were thus regarded with contempt. In the sixteenth century France became the center of legal humanism, and the *mos gallicus,* the new French approach, is contrasted with the old *mos italicus.* But it was early apparent that it was not enough to discard the accretion of later interpretation. The *Corpus juris* had been put together by the Byzantine Emperor Justinian and his helpers, but what the humanists rather wanted to discover was the Roman law, free from all later accretions, including those of Byzantium.

The most distinguished of the legal humanists was Jacques Cujas (1522–1590), professor first at Cahors but above all at Bourges. Among the earliest of his works are his notes on the *Pauli sententiae,* one of the very few pre-Justinianian Roman law books known at the time. He also edited with a commentary another such work, the *Ulpiani tituli,* likewise the *Consultatio veteris cuiusdam iurisconsulti.* Of much greater importance are his commentaries on the works of the great individual Roman jurists Paul, Neratius, Marcellus, Ulpian (only the *Responsa*), Modestinus, Cervidius Scaevola, Julian, Africanus, and above all, Papinian.

But the one work that best illustrates the connection between legal humanism and local institutes is the short *Antitribonianus* of another French jurist, François Hotman (1524–1590). The book was apparently written in 1567 but was first published in French after his death, in 1603, and the first Latin version appeared in 1647. It was republished many times.

Hotman begins with a declaration of the supreme importance of law and a statement that a part of the French youth are seriously engaged in the study of Justinian's law. "But if I draw a big distinction between the civil law of the Romans and the books of the Emperor Justinian, I do not think I am saying something remote from the truth." Hotman's procedure is, first, to proceed as if that method of legal study was the best regulated in the world and the books of Justinian were made in all perfection, and second, to investigate the quality of these books and their effects. He claims that at all times wise men have accepted that the laws of a country must be fitted to the state and form of the commonwealth, not the commonwealth to the laws. Among his illustrations is Rome, where as soon as kings were destroyed and the republic established, all effort for one hundred and fifty years was on making new laws fit for the democracy.

He then argues that the state of France is so different from Rome that nothing for France can be learned from Roman public law. Moreover, Roman public law of the republic and high empire cannot really be known from the *Corpus juris*.

Chapters 4–9 are devoted to showing how far Roman private law also differed from that of France. Hotman compares Roman and French legal education in chapter 10 but also draws more general conclusions. Thus, "And if one must speak of the civil law of the Romans, I will say further that it was never made or composed to serve as equity or natural reason, suitable to every nation without distinction, but only by a particular prerogative expressly invented to support Roman citizens, and in a higher degree and dignity than the other inhabitants of Italy." Again, "These two points have been sufficiently recognized; first that it is only very mistakenly that one calls the study of the books of Justinian the study of Roman law, since only a twentieth part has remained for us; second, that of the little which has survived to us, not even a tenth part can be used and put into practice in our France."

From chapter 11 onward Hotman deals with his second principal point, namely the quality of the *Corpus juris*. He notes the numerous disputes as to the law among the followers of the two Roman schools, Sabinian and Proculian, and implies that rescripts of notorious emperors such as Helagabalus, Commodus, Caracalla, and Diocletian would not be noteworthy for their equity. He stresses the iniquity of Justinian's chief minister, Tribonian, who according to Suidas despised God and all religions, especially the Christian, was so avaricious that he sold law and justice, and for money changed the tenor of the laws, and who according to Procopius did not let a single day pass without changing the law for the profit of an individual. Justinian, Hotman avers, was regarded as no better. Chapter 12 is devoted to a discussion of some peculiarities in the work of Tribonian. Having completed his work, for example, Tribonian suppressed and abolished all the old laws, the praetorian Edict, and the decrees of the Senate. While vaunting that he had left the expositions of the jurists, Tribonian actually suppressed the works of those great jurists who were truly Roman, such as the Catos and the Mucii, Manilius, Caecilius, and Servius Sulpicius, but retained the works of Greeks, Syrians, and Africans like Africanus, Tryphoninus, Modestinus, Javolenus, and Ulpian. Tribonian's work is composed of broken extracts, useless and out of context, and he has not kept to the original order, not even of statutes. Many contradictions remain, as well as many interpolations of Tribonian himself and many repetitions. Formalities of Roman law that had been abolished nonetheless appear throughout the work. Thus runs Hotman's criticism of Tribonian. The rest of Hotman's book then concerns the subsequent history of the *Corpus juris,* with chapter 18, the final one, expressing the hope of reform.

Even apart from Hotman's plea for a reformed attitude to law, the message of legal humanism for local law is plain. Roman law was not intended to be eternal or to serve as natural reason but was created for a particular people at a particular time: nor was it ever perfect for its purpose. Moreover, Justinian's law books do not really give Roman law, and they were the work of men famous for their iniquity. Respect for classical antiquity should therefore not lead to admiration of the *Corpus juris.* But if the *Corpus juris* does not give Roman law, if Roman law itself was never perfection and was intended only for a particular people and place and is no longer much in use, and if, as Hotman insists, good law is of great value, it follows that encouragement should be given to the study and improvement of law adapted to local conditions. Thus, legal humanism leads, *inter alia,* to the intellectual respectability of local law and its study. It is perhaps not entirely fortuitous that, on the one hand, France was the main center of legal humanism, followed in the seventeenth century by the Netherlands largely as a result of the flight there of eminent French Huguenot legal scholars, notably Hugo Donellus, and that, on the other hand, both these lands were prominent in the production of local institutes.[19] Institutes of local law are an unexpected by-product of legal humanism. Hence one can account for the time at which they became common.

On the relation between legal humanism and local institutes, Germany presents for the seventeenth century rather an exception, but an illuminating one. The Holy Roman Empire had accepted Justinian's *Corpus juris* as a whole as the law of the land, but as subsidiary law, in what is known as the "theoretical Reception," and had also accepted as primary law various and numerous individual principles and institutions of Roman law as transmitted through Italian scholarship and judicial practice, in what is known as the "practical Reception." The practical Reception was particularly strong in Germany. Side-by-side with this Roman law existed much surviving old German law which, however, lacked scientific treatment. This German law was regarded as "legal usage that had crept in," as divergences from the Roman law, and hence to be inter-

19. See e.g. Wieacker, *Privatrechtsgeschichte,* pp. 168f; R. Feenstra and C. J. D. Waal, *Seventeenth Century Leyden Law Professors* (Amsterdam, Oxford, North-Holland, 1975), p. 16f.

preted narrowly.[20] In this situation it was difficult for legal humanism to have much immediate impact or for institutes of local law to emerge.

Not that there was a shortage of legal humanists. Indeed, Udalricus Zazius (1461–1535), who became a professor in Freiburg-in-Breisgau in 1503, is widely regarded as one of the earliest and greatest of their number. Much more than the Dutch universities, the German Protestant faculties attracted the Huguenots: Franciscus Balduinus to Heidelberg from 1556 to 1561; Hotman to Strassburg from 1556 to 1559 (later to Switzerland); Hugo Donellus to Heidelberg in 1573, and to Altdorf in 1588. But as Franz Wieacker observes, this immigration by and large had no intellectual consequences.[21] Nor is this surprising. The great success of the practical Reception meant that what a German lawyer wanted for practice was a thorough grounding in the legal rules of both the *Corpus juris* and later developments as well as an understanding of the modes of legal argument developed by the glossators and later commentators. There would always be many professors willing to give this training in the *mos italicus* who would be skeptical of the value of a more academic legal training.

Nonetheless, the very calling of the French humanists to the German universities indicates a recognition that not all was well with the teaching of the *mos italicus.* The prolixity of the old method meant that only a few passages of the *Institutes* or *Digest* were commented on in a year, and that after five or six years of study the student had only a fragmentary knowledge. Moreover, the passages selected for study were not necessarily the most useful for practice. Consequently many Germans had already gone to France to study law, and in Germany itself unofficial courses of teaching developed.[22] From the beginning of the seventeenth century there were signs of a new movement toward freeing the universities from the *mos italicus,* but a movement that was essentially practical in its orientation. The aims of this movement were to give a coherent account of individual legal institutions rather than explicating only particular texts, and to concentrate on the *usus modernus pandectarum,* the modern understanding of the Roman law, getting away from the difficult and often outdated apparatus of the *Gloss.* A leader here was the University of Heidelberg, whose reform statute dates from 1604 under the influence of the French jurist Dionysius Gothofredus the Older, who moved there in the

20. Hans Thieme, s.v. Deutsches Privatrecht, in *Handwörterbuch zur deutschen Rechtsgeschichte* ed. A. Etler and E. Kaufmann (Berlin, Schmidt, 1964), I, 702ff.

21. *Privatrechtsgeschichte,* p. 168.

22. See e.g. *General Survey,* pp. 393ff. See also Koschaker, *Europa,* pp. 105ff.

same year.[23] According to the Strasbourg laws of 1634, the first professor of the Pandects should read "the materials which are most useful and in daily service," take account above all of the most recent law, and fit the texts "as much as possible to the use of the present century" so that the hearer learns "what is especially contained in each title and is particularly to be noticed." The lectures on the *Code* are expressly stated to be on the subject of procedure and feudal law. As was the case in other countries, university teaching concentrated on Roman law and, to a lesser extent, on canon law. The first university lectures on German private law were given in 1699 to 1701 by Christian Thomasius in Halle.[24] He was followed in 1707 in Wittenberg by Georg Beyer, one of his pupils.

The position was complicated by the existence inside Germany of a great many states—some large, some merely cities—of various types—princedoms, dukedoms, merchant oligarchies—and of differing religious persuasions—Catholic, Lutheran, Calvinist. Some of the old German private law applied throughout the Empire, some only in particular areas. Legislation might be imperial, or it might be for only one territory or city. Inevitably changes of various kinds would occur at different speeds in the states. For instance, early reform of the law syllabus in universities was particularly noticeable in southwest Germany.

Law books were produced in a bewildering array of types.[25] They ranged from straight commentaries on the *Institutes* or *Digest* to monographs, to commentaries on the law of a particular territory, such as the one for the city of Lübeck by David Mevius or that of Benedict Carpzov for Saxony.[26] Carpzov's work sets out a Saxon constitution with facing translation into Latin, followed by a commentary in the form of the numerous definitions relating to the mixture of Roman and Saxon law in force that can be deduced from the constitution.

To come now to institutes of local law, editions of Justinian's *Institutes* with a commentary concentrating on the *usus modernus* hardly qualify, for they are descendants of the glossed *Institutes.* Nor do com-

23. See e.g. Wieacker, *Privatrechtsgeschichte,* pp. 208ff.

24. See K. Luig, "Die Anfänge der Wissenschaft vom deutschen Privatrecht," *Ius Commune* 1 (1967): 203f.

25. See e.g. A. Söllner, in Coing, *Handbuch* 2.i, pp. 501ff.

26. Mevius, *Commentarius in ius Lubecense* (Leipzig, 1642/43), which contains numerous references to both the *Corpus juris* and later commentators; Carpzov, *Definitiones forenses seu iurisprudentia forensis Romano-Saxonica ad constitutiones Saxonicas* (Frankfurt-am-Oder, 1638; frequently republished until 1721). A very different work for Silesia is *Jus Silesiacum secundum usum modernum illustratum* (1736), which is a collection of dissertations.

mentaries devoted to the *usus modernus* qualify, for they are not designed for a particular locality and pay insufficient attention to German private law. But there were a few real institutes of local law. Sebastian Khraisser, *Institutiones iuris Romano-Bavarici electoralis* (1644), is one, for after a discussion of each title of Justinian's *Institutes* with references to much later jurists it usually includes a very brief treatment of the particular law of Bavaria. Another example is Samuel Stryk, *De iure Lubecensi ad methodum institutionum* (1674), for the city of Lübeck. Nonetheless such local institutes were relatively uncommon.

The most important institute is Georg Adam Struve, *Jurisprudentia Romano-Germanica forensis* (1670). It does not quite live up to its title, since it sets out much of the law in Justinian's *Institutes* that was no longer in use. But Struve does attempt to give German private law as well as the *usus modernus* (contemporary usage), with Germanic institutions such as *unio prolium* (1.11.6) and, above all, procedure. And the scope of the work is not restricted to one or a few German states. The work has the full institutional form, appearing in four books. Book 1 deals with law and justice, then with persons; book 2 is on the law of things, including succession both testate and intestate; book 3 concerns obligations; and book 4 is on procedure. Other such works are J. Philippus, *Usus practicus institutionum Justinianearum* (1665); J. F. Rhetius, *Meditationes academicae ad institutiones juris civilis Justinianeas praxi forensi et usui Imperii Romano-Germanici accommodatae* (1688); and the very different B. C. C. Hofacker, *Principia iuris civilis Romano-Germanici* (1788, volume two published posthumously in 1794).

Though not quite an institute of local law, Johann Schilter, *Institutiones juris ex principiis juris naturae, gentium & civilis, tum Romani, tum Germanici, ad usum fori hodierni accommodatae* (1685), gives the text of Justinian's *Institutes* with a commentary on it, drawn from the contemporary law of nature, international law, and civil law, the last term being used here both of modern Roman law and of German law. The nature of the work as a commentary on the text of Justinian inevitably affects the balance and prevents Schilter from giving a full, systematic picture of the existing law. A surprising amount of German law can be included, such as on hunting, but some topics, such as the various grades of free Germans, are ignored.[27]

But the most striking development for Germany is of institutes of German private law which exclude the treatment of Roman law and its contributions to the *usus modernus*.[28] An essential first step was a work

27. 11.1.16ff.

28. See also Luig, "Anfänge," pp. 195ff.

such as Hermann Conring, *De origine juris Germanici* (1643), which was the first pragmatic history of the Reception and refuted the "Lotharian legend." Wieacker finds its date significant: the collapse in the Thirty Years' War of the idea of a universal empire brought with it the fall of another idea, that of a universal law, to which Roman law had been indebted for its metaphysical legitimation.[29] This is not a full explanation of the emergence of a work such as Conring's since the very concept of German private law itself carries with it the notion that the local laws of the different German states contained principles which were originally German and once at least were valid everywhere in German territories.[30] The idea of a universal Germany is still there, even if in an attenuated form, with the authority of the emperor greatly reduced, and with no belief that the Holy Roman Empire is a continuance of the ancient Roman Empire. Some credit, in fact, must again be given to the humanists for making patent that much of the law in force was not to be found in the *Corpus juris,* that some living law was independent even of subsequent interpretation, and above all that unqualified esteem of the classical world could not be extended to the *Corpus juris* as, in large part, a Byzantine production. In Germany, too, legal humanism cleared the way for the intellectual respectability of local law. Johann Schilter (1632–1705), himself a humanist—as witness his book on the Roman jurist *Herennius Modestinus* (1687) and his *Praxis artis analyticae in jurisprudentiam,* published with *Diatribe logica de syllogismis ex hypothesi, secundum Aristotelem* (1678)—and a writer on Roman, feudal, and German law alike, gave impetus to the study of German private law by his doctrine that Germany possessed two common laws, a German that was native, and a Roman which was foreign.[31]

The earliest institute of German private law seems to be the *Delineatio juris Germanici* of Georg Beyer (1665–1714), which was first published in 1718, four years after his death. This sets out to be a systematic account of general German private law, although local rules of, say, Saxony or Brandenburg are at times noticed. Rules of Roman law as received in Germany are generally omitted. Nor is there much sign of the *Corpus juris* being acceptable as authority. Where a rule is the same in German law as in Roman law, the authorities adduced relate only to the German. At times the work expressly remarks that the *Corpus juris* has *wrongly*

29. *Privatrechtsgeschichte,* p. 206.

30. See e.g. Luig, "Institutes," p. 207.

31. See *Institutiones juris ex principiis juris naturae, gentium et civilis, tum Romani, tum Germanici, ad usum fori hodierni accommodatae* (1685), 1.2.17 (on *J*.1.2.10). The title of the work is itself of prime significance.

been adduced as the source of a rule, or that the rule accepted differs from that of the *Corpus juris.*[32] Nonetheless what is striking is the overall influence of Justinian's *Institutes* once again on the form of the entire work. Book 1 is the law of persons; book 2 is real rights, including succession; and book 3 is obligations.[33] A specific treatment of actions is excluded, as often happens. At least some editions, such as that edited by C. G. Hoffman and published in Leipzig in 1740, also contain introductory material on matters such as the sources and origins of German law and the utility of university lectures on German law. It is not a coincidence that the author of the earliest institutes of German law was almost the first person to lecture on German law. Beyer was also skilled in Roman law. In 1706 he became professor of the *Institutes,* namely of Justinian, at Wittenberg and in 1713 was elected to the third professorship, that is, of the *Digestum vetus.* The fame of the *Delineatio juris Germanici* has obscured his other works, but his *Delineatio juris civilis secundum institutiones et pandectas atque feudalis ad fundamenta sua revocati et ad seculi usum accommodati* (first published in 1704) was very popular. For instance, a fifth edition appeared in 1738. The title is indicative of the scope: "Delineation of the civil law according to the *Institutes* and *Digest* and of feudal law, restored to their basis and adapted to the use of this century." Beyer also produced a *Delineatio* of criminal law, one of feudal law, and one of divine law.

A much larger work is J. G. Heineccius, *Elementa juris Germanici tum veteris tum hodierni* (1735/36). As the title suggests, this is also a historical account. There are references to Tacitus writing on the ancient Germans, and much is made of the laws of the Visigoths and others. The *Elementa* are divided into three books: book 1 deals with persons; book 2, on the law of things, is subdivided into parts, of which the first deals with property, succession (intestate and testate), and contractual obligations, and the second with delicts and crimes; book 3 treats the law of actions. Thus, the arrangement is very much that of Justinian's *Institutes,* but the contents are determinedly Germanic. References to the *Corpus juris* do exist, but they are relatively rare and usually have the purpose of pointing a contrast.[34] A similar work in its emphasis on legal history is the slightly earlier *Systema jurisprudentiae civilis Germanicae antiquae* (1733) of J. F. Polac. This is in four books which betray the influence of Justinian's *Institutes.* Book 1 is persons; book 2 things, including con-

32. See e.g. 1.25.8, 2.5.25ff, 2.10.12, 3.1, 3.2.19, 32ff, 3.4.15ff.
33. See Luig, "Institutes," p. 210.
34. See e.g. 2.5.131 and 135.

tracts; book 3 delicts; and book 4 procedure. J. S. Pütter, *Elementa juris Germanici privati hodierni* (1748), contains long prolegomena on German law and its history, which are a common feature of such works, then a first part called "Theoretical First Part of German Law", which has two main subdivisions, persons and property, then a second part on procedure. The treatment of procedure is brief, but the division into theoretical law and procedure was to play an important role among the Pandectists, who taught the *Digest* interpreted for nineteenth century needs, and most notably for Karl Salomon Zachariae. J. H. C. von Selchow, *Institutiones jurisprudentiae Germanicae* (1757, then from 1762 republished as *Elementa juris Germanici hodierni*), also deals with procedure, again very briefly, in book 5. The same is true of J. F. Runde, *Grundsätze des allgemeinen deutschen Privatrechts* (1791), though his arrangement is rather different.

The question must be put: Why should there appear in Germany institutes of local law which as far as possible exclude treatment of rules deriving from Roman law? What was the practical, educational, or emotional need? There cannot have been a direct practical need, since what was wanted for practice was a work that gave living private law in its entirety, modern Roman law and German rules alike. This need was precisely filled by Struve, *Jurisprudentia Romano-Germanica;* hence its numerous editions until 1771 and its enormous popularity. It was said in the eighteenth century that many a lawyer needed only the "little Struve" for his practice.[35] In 1737, G. Schaumburg published at Jena his notes on Struve: *Annotationes ad. B. Georg Ad. Struvii iurisprudentiam Romano-Germanicam forensem.* This was intended for students for whom Struve was not entirely, in the author's opinion, a complete diet. Yet as he says in the preface: "You love Struve, you choose him as your guide in the study of civil wisdom, you move every stone to turn Struve's *Jurisprudentia* into juice and blood. And not without good reason."

The need, then, for books excluding Roman law was more emotional, rooted in the tradition of the German educational system. Even after the recognition of the existence of indigenous German private law, the universities continued to teach only Roman law, the *usus modernus,* and canon law. Books on living law would reflect the university bias, concentrate on *usus modernus,* and hence play down the role of German law. The natural reaction, indeed the simplest way to emphasize the continuing importance of German law, was the production of systematic treatises of German law, ignoring the contribution of Roman law. That

35. Wieacker, *Privatrechtsgeschichte,* p. 219n19.

such treatises appeared in Germany and not, for example, in France, Holland, or Scotland is to be attributed to the very strength of the Reception in Germany. The authority of Roman law there was so high that a special effort was needed to make heard the voice of indigenous law.

Finally, institutes of local law were produced in lands with a derived civil law system. Insofar as they are true institutes of derived local law, they cite as authority not so much the *Corpus juris* as the sources of the territory from which they derive. Again they may contain discussion on legal topics that appear in Justinian's *Institutes* but had disappeared from western Europe. Slavery is the obvious example.

The most successful was the *Instituciones de derecho real de Castilla y de Indias,* by Jose Maria Alvarez, a native of what became the Central-American Republic. Alvarez's chair at the University of Guatemala was for the "Institutes of Justinian". The book was first published in Guatemala in 1818–1820; a second edition appeared in Mexico in 1826; and there were numerous reprintings, as in New York in 1827, Havana in 1834 and 1841, and Guatemala in 1854. The author died in 1820. With the various editions the notes increased, and the later printings have a considerable citation of authority. The writer states in the prologue that he has followed the order of the Roman *Institutes,* although he could have adopted another better one, and that he has tried to adapt himself to the definitions, principles, and conclusions of the *Recitationes* of Heineccius (1681–1741). In addition to that famous scholar, another expert modern commentator of Justinian's *Institutes* who is frequently cited is the Dutchman Vinnius (1588–1657). A few other jurists are occasionally cited, but by far the greatest number of references are to Spanish laws or legal collections, such as *Las siete partidas, Nueva recopilacíon de Castilla, Novissima recopilacíon,* and *Recopilacíon de Indias,* as well as subsequent statutes pertaining to Central America. There are also references to canon law, but none to Justinian's *Corpus juris.*

VII
The Law of Reason

THE LEGAL tradition can be substantially affected by a general intellectual trend, such as humanism. Since law exists in the world of affairs as well as in the realm of ideas, the intellectual trend may have very practical, possibly unexpected, effects on the growth of the law. Thus, legal humanism largely brought about the intellectual and academic respectability of contemporary local law and was the prime cause of the widespread emergence at that time of institutes of local law, though the appearance of such institutes was, at some period or other, virtually inevitable.

Civil law systems are particularly open to philosophical influence, relative to common law systems. The reason is twofold. To begin with, Justinian's *Institutes,* backed by the remainder of the *Corpus juris,* and local institutes provide a simple account of the law and enable philosophers to feel that they know the law and what it is about, and that they can discuss it comfortably. Leibnitz is the obvious example. But also individual parts of Hegel's *Naturrecht und Staatswissenschaft in Grundrisse* show his knowledge of Roman law concepts, and the Introduction declares Hegel's familiarity with works such as J. G. Heineccius; *Antiquitatum Romanorum jurisprudentiam illustrantium syntagma,* and Gustav Hugo, *Lehrbuch der Geschichte des römischen Rechts.* In addition, the institutes with their obvious system are appealing to philosophers, not least because the clear defects in the system tempt them to offer improvements. In contrast, the common law with its mass of cases and its lack of system or theory, especially until the nineteenth century, is largely impenetrable to anyone not trained specifically in the common law.[1] Of the few great English philosophers who were interested in law, among whom perhaps Thomas Hobbes deserves pride of place, Bacon was himself a lawyer, and Bentham was implacably hostile to the common law.

Second, doctrinal advances in civil law systems, particularly before codification, lie largely in the hands of academics, whereas in common law countries they lie largely in the hands of judges. In general, one would expect university professors to be more interested in the overall systematic, philosophical, and structural side of law than are judges chosen mainly from among successful practitioners. Moreover, in their daily living, academics are in more contact with professional philosophers. Above all, however, the nature of the available source of legal development affects the degree of philosophical penetration, and here the academic treatise is ideal for setting out law based on a philosophical system. In contrast, a judge has to decide the case before him, one case at a time. However deeply held and carefully considered his philosophical views may be, he cannot usually set out the whole law in terms of them.

Thus, to speak broadly, the civil law is rather open to philosophical influence. Over a period of centuries natural law is a perennial, if not always the predominant, theory of law. Natural law appears in many guises; as the law of God, the law of reason, the law of living in harmony with nature, and so on. But the various forms of the developed theory have in common that they provide an external standard by which existing territorial law can be evaluated. It is largely from this that they derive the immense strength of their emotional appeal. Above all, theories of natural law are intended to have a practical effect—to influence legal reform or to persuade to obedience or disobedience of the territorial law.

So far as post-Justinianian civil law is concerned, natural law is endemic. This is not the result of the quality of Roman juristic thinking on the subject, which in fact remained rather unsophisticated and not worthy of Cicero, far less of the Greek philosophers.[2] The Roman jurists were always far too much concerned with explicating the practical living law to give natural law much more than lip service. Few texts in the *Cor-*

1. Yet in the twentieth century English philosophers have sometimes displayed more interest in the common law. Linguistic philosophers and common lawyers have a joint interest in interpretation and the meaning of words. Those interested in the philosophy of action are often intrigued by the untoward acts and legal rules uncovered in the courts of law and unraveled by the judges.

2. See *de leg.* 1.17–37; 2.8–15; *de re pub.* 3.21, 32–34; *de harusp. resp.* 32; the pseudo-Platonic dialogue, *Minos;* Plato, *Crito;* Aristotle, *Nichomachaean Ethics,* book 5.

pus juris civilis even mention natural law, such as

> D.12.6.64 (Tryphoninus, *Disputations,* book 7). If a master paid the debt he owed a slave to him after he had freed him, then even if the former master had believed himself liable to some action he can nonetheless not recover, because he recognized a natural debt: for just as freedom is part of natural law and slavery was introduced by the law of nations (*ius gentium*) so the question of whether there is a debt or not a debt is, for the action called *condictio,* to be interpreted naturally.[3]

The term *ius gentium,* which appears here and in many other texts, seems best translated by "law of nations." The Romans normally used the term with regard to legal rules that they considered were found in all societies. Long after Roman times the term came to have the sense of "public international law." One of the few other texts mentioning natural law is:

> D. 50.17.206 (Pomponius, *Various Readings,* book 9). By the law of nature it is fair that no one can be made richer by the loss and injury to another.

But leverage was given to natural law to penetrate civil law by the prominent position of a short treatment of it at the beginning of both the *Institutes* and the *Digest.* Thus in the *Institutes:*

> 1.2.pr. Natural law is that which nature instills in all animals. For this law is not peculiar to humankind but is shared by all animals which are born on land or in the air or sea. From it derives that association of man and woman that we call marriage; so also the procreation and rearing of issue; for we see that animals also are imbued with experience of this law. 1. Civil law and the law of nations, however, are distinguished in this way. All peoples who are governed by laws and customs use law which is in part particular to themselves, in part common to all men: the law which each people has established for itself is particular to that state and is styled civil law as being peculiarly of that state: but what natural reason has established among all men is observed equally by all nations and is

3. Other texts are *J.*1.2pr, 11; 2.1pr, 1,11,18,19,37,40,41; *D.*1.8.2; 1.8.3; 9.2.50; 16.3.31pr; 23.2.14.2; 43.18.2; 44.7.59.

designated *ius gentium* or the law of nations, being that which all nations obey. Hence the Roman people observe partly their own particular law, partly that which is common to all peoples. Which is which, we shall explain whenever it is desirable to do so. 2. However, civil law derives its name from each individual state, for example, Athens: for one would commit no error in calling the laws of Solon and Draco the civil law of Athens. In like manner, the law observed by the Roman people is termed Roman civil law or the law of *Quirites,* being applicable to *Quirites*—the Romans being called *Quirites* after Quirinus. However, whenever we do not add the name of a state, we are talking of our own (i.e. Roman) law; in the same way that, when we speak of "the poet" without adding his name, the Greek will understand that it is the great Homer, while we know it is Vergil. The law of nations, on the other hand, is common to all humankind. For, through force of circumstances and human needs, peoples have developed certain measures for themselves: wars have arisen with subsequent captivity and slavery—which is contrary to natural law (for, by natural law, originally, all men were born free). From the law of nations also come virtually all the contracts, such as sale, hire, partnership, deposit, loan and countless others.[4]

And in the *Digest:*

1.1.1.3 (Ulpian, *Institutes,* book 1) Natural law is that which nature taught all animals: for that law is not particular to humankind, but is common to all animals that are born in the land or in the sea and to birds. Hence comes the union of male and female that we call marriage, hence the procreation and bringing up of children. For we see that the other animals, even the wild beasts, are marked by knowledge of this law. 4. The law of nations (*ius gentium*) is that which all peoples use. It is easy to understand that it falls short of natural law since the latter is common to all animals, the former only to men among themselves.

2. (Pomponius, *Manual*). As, for example, religion towards god; or that we obey our parents and country.

3. (Florentinus, *Institutes,* book one) Or that we repel violence and wrong; for it is by virtue of this law that whatever a person did for the protection of his body is judged to be lawfully done by him;

4. *Institutes,* trans. J. A. C. Thomas, p. 4.

> and since nature has created a kind of relationship among us, it follows that it is sinfully wrong for man to ambush man.

So far as substantive law is concerned, this discussion of natural law is not very meaningful. The usage is clearly at variance with the two texts of the *Digest* previously quoted, as indeed with others in both the *Digest* and *Institutes*. But these texts provide a starting point for later civilians. For example, one of the earliest glossators, Rogerius, of whom a gloss can be dated to 1158, writes in his *Questions on the Institutes*, 1.2.1:

> We come next to natural law, the law of nations and the civil law. It should be noted here that the term "natural" law is multifarious. What is common to all animals is called "natural" as if from animal nature, as in this title. Further, what is common only to all men is called "natural" law from human nature, in which sense the law of nations (*ius gentium*) is called natural. Thus we say natural law teaches us to revere God and worship him and to keep faith in a promise. Another sense of "natural" law is the fairest law (*ius equissimum*), by which meaning even civil law can be called natural law. In this sense it is by "natural" law that minors who have suffered loss are to be restored to their previous position, that is those who were deceived by fraud or error, as in D.2.14.1pr, D.4.4.1pr and J.2.1pr, etc.[5]

Some of the inspiration for Rogerius' treatment here of the *Institutes* clearly derives from the *Digest* texts 1.1.1., 1.1.2, and 1.1.3.[6]

In the texts of the *Corpus juris* there is an awareness that the rules of positive law, of the *ius gentium* or *ius civile*, may conflict with those of natural law, but no indication of any weight being attributed to the latter. Indeed, J.1.2.3 reports that slavery is contrary to natural law, but certainly slavery existed as part of the established law.[7] At most the Roman texts suggest that an existing rule could be made to appear more authoritative by a reference to natural law or that, where the law was not quite settled, an argument for a particular decision might be drawn from natural law.[8] This extremely limited role of natural law is in marked contrast to its power in the pseudo-Platonic dialogue *Minos* or in Christian

5. See Hermann Kantorowicz, *Studies in the Glossators of the Roman Law* (Cambridge, Cambridge University Press, 1938), pp. 271ff; cf. the *Glossa magna*.

6. Cf. Kantorowicz, *Glossators*, p. 134.

7. Cf. *D*.1.5.4.1.

8. *J*.2.1.1. etc; *D*.12.6.64.

philosophers and theologians such as Francisco Suárez and, above all, Thomas Aquinas.

At least a respectable role was bound to be played by natural law in the subsequent civil law tradition. The opening passages of the *Institutes* and *Digest* meant that there was a place for discussing the nature of natural law; the power of the churches, canon law, and the opinions of philosophers meant that natural law doctrines would be one important focus for law reform; legal variations as they occurred from place to place and from time to time meant that at least occasionally justifications would be drawn from natural law. That what natural law was was a question to which different writers could give different answers was something that would only marginally diminish the influence of the idea of natural law.

But in actual fact, natural law was mightily to expand its influence in the seventeenth and eighteenth centuries, to such an extent that it must be regarded as a vital factor, separate from the *Corpus juris,* in the modern civil law tradition. The problem is to explain how radically different doctrines, on topics such as acquisition of ownership, formation of contract, paternal power, and the notion of marriage, could come into the tradition of private law largely determined by the authority of the *Corpus Juris.* Such an explosion could scarcely occur through the medium of writings on Roman law or local law: the changes in law are too numerous, the authority of the law is too different, and the reforms are too drastic. Nor could many of the doctrines be taken over directly from canon law, though admittedly canon law played its part; the doctrine of the Roman Catholic Church was too often denied, and even where papal dogma was accepted, papal authority need not be.[9]

The sudden upsurge of importance of natural law for the civil law dates above all to the seventeenth century. No overall satisfactory explanation can be drawn from religious, political, or economic factors. One cannot associate the trend with any increase in the authority of the Catholic Church; on the contrary, the upswing occurs after the Reformation and is particularly noticeable in Protestant countries. But one also cannot attribute the swing to a reaction against the Catholic Church; in fact, the natural law doctrines at this time frequently owe much, whether acknowledged or not, to such Catholic scholastic theologians as Aquinas, Francisco de Victoria, and Suárez. Nor does a close examination of the doctrines reveal a general bias in favor of or against any particular form

9. See Introduction by J. L. Barton to his edition of *St. Germain's Doctor and Student* (London, Selden Society, 1974).

of government, whether monarchy, republic, or oligarchy. One could not expect any, since the doctrines frequently develop from centuries of discussion by many jurists living under different regimes. Some doctrines, particularly those relating to contract, could facilitate commerce, but this by no means applies to all; nor were all the doctrines favouring commerce developed at a time of commercial growth, nor were they necessarily accepted as the law of a particular territory at such a time.

Of more significance was, first, the decline in authority of the *Corpus juris* with the advent of legal humanism and the growing acceptance of the respectability of local law. Natural law at this time represents in part an attempt to find a new authority for law which would justify at least some of the practical changes from Roman law, especially those that had not yet occurred or been accepted but seemed desirable. Second, and more significant, the natural law of the period is one aspect of the general intellectual movement known as the Enlightenment. With cause, Franz Wieacker calls the natural law of this time "the law of reason."[10] This law of reason can be crudely characterized as the law that may rationally and logically be derived from an understanding of the needs of man recognized to be above all a social animal. But the law of reason is almost the earliest manifestation of the philosophical, as distinct from the scientific, Enlightenment. The law of reason cannot be dismissed as an offshoot of the Enlightenment. The law of reason, indeed, owes much to preceding philosophy, in particular to the late Scholasticism of above all Spanish theologians and canon lawyers. Among the most influential were Cajetan, Covarruvias, Lessius, Molina, and Soto.[11] The issue here is to explain how a secular law of reason, with such forebears, could arise and penetrate the civil law tradition.

The force and upsurge of natural law in the early seventeenth century is in part due to general philosophical trends, but only in part. The vital factor is the always unexpected presence of a human genius, in this case Hugo Grotius, who cites but may not have read all the late Scholastic writers just mentioned. The presence of a second, slightly later, and very different genius, Leibniz, was finally to ensure the incorporation of the law of reason into territorial, namely local positive law: particularly into Prussia in the *Allgemeines Landrecht für die Preussischen Staaten*.

Grotius was not the first jurist outside of the main Scholastic tradition who wrote on the law of nature. There are, for example, Johann Ol-

10. *Privatrechtsgeschichte*, p. 249.

11. See e.g. *La seconda scolastica nella formazione del diritto privato moderno*, ed. P. Grossi (Milan, Giuffrè, 1973).

dendorp (1486 ?–1567) and Johannes Althusius (1557–1638).[12] These two writers do not set up a system of natural law that is independent of divine revelation. For instance, in his *Eisagoge seu elementaria introductio ad studium iuris et aequitatis* (1539), Oldendorp, *inter alia,* investigates the question why law seems so obscure compared with other arts, and he seeks to define natural law, law of nations (*ius gentium*), and civil law. At the end of title two, which is dedicated to establishing the meaning of "natural law," he says that the formulas of the laws or natural awareness are to be found "in the divine tablets," by which formulation he means the Ten Commandments. In the *epilogus* he asks how one can know whether rules of the law of nations or of civil law have been rightly received; and he answers that one must have recourse to the Ten Commandments. Almost one-half of the book is dedicated to showing that the Ten Commandments, which are natural law, are very much in harmony with Roman law and, in particular, with the Twelve Tables, the Roman codification of the fifth century B.C.

It would have been no easy matter to insert much natural law into works devoted to Roman or territorial law, a view confirmed by Grotius' *Inleidinge tot de Hollandsche rechtsgeleertheyd.* This work makes the typical enlightenment reference to mathematics in connection with the different senses of justice[13] and says much about natural law—a discussion largely deriving from Scholasticism—in the preliminary chapter 2 of book 1, "On the Distinction and Operation of Laws." But thereafter, in the actual discussion of the law of Holland, natural law is scarcely more prominent than it is in Justinian's *Institutes.*[14] The idea of natural law is used largely as authority for an explanation of the existing law, not to urge reform. In some senses the most interesting text of the *Inleidinge* in this context is 2.5.2:

> To acquire ownership by consent of the former owner it appears to be enough by the law of nature that the former owner should manifest his will that the ownership should pass and that this should be accepted by the other as a surely acquired right; and, acceptance following thereon, no more seems to be required. But the civil law having more power over each person's property than the owner himself, seeking to prevent all unconsidered alienations and to save people from regrets, has decreed that the first owner must put the

12. See e.g. Wieacker, *Privatrechtsgeschichte,* pp. 283ff.
13. 1.1.11 referring to 1.1.9,10.
14. Cf. Grotius 2.3.2,3; 2.5.2,3; 3.1.15,19,21.

> second in actual possession; this is called delivery or transfer: therefore, mere agreement cannot now make anyone owner or secure his title: likewise, no property can be made inalienable by contract, though by last will it may be. The same civil law has also not thought it enough to limit alienation as described, but has further decreed that the delivery should proceed from some cause, whether based upon benevolence, as gift, or upon contract, as sale, exchange and the like: which cause is called the title to the thing.[15]

Here it is emphasized that natural law is different from civil law—which in this context is the law of Holland—and yet the law described here as the civil law was also in force at Rome; and Justinian's *Institutes* 2.1.40 specifically describe the Roman rules as existing at natural law. But significantly, Grotius does not seek to change the local law; rather he justifies it, or at least explains it. The passage of Justinian's *Institutes* almost encourages contradiction:

> At natural law, we also acquire things by delivery (*traditio*), for nothing is more consonant with natural equity than that the will of an owner wishing to transfer his thing to another should be ratified. Accordingly, of whatever kind a corporeal thing may be, it can be handed over and, if this be done by its owner, alienated.[16]

Thus, the justification for the statement that ownership is acquired by delivery says nothing to the point about physical delivery but argues purely from the will of the owner wishing to transfer his thing. Moreover, the corresponding passage of the *Digest,* D.41.1.9.3, attributes the rule to the *ius gentium,* not to *ius naturale.* The text of Grotius, then, does not seem to be a pointer to an invasion of the civil law tradition by natural law. Its importance in this context is mainly its lack of significance.

Furthermore, a direct line of influence does not exist between Grotius' views on natural law on the one hand and the political and economic conditions of the time and Grotius' involvement in them on the other. There is a temptation to make such a claim, but it must be resisted. This systematic account of natural law in a private law context is found in Grotius, *De iure belli ac pacis,* which was first published in 1625. Scholars accept that the work derives in large measure from his earlier

15. *Jurisprudence of Holland by Hugo Grotius,* trans. R. W. Lee (Oxford, Clarendon Press, 1926), I, 93ff.

16. *Institutes,* trans. Thomas, p. 72.

Commentarius de jure praedae, which actually was not published until 1868 but the writing of which was completed in 1605. And the *Commentarius* owes its being to a prize case of 1604 in which Grotius was involved. It has even been suggested that Grotius wrote the *Commentarius* at the direct instigation of the Dutch East India Company.[17] But it would be a mistake to claim that Grotius' systematic treatment of natural law in the area of private law—which is where an invasion of the civil law tradition by natural law occurs—owes much directly to Grotius' involvement in individual legal cases, to the economic expansion of the Dutch East India Company, and to the corresponding political interests. This systematic treatment occupies book 2 of the *De jure belli ac pacis,* and there is nothing akin to it in the *Commentarius.* For the *Commentarius* it would also have been irrelevant, and it does not even fit neatly within *De jure belli ac pacis.* The connection of book 2, which is about as long as the other two books together, with any theme of war and peace or with the law between states is extremely tenuous, to the extent that more than once the suggestion has been made that the work is composite and that Grotius put together two independent manuscripts of his, one from the *Commentarius,* the other on natural law.[18]

The quality and the success of *De jure belli ac pacis* are both outstanding. A century and three-quarters later Sir James Mackintosh claimed that the work of Grotius "is perhaps the most complete that the world has yet owed, at so early a stage in the progress of any science, to the genius and learning of one man."[19] By the year 1700 there were already twenty-six editions in Latin of *De jure belli ac pacis;* translations had appeared in Dutch by 1626, English by 1654, French by 1687, and German by 1707.[20] Not only were there numerous editions of this work with learned commentaries by scholars of the stature of Jean Barbeyrac, but there were also institutes of natural and international law of which the contents were expressly drawn from *De jure belli ac pacis.* The *Institutiones iuris naturalis gentium et publici* of the Dutchman J. Klenckius, which went into several editions in the second half of the seventeenth century, is an example. In 1661 a chair of the law of nature and of na-

17. See e.g. A. Nussbaum, *Concise History of the Law of Nations,* 2nd ed. (New York, Macmillan, 1954), p. 102; cf. J. B. Scott, in *De jure belli ac pacis,* Classics of International Law (Oxford, Clarendon Press, 1925), II, xx.

18. See Nussbaum, *Concise History,* pp. 107ff.

19. *A Discourse on the Study of the Law of Nature and Nations* (Edinburgh, Clark, 1835), pp. 13f (first published in 1799); quoted by Scott, in *De jure belli ac pacis,* II, xliii.

20. See J. ter Meulen and P. J. J. Diermanse, *Bibliographie des écrits imprimés de Hugo Grotius* (The Hague, Nijhoff, 1950), pp. 222ff.

tions was created at Heidelberg for Samuel Pufendorf specifically to comment on and elaborate the teachings of Grotius. The work had a multifaceted success, since the chair was in the philosophical, not the law, faculty. Grotius' book was, in fact, to establish a close and long-lived, but not otherwise immediately obvious, connection between international law, the law of nature, and legal philosophy. In 1707 the chair of public law and the law of nature and nations was founded at Edinburgh University; the professor was long responsible for teaching international law, though now the chair is considered to be for legal philosophy.[21] Even in present-day Germany there is still in many universities a close tie between the teaching of international law and of legal philosophy. It would seem that a work solely setting out natural law arguments for substantive private law should have had more difficulty in penetrating the civil law tradition because it would have appeared remote from legal reality. The success here of natural law is due to the overall success of *De jure belli ac pacis,* which would never have been so great had the work not been so important for international law.

Grotius sets out his general view of natural law in the prolegomena. Man is a very superior animal, one of whose characteristics is an impelling desire for society, not society of any sort but peaceful and organized society according to the measure of his intelligence. It is not a universal truth that every animal is impelled by nature to seek only its own good (§6). Man, moreover, alone among animals, is endowed with the faculty of knowing and of acting in accordance with general principles (§7). The maintenance of the social order which is consonant with human nature is the source of law: hence come the legal obligations to abstain from anything that is another's, to restore to another anything of his that one has plus any gain one has received from it, to fulfill promises, to make good a loss suffered through one's own fault, and hence also the inflicting of punishment in accordance with deserts (§8). A more extended meaning of the term "law" flows from the above; as man has the power of discrimination, to act contrary to this discrimination is to act contrary to the law of nature (§9). To the exercise of such discrimination belongs the rational allotment to each individual or social group of that which is properly theirs; such as preference at times to the more wise over the less wise, to a kinsman and not to a stranger, to a poor man not to a wealthy man (§10).

All the foregoing, claims Grotius, would have some validity even if it

21. At least in theory; the chair has at times been treated as a sinecure. For the development of chairs on the model of that for Pufendorf see Tarello, *Ideologie,* pp. 90f.

is conceded—which it cannot, without great wickedness—that there is no God, or that men's affairs are of no concern to Him. The opposite of this view, namely the understanding that God exists, has been implanted in man, partly by reason, partly by tradition, and is confirmed by many proofs. Thus, all people must all render obedience to God their creator (§11). The free will of God is thus another source of law (§12). Again, to obey pacts is part of the law of nature, and this source of law gives rise to bodies of municipal law, since those who have associated with a group have subjected themselves to a man or men (§15). The principles of natural law, being always the same, they can easily be systematized, whereas elements of positive law are outside systematic treatment since they often undergo change and are different in different places.[22]

This theoretical discussion of the nature of law is carried further by Grotius in the body of the work, particularly at 1.1.2–1.1.15. At 1.1.10, for example, Grotius claims that the law of nature is unchangeable even in the sense that it cannot be altered by God. And again, some things are in accordance with this law not in a proper sense but "by reduction"; that is, the law of nature is not contrary to them. Presumably Grotius means here, as in prolegomena §15, that when established municipal law is not directly derivable from natural law but is not contrary to it, then it is in a secondary sense natural law "by reduction".

This theoretical foundation justifies the individual legal rules. Grotius does not set out either the Roman rules or local rules but by the use of reason attempts to deduce what the rules should be according to the law of nature. One example of the method is his account of contracts in book 2, chapter 12. Of simple acts, some are mere acts of kindness, others involve a mutual obligation (II). Of these acts that are reciprocal, some separate the parties, others produce a community of interests. The Romans rightly divide the former into three classes: I give that you may give; I do that you may do; I do that you may give. The Romans omitted from this classification the specific named contracts, not so much because they have a name but because their more frequent use gave them a certain force and character. But the law of nature ignores these distinctions (III). The law of nature requires that there be equality in contracts, and the party who receives less acquires a right of action from the inequality (VIII). Thus, a person making a contract ought to point out to the other any faults in the thing concerned in the transaction, but he need not disclose circumstances that have no direct connection with the thing (IX).

22. The terminology used here is adopted from the translation of F. W. Kelsey, in *De jure belli ac pacis*, II.

Equality is also required with respect to freedom of choice; no fear should be unjustly inspired for the sake of making a contract (X). Likewise, except in the case of beneficence, there should be careful observance that the exchange of considerations be equally balanced (XI). Finally, there should be equality in the subject matter of the contract, so that if subsequently an inequality, even one not due to the fault of a party, be spotted, it should be made good. The Romans properly established this rule not to apply to every inequality, since otherwise there would be a great many law suits, but it applies above one-half of the just price (XII). The most natural measure of the value of a thing is the need of it. But this is not the only measure. Desire, for instance for luxuries, sets a measure, and the most necessary things are of less value because they are abundant. The view of the jurist Paul is acceptable that the prices of things are not fixed by the desire or the use of individuals but by common estimation (XIV).

In the preceding chapter on promises, Grotius had already made other relevant points. For instance, the first requisite in a promise is the use of reason; hence the promises of lunatics, idiots, and children are void. But the promises of minors and women are not void since they have judgment, though it is rather weak. The time when a boy begins to exercise reason cannot be absolutely fixed but must be assumed from his daily behavior. Various states fix the commencement of capacity at different times, but this has nothing in common with natural law except that it is natural that the individual local rule be observed in the places where it is in force.

These particular points are part of a systematic and comprehensive treatment in which Grotius seeks to build up a structure of private law founded neither on Roman law nor on revealed religion. Certainly arguments are at times drawn from Roman law or religion, and either may even be cited occasionally as if it were of some authority. But the final product is far removed from the *Corpus juris*. Thus, quite gone is the Roman concentration on the individual contracts such as sale or stipulation, each with its emphasis on its own requirements. Instead, the omnium gatherum attributed to Paul—with the omission here of "I give that you may do"—comes to the fore although it has little prominence in the *Corpus juris* and was never part of the Roman contractual system. Formalities of contracting have disappeared, and the stress is on agreement. Even more striking is the emphasis on the equality of the agreement, including the equality of the prestation. Not only was the role of enorm lesion limited to sale in the *Corpus juris,* where it appears only in the *Code,* but many of the individual contracts such as stipulation are unilateral in form and theory, though in practice they might be balanced by a second stipulation.

In view of the nature of *De iure belli ac pacis,* the basic divisions, even as they relate to private law, are very different from those of Justinian's *Institutes.* Thus, instead of a division of contracts into the four genera each with its species, contractual obligation is treated in three chapters, 11–13, of book 2—on promises, contracts, and oaths.[23] Again, the overall arrangement is by no means the same as that of the *Institutes.* For instance, the first seven chapters of the book are titled: "The Causes of War: First, Defense of Self and Property," "Of Things Which Belong to Men in Common," "Of Original Acquisition of Things, with Special Reference to the Sea and Rivers," "On Assumed Abandonment of Ownership and Occupation Consequent Thereon: and Wherein This Differs from Ownership by Usucaption and by Prescription," "On the Original Acquisition of Rights over Persons: Herein Are Treated the Rights of Parents, Marriage, Associations, and the Rights over Subjects and Slaves," "On Secondary Acquisition of Property by the Act of Man: also Alienation of Sovereignty and of the Attributes of Sovereignty," and "On Derivative Acquisition of Property Which Takes Place in Accordance with Law: and Herein, Intestate Succession."

Though Grotius' main intention was undoubtedly different, the *De jure belli ac pacis* opened up the serious possibility of drastic reform of private law, of a system based not on Roman law but reason. The book presented an inspiration as well as a challenge. With hindsight, given the references to natural law in the *Corpus juris,* the general philosophical Enlightenment, and the genius of a Grotius expressed in a work such as *De jure belli ac pacis,* it would have been astonishing if natural law as the law of reason had not had a considerable effect on substantive private law. With the same hindsight, one can reasonably predict three aspects of the role of natural law. Inevitability of outcome is not being claimed here, but rather the likelihood of occurrences that actually did happen. This approach is similar to that of Thomas F. Torrance without the theological overtones.[24] In his view law, like everything in the universe, is neither a matter of chance nor determined: that a development is rational does not mean it is necessary. Thus, when a change has occurred, it is possible

23. Then come three chapters, on promises, contracts, and oaths of those who hold sovereign power; on treaties and sponsions; and on interpretation.

24. See his "Juridical Law and Physical Law: Toward a Realist Foundation for Human Law," in a forthcoming book edited by A. McCall Smith and T. Carty (Edinburgh, Scottish Academic Press, 1982); and his *Divine and Contingent Order* (New York, Oxford University Press, 1980).

to show that it was rational and caused, but it is not possible to predict the changes that will occur, since such changes are "contingent."

The first prediction is that natural law doctrines would have a peculiarly strong effect in Germany. Roman law had a particularly important role in Germany; hence any reaction against it, to be successful, also had to be of great force. Dissatisfaction with the sway of the *Corpus juris* is evident from the institutes of Germanic law. There was, even apart from natural law, going to be a battle over the role of Roman Law. Apart from its intrinsic charms, natural law was a weapon to be used, since it offered a new, nonforeign authority. Even where a rule of the *Corpus juris* and what could be deduced for natural law were the same, the legal proposition could now be maintained without invoking Roman texts. Natural law could equally be invoked in favor of a rule of German law. More to the point, however, natural law both "in a proper sense" and "by reduction" could offer a solution to an otherwise intractable problem every time there was a conflict between the *Corpus juris* and Germanic law: it would present itself as authority, moreover as a very rational and attractive authority, one outside of the conflict of rules, and of a higher ethical and philosophical standing.

The second prediction is that natural law, as it entered the sphere of practical private law, would be tamed. Courts enforce existing and established law. To have any practical impact, natural law doctrines would have to appear consonant with the law as seen by the courts and as taught in the universities. With regard to the latter, books would emerge setting out Roman law, Romano-German law, and natural law together, or reconciling Roman law with natural law. Books of both kinds are numerous. One example, remarkable only for its range, is D. H. Kemmerich (1677–1745), *Accessiones institutionum juris civilis ex jure naturae et gentium Romano et Germanico cum primis saxonico communi et electorali ad methodum quidem institutionum justinianearum, sed suppletis harum defectibus, et materiis juris in ordinem redactis, concinnatae, in usum academiae et fori* ("Additions to the Institutes of Civil Law from the Law of Nature and Nations, from Roman and German Law, (Especially Saxon, *ius commune* and Electoral) According to the Method of the Justinianian *Institutes* but with the Defects Corrected and the Legal Materials Brought into Order, Harmonized, and for the Use of Universities and the Law Court"). In addition, books on natural law itself that treat it as in any sense law that was or could come to be the law of a territory will bring it more into line with Roman law. This is true of the work of the second great natural lawyer of the period, Samuel Pufendorf (1632–1694), who sought to give a detailed practical content to the subject. His

De iure naturae et gentium (of 1672) abounds in reference to Roman law sources where that system is regarded as authoritative.

The third prediction is that there would be attempts to establish a new, systematic arrangement of legal topics. Justinian's *Institutes* with all their advantages of structure could not be said to be firmly established on a basis obvious to reason. Grotius' *De jure belli ac pacis* already indicates the need felt for a different arrangement there. Another case in point is the Dedication by Elie Luzac to his 1772 edition in French of Christian Wolff, *Institutiones juris naturae et gentium,* which had been first published in 1750. The Dedication gains in significance because Luzac, not being the author of the *Institutiones,* had no personal axe to grind, and because in general he was not an intellect of the first rank. Having objected *inter alia* that the *Digest* and *Code* contain few general principles, and these without noticeable order, he continues: "I believe . . . that the *Institutes* of Justinian could have provided some sort of remedy if they had been composed in a more natural and more methodical order, if the definitions had always been exact and illuminating . . . But despite that, I do not see that one can conclude that it is pointless to work for the perfection of law, and that the study of Roman law cannot contribute to this." The implication is that in the context of natural law attempts should be made to find a methodical arrangement of law; this methodical arrangement, suggests Luzac, does not exist in Justinian's *Institutes,* but a study of Roman law and particularly of Justinian's *Institutes* could help in discovering the perfect arrangement. Wolff's arrangement derives basically from that of Pufendorf; and in its turn it was to serve as the structural model for the *Allgemeines Landrecht für die Preussischen Staaten.*[25]

Wolff's *Institutiones* are in four parts. Part 1, "On the Law of Nature in General, and Duties Toward Oneself, Toward Others and Toward God," deals with general obligations and duties. Part 2, "On Ownership, and Rights and Obligations Arising Therefrom," contains a treatment of the acquisition of property, individual contracts, quasi-contracts, and other matters. Part 3, "On Empire, and Obligations and Rights Arising Therefrom," is in two sections. Section one, "On Private Empire," deals with marriage, relatives, paternal power, and succession. Section two is "On Public Empire or the Law of the State." Part 4 is "On the Law of Nations."[26]

25. See also Koschaker, *Europa,* pp. 245ff; Tarello, *Ideologie,* pp. 94ff, 98ff, 104ff.
26. See Tarello, *Ideologie,* pp. 110ff.

VIII
Successful Modern Codification

In developed Western systems of law there is habitually to be found a drive toward codification.[1] The drive is not always powerful, nor is it always well directed, and it may meet emphatic opposition. The drive may be official or unofficial; it may be realistic, idealistic, or even cosmetic. Consequently it is probably not very meaningful to inquire into the circumstances in which codification is demanded.

Moreover, what may be envisaged as a code can vary enormously, even within the Western tradition. At one end of the scale are the short and succinct Roman Twelve Tables of the fifth century B.C., which do not set out the law comprehensively within the sphere of law treated.[2] For the inclusion of a clause in that code, there apparently had to be a particular reason, such as innovation, in addition to the mere fact of stating the law. At the other end of the scale is Justinian's *Corpus juris civilis,* which is enormous. Collections of statutes in force, where the individual obsolete clauses are omitted, may also be included within this category, as likewise the *Corpus juris canonici.* Moreover, collections of legal materials, which may well be classified as codes, have studded the development of law in Spain. Consequently, without a very detailed preliminary classifi-

1. For a recent expression of this drive see A. Watson, "Two-Tier Law—A New Approach to Law-Making," *International and Comparative Law Quarterly,* 1978, pp. 552ff.

2. See e.g. A. Watson, *Rome of the XII Tables* (Princeton, Princeton University Press, 1975).

cation, it would not be possible to investigate the circumstances of successful official codification in past ages.[3]

An investigation is possible, however, into the circumstances of successful modern Western codification, because of the similarities of these codes. By "code" is meant here primarily a written work that is intended to set out authoritatively at least the principles and basic rules of a wide field of law, such as the whole of private law, commercial law, or criminal law, or of criminal or civil procedure. Such codes are extremely numerous. Their introduction contains two implications.

First, since they are of necessity official, they require considerable political backing or at least consent. Thus, political factors are inevitably important for codification, and the political circumstances must be right at the moment of introduction. In view of the fact that codification has been very common in modern times, it must be that either very differing political conditions favor or at least allow codification, or the necessary political conditions are a common occurrence. One would expect greater political involvement for the earlier of the modern codes.

Second, virtually all modern civil law systems are codified. South Africa is perhaps the main exception, although most scholars would classify it as a "mixed" system. But codification, especially of private law, is relatively rare in common law countries. Law is not codified in the United Kingdom, Ireland, Canada (outside of civil law Quebec), Australia, New Zealand, and in general in the United States. Some codes were prepared for Anglo-India, and others are found in the United States, particularly in the West, most notably California. The contrast in this regard between civil law systems and common law systems is so great that much effort is expended by comparative lawyers to rebut the fallacy that the difference between the two types is that the former are codified and the latter are not.[4] Yet if codification is such a feature of civil law systems as distinct from common law systems, then there must be something inherent in the civil law tradition, whether with regard to the legal profession, the substantive law, the structure of the system, or attitudes to law, that favors codification. One cannot attribute the successful predilection for codification to political factors overall, because then it would be incomprehen-

3. See e.g. J. Vanderlinden, *Le concept du code en Europe occidentale du XIIIe au XIXe siecle: essai de définition* (Brussels, Université Libre de Bruxelles, 1967); S. A. Bayitch, "Codification in Modern Times," in *Civil Law in the Modern World,* ed. A. N. Yiannopoulos (Baton Rouge, Louisiana State University Press, 1965), pp. 161ff; F. H. Lawson, "A Common Law Lawyer Looks at Codification," in *Many Laws* (Amsterdam, North-Holland, 1977), I, 43ff.

4. Cf. Lawson, *Common Lawyer,* pp. 47ff.

sible that the factors were not present to the same extent in the countries of the common law tradition. Likewise, the extent to which the division codified-noncodified corresponds to civil law-common law systems means that one can exclude as the determining factor the prevalent social or economic conditions, other than possibly the social or economic conditions of the lawyers.

Successful modern codification leads to four subsidiary conclusions about legal development. First, successful codification was not simply the response to a felt need for it in the sense that the greater the complexity of the law and the difficulty in finding the law, the greater the demand for simplification, hence codification. Certainly, one strong impulse toward codification has frequently been the complexity and amount of the existing law. According to Suetonius, Julius Caesar formed the project "to reduce the civil law to fixed limits, and from the enormous and prolix mass of laws to place only the best and necessary in a few volumes."[5] As a motive for his *Digest,* Justinian alleges that "we find the whole course of our statutes, such as they come down to us from the foundation of the city of Rome and from the days of Romulus, to be in a state of such confusion that they reach to an infinite length and surpass the bounds of all human capacity."[6] The publication regulations (*Publikationsprotokol*) of March 20, 1791, of the *Allgemeines Landrecht für die Preussischen Staaten* declare "that the whole law will be produced in a coherent order, in the language of the nation and presented in a generally understandable way so that any inhabitant of the state, whose natural capacities have been trained through education even only to a moderate standard, may be himself able to read the laws in accordance with which he should conduct his dealings and be judged, to understand them and in future cases be attentive to their provisions."[7]

However great was the difficulty of finding and understanding the law in continental countries, it can scarcely have been greater than in England, where the law was not systematized, even after the appearance of Blackstone's *Commentaries on the Laws of England* in 1765–1769, where different courts enforced common law and equity, where local custom remained important, and where much law was hidden in inaccessible law reports. Yet English law was not codified, nor was there ever much chance of it.

5. *Divus Iulius* 44.2.

6. *C. Deo Auctore,* 1.

7. Cf. the prefatory remarks of Franz I of Austria to the *ABGB* of 1811 that the law should be in an understandable language and in an orderly collection.

Second, the introduction of "original" codes, namely those prepared fresh without deriving in structure and content from an existing code, is not sufficiently explained by social upheaval or complexity, as Frederick H. Lawson argues: "All the original codes have been in countries which have just undergone a revolution and wish to recast their law quickly from top to bottom, or in countries which had in the past suffered from a diversity of legal systems or had just found themselves in that position because they have incorporated new territories or had come into existence by a union of territories governed by different laws. One or the other of these factors must be at work if the lawyers of a country are willing to undergo the immense trouble and inconvenience of transforming their law and learning it afresh."[8] Lawson is right in stressing the difficulty of successfully preparing and introducing an original code.[9] But he does not take sufficient account of the eighteenth century codifications in Bavaria, which he describes as "too old-fashioned to fit into the movement" of codification.[10] Work on codification in Bavaria was in fact begun in 1750, and the code of criminal law, *Codex iuris Bavarici criminalis,* was issued in 1751; of procedure, *Codex iuris Bavarici judicialis,* in 1753; and of private law, *Codex Maximilianeus Bavaricus civilis,* in 1756. Historically this codification is undoubtedly part of the general movement and was inspired by initiatives already taken in Prussia. Moreover, the Bavarian civil code is thoroughly modern in its arrangement. Above all, whether the Bavarian codification was or was not old-fashioned is irrelevant, for the codes are original, despite the fact that neither of the factors postulated by Lawson for the appearance of an original code was present to any important extent. Furthermore, the emphasis on social upheaval does not explain why there was no really successful codification in the United States after the Revolution or the Civil War. The power of the individual states of the Union cannot have precluded codification, for Germany, which introduced the *Bürgerliches Gesetzbuch,* was and still is a federation; and other countries, notably Switzerland, that have civil codes are also federal. Still another federation that has codes is Mexico, but here the individual states have each their own civil codes.

Third, the introduction or nonintroduction of a code in a particular territory cannot be attributed to the power or persuasiveness of one individual. Thus, no doubt Napoleon's energy and power counted for much

8. *Common Lawyer,* p. 49.

9. Cf. Watson, "Two-Tier Law," p. 574.

10. *Common Lawyer,* p. 48n13. See also A. T. von Mehren and J. R. Gordley, *Civil Law System,* 2nd ed. (Boston, Toronto, Little Brown, 1977), pp. 59f.

in the promulgation of the *Code civil,* but in the French Revolution there had already been attempts at codifying the law. Despite all his persuasiveness, learning, and political power, Friedrich von Savigny could, at the most, greatly delay the preparation of a code for Germany, most noticeably by his *Vom Beruf unsrer Zeit für Gesetzgebung und Rechtswissenschaft,* first published in 1814. And in non-civil law countries, Jeremy Bentham could not move the English to codification, nor could David Dudley Field move the Americans in the populous East.

Finally, even for civil law countries, systematic codification of private law is a relatively modern phenomenon. The earliest codification is that of Bavaria in 1756. In any account of codification as a phenomenon related more to civil law than to common law systems, this matter of dating also requires explanation. The success of codification in the civil law systems and its relative failure in common law systems is explained primarily by general factors in the legal systems themselves.[11] The distinctive element of civil law systems is the acceptance, past or present, of the *Corpus juris* or part of it as authoritative. This acceptance has profound consequences for the legal system, apart even from the acceptance of individual legal rules. But these consequences do not appear immediately or all at the same time. They include an academic and systematic, as distinct from a practical and pragmatic, emphasis on law. Roman law dominates legal education, and particular prominence falls on Justinian's *Institutes,* because it is both the fundamental book for beginners and is the authoritative attempt to give a systematic structure to law. When the insufficiency of Roman law for contemporary needs becomes apparent and respectable to notice, books on local law then emerge. These books are of various kinds and of different scope. But Justinian's *Institutes* show that it is possible to set out the basic rules of even a complex system in a comprehensive and organized way. This leads to a desire likewise to set out in one work the basic rules of a local system. Almost inevitably, these books model themselves in length and arrangement on Justinian's *Institutes,* though with variations. The role of Justinian's *Institutes* in legal education increases the influence of such local institutes vis-à-vis other books on contemporary law. In addition, a system in which the *Corpus juris* is authoritative is more open than is a common law system to the influence of powerful general intellectual currents, such as the Enlightenment. A great boost was given to natural law's capacity to influence private law

11. The position is very different where codification may be imposed by an absolute autocrat like Ataturk in Turkey, or by a foreign conqueror, or is intended for a territory where there is no deeply established legal tradition.

by the genius of Hugo Grotius. The Enlightenment led to the belief that law can be established on the basis of reason, and this intellectual impetus toward reform, married with the civil law tradition, led on to official codes of law. With the coming of institutes of local law and of natural law, the civil law tradition became more receptive to the idea of codification. Justinian's *Institutes* show that it is possible for a brief outline of the law to have legislative effect. But successful codification in the civil law tradition, at least in the forms that the codification takes, has to wait for the emergence of institutes of local law.

Proof that codification can be regarded as the natural product of the civil law tradition is two fold. First, no explanation, other than one based on legal tradition itself, can account for codification flourishing in civil law systems to a degree unknown in common law systems. "Many of the most civilized modern societies have felt the need to codify their laws. One can say that it is a periodical necessity for societies"—so begins the message of the executive to the Congress in Chile, proposing approval of the Chilean civil code in 1855. But these "most civilized modern societies" are in the main only those of the civil law tradition. The second proof is the similarity between institutes, whether of Justinian or local law on the one hand and of civil codes on the other. Many oddities of construction of modern codes can be explained only by reference to these institutes. More particularly, modern scholars profess to see two different "families" among civil law systems or two branches of the civil law "family," one deriving from the Germanic sphere of influence, the other from the Latin or, more particularly, the French. This distinction is best explained in terms of the preceding civil law tradition, the juristic reaction to it, and the penetration of it by natural law.

In Bavaria, the impetus to the three codes of the 1750s came from the cabinet order of December 30, 1746, of Frederick the Great of Prussia to his chancellor, Samuel Cocceji, and their intention was to unify the territorial law and to settle legal disputes of the *ius commune.*[12] The civil code, *Codex Maximilianeus Bavaricus civilis,* had only subsidiary validity, because the previous statutes continued in force. It is divided into four parts which follow the order of Justinian's *Institutes.* Thus, the first part consists of eight chapters, covering the nature of law and justice, kinds of laws, rights and duties of persons with regard to their status,

12. See e.g. Conrad, *Rechtsgeschichte,* II, 386f; Wieacker, *Privatrechtsgeschichte,* pp. 326f. The so-called *Codex Ferdinandeo-Leopoldino-Josephino-Carolinus* for the hereditary Kingdom of Bohemia and other territories is not a code but a collection of privileges, rescripts, and other statutory or quasi-statutory material, collected by J. J. Weingarten and published in 1720.

family status, paternal power, marriage, guardianship, and bondage. The second part has eleven chapters on the rights and duties relating to property in general, ownership, acquisition of ownership, prescription, possession, real security, servitudes in general, praedial servitudes, usufruct, tiends, and services due from country dwellers. The third part has twelve chapters on succession, the last on intestate succession. The fourth part has eighteen chapters on agreements in general, real contracts, consensual contracts especially sale, right of preemption, hire, emphyteusis, partnership, mandate, verbal contracts including personal security, literal contract, innominate contracts, quasi-contracts, performance, other forms of discharge of obligation, wrongdoing and the obligation arising therefrom, defamation and injury (*iniuria*), and feudal law. The contents in general correspond closely to those of Justinian's *Institutes* but, following the pattern established by so many institutes of local law, procedure and crimes are omitted. The substantive rules also show great Roman influence. The influence of natural law, however, is particularly noticeable in the use of a clear, matter-of-fact German and in the legal decisions often based on Reason.

The Prussian codification took almost a century to reach fulfillment, and it provides a clear insight into the growing influence of natural law.[13] At the beginning of the eighteenth century the numerous and scattered Brandenburg territories involved a multiplicity and diversity of laws. Frederick William the First's desire to bring these laws together appeared immediately after his accession in his edict of June 21, 1713, §156, and the cabinet order of June 18, 1714, to the law faculty in Halle. "Sound reason" was to be taken into account in the consolidation program, and the natural lawyer Christian Thomasius was to direct the project. Thomasius' fundamental objections blocked the plan.

The next step came from the initiative of the Enlightenment philosopher Frederick the Great, who was much influenced by Voltaire and Montesquieu. Frederick had as collaborator his Chancellor Cocceji, who is usually rated as a student of the *usus modernus* but must also be counted as a natural lawyer. Thus, his doctoral dissertation was on natural law, and he produced the *Grotius illustratus* (1744), which contains not only the apparatus of the most distinguished commentators, especially of his father, on *De jure belli ac pacis* but also twelve introductory essays. The cabinet order of December 30, 1746, to Cocceji formally requests that the law have rationality and clarity and be based as to sub-

13. See Conrad, *Rechtsgeschichte,* II, 387ff; Wieacker, *Privatrechtsgeschichte,* pp. 327ff; Tarello, *Ideologie,* pp. 252ff, 290ff, 312ff.

stance in natural reason and the constitutions of the various territorial parts. Here there is emphasis both on natural law by itself, and on natural law by reduction, namely local private law that is not contrary to the law of nature. This approach to natural law goes back to Thomasius as well as Grotius, though Montesquieu is a more direct influence on Frederick. The program was called "Das Project des *Corpus juris Fridericiani*, d.h. S.M. in der Vernunft und Landesverfassungen gegründetes Landrecht, worin das Römische Recht in eine natürliche Ordnung und richtiges Systema nach denen dreyen Objectis juris gebracht (The Project for the *Corpus juris Fridericiani*, That is, the Territorial Law of His Majesty, Founded on Reason and the Territorial Constitutions, in Which Roman Law Is Brought into a Natural Order and Right System in Accordance with the Three Objects of Law)" and was published in Halle in 1749–1751. This was simply *ius commune* arranged in the order of Justinian's *Institutes*. Because of the Seven Years' War it was never put into effect.

The move toward codification began again in 1779 under the influence of C. von Carmer, G. Suarez and E. F. Klein, all three learned in natural law. The cabinet order of April 14, 1780, for an *Allgemeines Landrecht*, a common law for the Prussian territories, demanded the implementation of natural law with completeness and exhaustiveness and the resolution of doubts not by the judge but by the legislative commission. The draft was published in 1789, and a prize for suggested improvement was offered to "philosophical jurists" even of other parts of Germany, and to the Prussian governments and estates of the realm. Many suggestions from philosophers and members of the general public were carefully examined by Suarez from 1787–1790, and the final version, the *Allgemeines Landrecht für die Preussischen Staaten*, was published in 1789–1792. Political difficulties delayed its coming into effect until 1794. It remained in force in the old Prussian territories until January 1, 1900, and was introduced in 1814 into the Westphalian territories then united with Prussia, though not into the new Rhineland territories.

This codification is above all of natural law rather than of civil law. The stress on law as education reinforces this fact. Historical natural law is presented as able to give the right concrete decision even in the smallest detail, an approach that goes back to Christian Wolff. The codification contains all the law, criminal, public, and commercial as well as private. The structure also derives from natural law ideas, largely from Wolff and ultimately from Pufendorf. The introduction on laws in general and the first eight sections of the first part, on persons and related rights, things and related rights, transactions and resultant rights, declarations of intention, contracts, rights and duties that result from illicit acts, custody and possession, and ownership, sound like a "general part" and are called in fact "General Truths."[14] Then comes the law of things, which here means the property rights of individuals. The provisions, arranged organically, involve direct methods of acquiring ownership; indirect methods, including the law of obligations; acquisition of ownership on account of death, or law of succession; retention and loss of ownership; common ownership; and real and personal rights to things.[15] The basic divisions in the second part on "unions" or "associations" are rights that establish household standing, namely family law, family property law, the law of the kin; laws relating to the various estates in the state; and rights and duties of the state against its citizens, namely constitutional and administrative law.

The *Allgemeines Landrecht* marks a high point of legal culture. But it remains without direct descendants for a number of complex reasons. First, it was very much rooted in its place and age, in Prussian and Enlightenment absolutism. Its very wealth of detail thus worked against its being copied elsewhere. Second, its modern use of German restricted its impact outside German-speaking territories.[16] Third, the French *Code civil* of 1804, constructed on very different principles, was destined for enormous success—partly because it was much shorter and more abstract, therefore less tied to one place and time; partly because it followed a pattern derived from Roman law and hence was more widely acceptable in civil law countries generally; partly because Napoleonic victories imposed it on many parts of Europe; and partly because of the subsequent prestige of France. Likewise, the Austrian code of 1811 reverted to a construction modeled on Justinian's *Institutes.* The influence of the *Corpus juris* was not to be easily ousted. Fourth, academic lawyers, always powerful in the civil law tradition, often resented the *Allgemeines Landrecht,* largely because of its enormous detail and also because it left little scope for initiative by judge and jurist. Friedrich von Savigny called it "a filthy work in form and content," and more recently Wolfgang Kun-

14. See e.g. A. B. Schwarz, "Zur Entstehung des modernen Pandektensystems," *ZSS* 42 (1921): 605; Tarello, *Ideologie,* pp. 316ff.

15. Cf. Wieacker, *Privatrechtsgeschichte,* p. 332.

16. A French translation by various hands appeared at Paris in 1798–1799: *Code général pour les états prussiens* (Imprimerie de la République). Even earlier translations had appeared of Frederick the Great's *Project:* into French, with no date or place, by A. A. de C.; into English from the French, anonymously, in 1761 at Edinburgh.

kel called it "a monstrous anti-intellectual undertaking."[17] It may not be accidental that much of this hostility has come from enthusiasts for Roman law.

The codification movement in Austria began around the middle of the eighteenth century and encompassed private law, criminal law, and procedure.[18] The intention was to unify the territorial law and to settle legal disputes of the *ius commune.* The first tangible success was in criminal law, with the codification of Maria Theresa, the *Constitutio criminalis Theresiana* of 1768, which was replaced in 1787 by that of Joseph II, the *Allgemeines Gesetz über Verbrechen und derselben Bestrafung.* Both criminal codes are products of the Enlightenment.[19] Procedure was codified, appropriately for the period, in the *Allgemeine Gerichtsordnung Josephs II* of 1781.

More difficult was the codification of private law, which went through various stages. At first the predominant aim was to unify the territorial laws, but later greatest weight was attributed to giving a new form to the law in force. A commission was established at Brünn in 1753 to make a code, then called *Codex Theresianus juris civilis,* of unified private law for the hereditary Austrian territories, namely Austria, Styria, the Tyrol, Vorderösterreich (territories in western Europe outside of Austria), Bohemia, Moravia, and Silesia, based on a choice of the most natural and fairest rules, filled out by general natural law and the law of nations. The first draft was replaced by a second which was put together by a commission at Vienna. This second draft, which filled eight folios, was arranged in the order of Justinian's *Institutes.* The draft was rejected by the empress because of its prolixity and lack of clarity, and a new commission was set up in 1772. The code was to be short, unambiguous, marked by simplicity and "natural equity," in contrast to the detail and *ius commune* traditionalism of the previous drafts.

A first part, dealing with marriage and succession, was published in 1786 as the *Josephinisches Gesetzbuch.* A new high commission was set up under Martini, a natural lawyer, in 1790, and a very short draft in three parts, heavily influenced by Roman law, was produced in 1796. In 1797 a slightly modified version, known as the *Westgalizisches Gesetz-*

17. Savigny to Arnim, 1816, in A. Stoll, *F. C. von Savigny* (Berlin, Heymann, 1929), II, no. 319; Kunkel review of Wieacker, *Privatrechtsgeschichte,* 1st ed., *ZSS* 71 (1954): 534. In contrast, Wieacker thinks highly of the codification: *Privatrechtsgeschichte,* pp. 333f.

18. See e.g. Conrad, *Rechtsgeschichte,* II, 391ff; Wieacker, *Privatrechtsgeschichte,* pp. 335ff; Tarello, *Ideologie,* pp. 332ff.

19. See e.g. Conrad, *Rechtsgeschichte,* II, 441ff.

buch, was introduced as an experiment in the recently annexed West Galicia, and then later in East Galicia. Opinions were sought from provinces, university faculties, and commissions of knights. A further commission was set up whose expert adviser and intellectual leader was F. von Zeiller, who had been first a pupil of Martini, then his successor as professor of natural and Roman law, before entering government service in 1794. The commission eventually, after drawing up another draft based on the *Westgalizisches Gesetzbuch,* published in 1811 the *Allgemeines Bürgerliches Gesetzbuch* (*ABGB*), which came into force on January 1, 1812. In the permission to publish, the emperor declared that the code was issued "In the consideration that, to provide citizens with complete tranquillity in the secure enjoyment of their private rights, the civil laws should be determined in accordance not only with the general principles of justice, but also with the particular circumstances of the inhabitants, made known in a language intelligible to them and kept steadily in the memory by means of a reasonable collection." The *ABGB* brought unity of law within Austria; and its operation was eventually introduced in Austrian territories outside of the German hereditary lands.

The *ABGB* is thoroughly modern in its construction. It has an introduction and three parts. The introduction, §§1–14 is on civil laws generally. Here "laws" (*Gesetze*) means officially pronounced rules, namely code provisions or statutes. It is declared in §10 that custom can be taken into account only when it is referred to by a law, and in §12 that judicial decisions never have the force of a law and cannot be extended to other cases or to other persons. However much inspired by natural law this codification may be, the idea of natural law does not appear *prima facie* in the finished work. Natural law is not expressly mentioned in the Introduction. There is no definition of it nor, more surprisingly, is there a general definition of law. What does appear, at §1, is a definition of civil law, where *Recht,* "law," can mean either "law" in the sense of the Roman *ius* or "right" in the sense of what is correct or proper. The definition reads: "The totality of laws [*Gesetze,* statute-law or Roman *leges*] by which the private rights and duties of the inhabitants of the State are fixed with regard to one another, constitutes the civil law." This is a far cry from the so-called *Ur-Entwurf,* "original draft," of 1797, as shown by the first nine sections of the first part of that earlier work:

> §1. Law [or right] is everything which is good in itself, which contains or brings out some good in its relations and consequences, and contributes to the general well-being.
>
> §2. Out of that which is right [or law] are drawn the rules which

should serve man as a plumb line in his acting and refraining from acting.

§3. In addition, the word law [or right] is also taken in a double sense; by it one understands the rule itself that prescribes what is right [or law], and also the natural freedom or the authority to transact that every person has when he arranges his transactions in accordance with these rules.

§4. Rights [or laws] and duties are either based solely on the nature of man, and then they are called natural and innate rights [or laws] and duties, or they are based on a particular society, and then they are called positive rights [or laws] and duties, that is, having arisen by dint of social life.

§5. Persons who join with one another in accordance with fixed principles in order to reach a common end are called a society.

§6. The state is a society that is united and bound under a common sovereign in order to achieve a final appropriate and unalterable goal determined by man's nature.

§7. This final goal is above all the general well-being of the state, that is, the security of the persons, of property, and all the remaining rights of its members.

§8. The sovereign of the state issues the prescriptions or rules necessary to achieve this final goal, and they are called statutes.

§9. The aggregate of these statutes, by which reciprocal rights and duties of the inhabitants of the state among themselves are determined, constitute its own civil private law. This private law is contained in the present code.[20]

Of the *ABGB* itself the first part is the law of persons and has four major divisions: the rights relating to status, marriage law, rights between parents and children, and guardianship and curatorship. The second part, the law of property, has an introduction on things and their legal distinctions, then two major subdivisions. The first concerns corporeal things and includes possession, right of ownership, acquisition of ownership, real security, servitudes, succession testate and intestate, and common ownership and other property rights. The other subdivision treats personal property rights, contracts and legal transactions generally, gifts, the individual contracts (including marriage settlements), and delict. The third part deals with rules that are common to the law of persons and of things: surety and guaranty, modification and termination

20. See *Der Ur-Entwurf und die Berathungs-Protokolle des oesterreichischen allgemeinen bürgerlichen Gesetzbuches,* ed. J. Osner (Vienna, Holder, 1889), vol. 1.

of rights and obligations, and prescription. The parts are of unequal length, the second part being considerably more than twice as large as the first and third put together.

The form of the *ABGB* is very Roman. In length, as in general arrangement, the whole work is reminiscent of Justinian's *Institutes.* Both have in common the sequence: sources, persons, property, testate succession, intestate succession, contracts, delicts. The *ABGB* has no sign of the natural law influenced structure of a "general part" and of property preceding persons. Again the scope of the ABGB is restricted to that of Justinian's *Institutes.* It contains only private law and, at that, significantly leaves out commercial law. From the contents of the *Institutes* the *ABGB,* like other books of local law, leaves out both criminal law and procedure.

Austrian law, as presented by the *ABGB,* is also very Roman in its contents. For example, Austria is one of the few jurisdictions to retain three classes of persons who, because of their age, lack full capacity: children under 7, children under 14 (*Unmündige* or *impuberes*), and minors under 21. One further characteristic of the code, resulting from the concern to make the code of use to nonexperts, is the frequency of cross-references and of paternalistic advice. Thus, §580 reads: "A testator, who cannot write, must, in addition to observing the formalities set out in the preceding article, place his mark, instead of his signature, with his own hand, and that in presence of all three witnesses. To facilitate lasting proof as to the identity of the testator it is also prudent that one of the witnesses should add the name of the testator, indicating that he has signed for him."[21] This characteristic, along with others, such as the extremely brief treatment of delict that is normal in a civil code, are indications of enduring natural law influence.

In France, the *Institution au droit français* of Argou, which was first published in 1692 and had reached its eleventh edition by 1787, was similar in construction to Napoleon's *Code civil.*[22] But the honor of determining the arrangement of the *Code civil* is now often given to a book which until recently was little known, François Bourjon's *Le Droit commun de la France et la coutume de Paris reduits en principes, tirés des loix, des ordonnances, des arrets des jurisconsultes et des auteurs, et mis dans l'ordre d'un commentaire complet et méthodique sur cette coutume: contenant dans cet ordre, les usages du châtelet sur les liquidations, les*

21. See e.g. §578.

22. See e.g. Conrad, *Rechtsgeschichte,* II, 394ff; Wieacker, *Privatrechtsgeschichte,* pp. 339ff; *General Survey,* pp. 251ff; A.-J. Arnaud, *Les origines doctrinales du code civil français* (Paris, Pichon & Durand-Auzias, 1969).

comptes, les partages, les substitutions, les dîmes, et toutes autres matieres, first published in 1743, whose third and final edition appeared in 1773.[23] A comparison by André-Jean Arnaud of the provisions of Bourjon, *Droit commun,* and of the *Code civil* shows that the three books of the *Code* correspond closely in arrangement to the first three books of Bourjon. This is most easily seen in the major arrangement. Thus in both cases the title of the first book is "Des personnes (persons)"; for the second book, Bourjon has "Des biens (things)," the *Code* has "Des biens et des differentes modifications de la proprieté (things and the various modifications of ownership)"; for the third, Bourjon has "Comment les biens s'acquierent (the acquisition of things)," the *Code* has "Des differentes manières dont on acquiert la propriété (the different ways of acquiring ownership)." Although Bourjon's work is in six books, the contents of the last three fit into the general structure of the *Code civil.*

Arnaud also makes a direct comparison of contents: the feudal matters in Bourjon do not appear in the *Code civil,* since feudal incidences and distinctions had been abolished; whereas in addition to what is in Bourjon, the *Code* contains only one title (I.8) on adoption, a subject that was introduced into French law by Napoleon; one (II.2) on property; and one (III.3) on the general theory of contract.[24] For Arnaud, the omission from Bourjon of a theory of property and a general theory of obligations indicates that he is still bound to the letter of the Custom of Paris. The omissions also indicate the lack of the influence of doctrines of natural law. Although the three books of the *Code civil* correspond closely to the first three books of Bourjon, nonetheless the actual arrangement of the individual provisions of the *Code civil* seems rather closer to the arrangement of the chapters of the four books of Argou. Given the enormous popularity of Argou, as evidenced by the number of editions, this cannot be a matter for surprise.

The movement in France for codification had begun long before the rise of Napoleon. Charles VII's *ordinance* of 1454 at Montil-les-Tours marks the beginning of the undertaking to write down the various regional customs. Then the mandate of Louis XI to the bailiwick of Sens in 1481 represents in one view the intention to consolidate and unify customary law.[25] This unification of customs was also the ideal of Charles

23. See Arnaud, *Origines doctrinales,* pp. 159ff; R. Martinage-Baranger, *Bourjon et le code civil* (Lille, Klincksieck, 1971).

24. One example of the influence of Bourjon is the formulation of the *Code civil* (art. 2279), "En fait de meubles possession vaut titre."

25. See e.g. *General Survey,* p. 279; Vanderlinden, *Concept du code,* p. 26. For the mandate see R. Gandilhon, "L'unification des coutumes sous Louis XI," *Revue historique,* 1944, pp. 322f; cf. Vanderlinden, *Concept du code,* pp. 286f.

Dumoulin. In 1576 the States-General, meeting at Blois, expressed itself in favor of codifying both royal legislation and customary law. The task was entrusted in 1579 to Brissonius, but only with regard to legislation. The result was the *Code du roi Henri III*, published in 1587 but never promulgated, since Henri died in 1589. Under Louis XIV, Colbert again brought forward the idea of codification, but success was limited to certain great ordinances: of civil procedure (1667), waters and forests (1660), criminal procedure (1670), commerce (1673), and maritime law (1681). Lamoignon (1617–1677), who was chief president of the court of the parlement, set out as a code in a private work the principles of customary law, and the Chancellor D'Aguesseau (1668–1751) was responsible for three great ordinances that were in effect codifications of wills, gifts, and entails and were influential for the *Code Napoléon*.

With the coming of the French Revolution, the Constituent Assembly voted on October 5, 1790, that a general code should be prepared, and this promise was renewed in the first written constitution of France in 1791. The Constituent Assembly had no time to see to the preparation of the code, nor indeed really had the Legislative Assembly. But the Convention in 1793 ordered its legislative committee to present a draft code within one month, and this order was complied with. In the month of August of that year Cambacérès presented his plan for an exceptionally short code containing only 695 articles. In a speech delivered on the occasion Cambacérès declared that civil legislation should be "an edifice simple in its structure, but majestic through its proportions; great through its very simplicity, and so much the more solid in that not being built on the moving sand of systems, it will arise on the firm earth of the laws of nature and on the virgin soil of the Republic." He declared it was a chimerical hope to have a code that would provide for all cases and accepted the view that many laws made a bad republic.[26] Revolutionary though this plan was, it was not sufficiently so for the Convention, which rejected it. The Convention, which had expressed contempt for both Roman law and the customs and wished for a code that was simple, democratic, and accessible to every citizen, voted for a committee of philosophers to prepare a new draft. Nothing came of this plan, and Cambacérès presented a new, even shorter draft, of 297 articles, after the fall of Robespierre. Little likewise came of this plan. Again, under the Directory which commissioned a civil code, Cambacérès presented a third draft, but this also came to nothing.

Napoleon as first consul appointed a committee of four on August

26. See P. Fenet, *Recueil complet des travaux préparatoires du code civil* (Paris, Ducessois, 1827), I, 2f.

13, 1800, to draft a civil code. The members were Tronchet, president of the Court of Cassation; Bigot du Préameneux, government commissioner in that court; Malleville, a judge in the same court; and above all, Portalis, government commissioner in the Prize Court. Thus, all the members were practical lawyers and not academics. Each member prepared a part, and the draft was completed in four months. It was then presented for comments to the Court of Cassation and the Court of Appeal. After considerable political opposition in the Tribunate, where the code was declared a servile imitation of Roman law and the customs, and the purging of the Tribunate by Napoleon, the draft civil code was enacted by thirty-six laws between March 1803 and March 1804.[27]

This most influential of all civil codes is in the tradition of Justinian's *Institutes* and the institutes of local law. To some extent, the attractiveness of the *Code civil* is to be attributed to the familiarity of its arrangement. Ambroise Colin and Henri Capitant explain the absence from the *Code civil* of the general part that is found in some more modern codes, such as that of Germany and Brazil, by the essentially practical character that the draftsmen wished to give the code; thus, the code regulated different kinds of incapacity (of a married woman, minor or interdicted person) without presenting a general theory of incapacity.[28] But this explanation is unhistorical. The absence of a general part in the *Code civil* and its presence in the German *Bürgerliches Gesetzbuch* (*BGB*) is the direct consequence of the existing legal tradition. French juristic writings before the *Code civil* contain nothing akin to the general part; German juristic writings before the *BGB* do. So, indeed, does the civil code of Saxony, the *Bürgerliches Gesetzbuch für das Königreich Sachsen,* which came into force in 1865 and of which the draft, the "Entwurf," was published in 1853. The gradual development of a general part, which has been traced by A. B. Schwartz, owes much to the natural law tradition which despite Montesquieu and the French revolutionaries had never really penetrated the French legal tradition.[29] The French legal tradition was still very much that of civil law as distinct from natural law. It is true that the codification movement in the eighteenth century was directly inspired by natural law, that the revolutionaries spoke of natural law, and that the Dec-

27. The code was published under the title *Code civil des Français,* but the name was officially changed in 1807 to *Code Napoléon.* The original title was resumed in 1814 and 1830, but the accepted title since 1870 is *Code civil.* For convenience, the code as it was enacted is usually termed *Code Napoléon.*

28. *Traité de droit civil,* remodeled by L. Juliot de la Morandière (Paris, Dalloz, 1957), I, 131.

29. "Zur Entstehung."

laration of the Rights of Man of 1789 is very much a product of the law of nature. But the issue is more complicated than that.[30] There is, independently of natural law, a strong tendency toward codification of private law. Thus, before the Enlightenment, Dumoulin in France had already expressed the ideal of a short, unified compilation of customary law. In addition, the writers of local institutes had pointed the way for a codification that was not based on natural law, though this contribution has been generally ignored.[31]

The basic structure of the *Code civil* is that of the institutional tradition; and it can even be described as unnatural. Thus, unlike the *Code civil,* natural law codes stress the importance of the state for human society and emphasize the legal relationship between the individual and the state. Other omissions from the *Code* are inexplicable on any notion of a law of reason. The most striking of these omissions is commercial law, which became the object of its own code, the *Code de commerce,* which came into effect on January 1, 1808. On any normal understanding, commercial law is a part of private law, the law between citizens. And the incorporation of commercial law into the *Code civil* would have been particularly easy, given the existence of what was in effect a code of commercial law in Colbert's ordinance of March 1673, which was followed in 1681 by a similar ordinance for mercantile law. Moreover, the hostility of the revolutionaries to the commercial class ought logically to have brought about the disappearance of any separate commercial law and the incorporation of rules appropriate to all transactions and classes of the people in the *Code civil.*[32] The explanation for the omission of commercial law from the code is simply that commercial law was not thought of as "civil law," and the explanation for that is that commercial law formed its own distinct legal tradition, had no obvious forerunners to

30. Zweigert and Kötz, *Introduction,* p. 80, stress that, as compared with the earlier versions, the final *Code* was less a product of natural law and that, as it took shape, the value of historical continuity was increasingly recognized.

31. See e.g. Zweigert and Kötz, *Introduction,* p. 73; Brissaud, *General Survey,* pp. 251ff; Colin and Capitant, *Traité,* pp. 116ff; Wieacker, *Privatrechtsgeschichte,* pp. 339ff; Conrad, *Rechtsgeschichte,* pp. 394ff. K. Sójka-Zielińska, "Le droit romain, et l'idée de codification du droit privé au siècle des lumières," in *Le Droit romain et sa réception en Europe,* ed. H. Kupiszewski and W. Wolodkiewicz (Warsaw, Université de Varsovie, 1978), pp. 181ff, does stress the hostility toward Roman law expressed by some natural lawyers and emphasizes that this hostility was tempered, especially during the course of codification; but no word is said about the role of Justinian's *Institutes* and of local institutes in framing the modern codes.

32. See e.g. J. Hamel and G. Lagarde, *Traité de droit commercial* (Paris, Dalloz, 1954), I, 30.

which it could be attached in Roman law, and above all was not to be found in Justinian's *Institutes* and hence not in the institutes of French law. The same explanation applies to the same omission from the Austrian *ABGB* and the German *BGB*.

The claim that the modern codification movement in France or elsewhere resulted from natural law is further undermined by the fact that codification is primarily a phenomenon of the civil law tradition and is rare in the common law. More specifically, there was no successful common law codification in the heyday of natural law. These facts make sense only on the assumption that, however important natural law may have been, the civil law tradition was also basic for codification. The fact that natural law theories were never so prominent in the common law world as they were in that of the civil law is irrelevant, since in spheres other than law the common law countries played a full part in the Enlightenment.

Admittedly natural law had to some extent penetrated French law, but this was in the typical form that may be designated "pre-Grotian" and which was in addition much Romanized. Thus, Jean Domat (1625–1696) in the preface to *Les loix civiles dans leur ordre naturel* observes that in the works of Roman law one can admire the light that God gave the infidels "whom he wished to make use of to compose a science of natural law." He insists that though other rules have been necessary where natural law did not determine precisely what was just, Roman law contains few of these arbitrary rules and consists almost entirely of natural law. Henri-François D'Aguesseau (1668–1751) advises the beginning law student first, to choose to examine the most common matters where it is easiest to see the first rules of natural law that distinguish Roman jurisprudence from all others and, second, to choose as guide that person, namely Domat, who treated such subjects most methodically and always with the intention of reducing them to this "primitive law which should be as common to all nations as justice itself."[33] Thus, D'Aguesseau holds that the principles of natural law are most evident in Roman law and that these principles are most clearly brought out by Domat. For his part, Robert Joseph Pothier (1699–1772), who frequently cites Hugo Grotius, Jean Barbeyrac, and Samuel Pufendorf, nevertheless seems much closer to the tradition of Thomas Aquinas, on whom he also relies, and of the canonists generally. For example, in the preliminary article of his *Traité des obligations,* he observes, "The *obligation* which is purely *natu-*

33. *Quatrième instruction sur l'étude et les exercises qui peuvent préparer aux fonctions d'avocat du roi* (Paris, 1787), I, 389.

ral, which is a *bond of equity alone,* is also, though in a less proper sense, a *perfect obligation* since it gives the person toward whom it is contracted the right to demand its accomplishment, if not in the exterior forum, at least in the forum of conscience; whereas an imperfect obligation does not give this right." This remark leads Jean-Joseph Bugnet to note, "Pothier too often distinguishes the exterior forum and the interior forum (or the forum of conscience)."

The French *Code civil* is certainly not of pure Roman descent, in either substance or form. The *Code* rather represents the civil law tradition as it had developed in France. Its form is a development from the institutes of French law; and its substance is a mixture of Roman and customary law, with Roman law predominant in contracts, both in the general provisions and in the specific contracts, and in ownership. Although one must not ignore the contributions of customary law, royal ordinances, and revolutionary laws, one must not play down the contribution of Roman law, as in Jean Brissaud's remark: "There were two general currents of law at the time of the unification of the French law: the Roman spirit and the Customary traditions. It was the latter that prevailed."[34]

One curious event reveals the actual strength of the Roman spirit in the *Code*. The influence of French law came to Italy with the French armies in 1796, and the *Code civil* in Italian translation was promulgated as law in the Kingdom of Italy in 1806. By a vice-regal decree of November 15, 1808, this code was always to be taught in conjunction with Roman law.[35] Indeed, the chairs of Roman civil law were to be converted into chairs of the Code Napoleon Compared with Roman law. The idea that such a comparison was possible as well as desirable implies a belief in the continuing importance of Roman law and, more significantly, in the predominance of Roman law principles in the *Codice civile di Napoleone il Grande.* Indeed, this belief in the predominance of Roman law principles was at times spelled out. Thus, in his edition of the *Codice,* Onofrio Taglioni remarks: "All the peoples of Europe have tried hard and long to form their own legislation; but in the end the greater part of them have recognized that the law of Rome suited them, and they have, therefore, embraced it. Although the successive variation of circumstances and time, with which every people have been involved, made them feel the need to make some change, no change of circumstances or time has ever demonstrated the need to alter the principles. This sole ar-

34. *General Survey,* p. 286.

35. This requirement is set out more clearly in the decree of October 11, 1811, tit. 2, §18.

gument is enough to show that it [Roman law] is better than all the others. In fact it could not be otherwise since it is the cumulation of wisdom of the wisest two nations [Greece and Rome] that the world has ever seen. Nonetheless there are those who could wish to condemn this law to oblivion as not being, they say, fitted to our time, to our customs. . . The *Codice civile* conforms for the most part to these Roman legal rules, a fact which their superficial readers would deny: most of the time, moreover, the *Codice* necessarily presupposes the knowledge of Roman law principles, without which it would not be understood in the way that it should be."[36] However chauvinistically proud of Roman law Taglioni may have been and however one-sided his view, these remarks could not have been made by any learned man, as Taglioni certainly was, unless the *Code civil* was largely a product, in substance as in form, of the Roman law tradition. More to the point, if there had not been a heavy reliance on Roman principles in the *Code,* he could not have made the direct comparison, article by article, with the corresponding and contrasting Roman texts, though not every article permits such comparison.

The French *Code civil* did not stand by itself in that country but was rapidly followed by the *Code de procédure civile,* the *Code de commerce,* the *Code de procédure pénale,* and the *Code pénal.* These codes are very inferior to the *Code civil* both in drafting and in the quality of the rules. Brissaud explains the inferiority primarily by the fact that the authors of these codes had few or no models to follow, whereas for the drafting of the *Code civil* much of the work had been done in advance by earlier generations of jurists.[37] Surprisingly Brissaud fails to identify more precisely the models that existed for the drafting of the *Code civil* or to explain why models existed for that code but not for the others.

The question arises why the force of Roman law for the structure and principles of modern codes, especially for the *Code civil,* has been underestimated, and why the role of natural law and, for France, of the customs has been overestimated. This underestimation of the Roman law contribution is surprising, since the force of the Roman law that has been neglected is obvious. Any explanation must be couched in psychological terms.

One of the most striking features of a code is that it marks a new beginning. In most countries, a basic idea is that all preceding law is abrogated by a code; one cannot go back historically beyond the code to

36. *Codice civile di Napoleone il Grande col confronto delle leggi romane* (Milan, Sonzogno, 1809), I, pp. V, IX.

37. *General Survey,* p. 293.

interpret its provisions. In many ways this is a very proper and reasonable attitude and, on one level, makes for simplicity and clarity in the law. But jurists, faced with questions of interpretation, have a tendency to rely on authority, which means in the context of a new code to look at the preceding law. The success of the code as the whole law, which lawyers presumably desire, depends on eradicating this tendency; hence the strenuous effort made both consciously and unconsciously to distance the code from its historical roots. It is in this light that the remark of Bugnet, one of the early commentators, should be seen: "I know nothing of civil law; I teach only the *Code Napoléon.*"

But why is the Roman law influence in particular underplayed? The answer is that the danger feared in the interpretation of the *Code* comes particularly from Roman law. Roman law principles and structure have been and even now remain so much a part of the educational tradition that it is easier to envisage recourse to that system rather than to natural law or the customs for arguments as to interpretation, especially since the formulation of Roman law principles has been so much more precise. Because the danger of recourse to arguments from Roman law is greatest, its role in forming the *Code* must be underemphasized. This argument is reinforced by David Daube, a jurist and linguist. When Daube, who does not read Bulgarian, received a book in that language on Roman law, he consoled himself with the thought that the book probably contained little that was new. What one cannot easily understand, he observes, one depreciates.[38] In a similar way, when one fears the continuing influence of something, one depreciates past reliance on it. This tendency helps explain why succeeding generations continue to downplay the importance of Roman Law for the formation of the *Code.* Roman law continues to be taught for its own sake and enjoys high prestige. In general in civil law countries there is less teaching of other history of law before codification and virtually none of natural law, and the scholar of present-day law is expected to know more about Roman law than about other legal history or natural law. In practice, however, most writers on modern law have only the sketchiest knowledge of Roman law. To acquire enough knowledge to make full use of Roman law requires much effort; hence it is simpler and more satisfactory not to recognize the utility of the knowledge and to downgrade the contribution of Roman law.

Finally, emphasis should again be placed on the striking importance of Roman law in the *Code civil.* Before codification, France was excep-

38. "Fashions and Idiosyncracies in the Exposition of the Roman Law of Property," *Theories of Property,* ed. A. Parel and T. Flanagan (Waterloo, Canada, 1978), p. 43.

tional in continental Europe for the extent to which the *Corpus juris* was not authoritative in the northern "pays de droit coutumier". Given the relative weakness of the civil law tradition in northern France, it is not surprising that, atypically, all the draftsmen of the *Code civil* were active in practice and were not academic lawyers. Moreover, the main source for the substantive law in the *Code* is Pothier (1699–1772), who had written extensively on the customs, as well as on obligations, and who had been so dissatisfied with the arrangement of texts inside each *Digest* title that he prepared his own edition with a different arrangement.[39] In view of this background and of the rationalist element of the Revolution, the great extent of Roman law influence in arrangement and substance is particularly significant.

The modern codification movement can be divided historically in two parts, the first terminating with the codes of France and Austria, and the second beginning with the spread of the French *Code civil* and with codes derived from it. The rationale for this division is not just the prevalence after the break of the use of the *Code civil* in territories for which it was not designed, and of numerous codes even outside Europe that are heavily indebted to the *Code civil* in form and content. It is also that in this period the original codes of, say, Chile, but more especially of Germany and Switzerland, are framed in a full awareness of the existence and operation of earlier codes. The distinction must not be exaggerated. The draftsmen of earlier codes, too, were aware of foreign precedents, but now it is as if a critical mass of excellent codes has become available as a quarry. Legislators and draftsmen from this point on have three choices. First, they can accept an existing code in its entirety or with minimal changes. Second, they can prepare a national code in the light of an existing foreign code that provides the basic model for substance and structure. Third, with experience of the advantages and disadvantages, theoretical and practical, of foreign codes, the legislators and draftsmen can determine to produce their own "original" code. Such a code always involves a response, favorable or unfavorable, to existing great codes.

This second phase of codification has two peculiarities. First, a marked feature of the civil law tradition before codification is that it is international in character, in judicial decisions and juristic writings alike. With the advent of codification, that feature undergoes change, though it

39. See the eloge pronounced upon his death by the king's advocate, Le Trosne, in Pothier *Treatise on the Law of Obligations,* trans. W. D. Evans (London, Strachan, 1806), I, 1ff.

does not necessarily disappear. After the first few codes are produced, the adoption of a national code itself is an act of comparative law.

Second, one of the most impressive features of this phase is the reception of the *Code civil*. Although this reception is prominent even in countries that previously were outside of the sphere of French legal interest, such as much of Latin America, the reception nonetheless occurs only in civil law countries. However easy it might have been there to accept a code that contained many rules deriving from French customary law and which were novel for the adopting territory, nonetheless the *Code civil* did not prevail in countries of the common law. Whatever explanation may be offered, the contrast is instructive for any understanding of the role of legal tradition in legal growth.

The first steps in the reception of the French *Code civil* were the direct result of Napoleon's conquests.[40] Belgium was incorporated into France in 1797, and the *Code civil* automatically came into force in 1804, remained in force despite Napoleon's fall, and so remains. The Netherlands, despite their neutrality, were forced more and more into the French sphere of influence, and in 1806 the Dutch were forced to accept Napoleon's brother Louis as king. In 1809 Napoleon compelled them to accept a version of the *Code civil* that was slightly altered to take account of some Dutch legal practices. In 1810 Napoleon annexed the Netherlands, and the original *Code civil* was introduced. After Napoleon's fall, Belgium and the Netherlands were united. The *Code civil* was to remain in force until a fresh code could be issued, but Belgium separated in 1830, and a new Dutch commission was appointed, whose proposed code, the *Burgerlijk Wetboek*, came into force in 1838. The *Burgerlijk Wetboek* is itself strongly based on the *Code civil*, and indeed the majority of provisions are straight translations. There are, however, changes in structure. This code is in four books. The first deals with persons, and a significant change is that matrimonial property appears here sandwiched between marriage and divorce, whereas in the *Code civil* the subject is treated in book 3. Book 2 concerns things, including—unlike the *code civil*—succession. Book 3 concerns obligations, and book 4 is proof and prescription. Procedure and commercial law are excluded, as they are from the *Code civil*. In contrast to Justinian's *Institutes*, book 4 is much shorter than the others. Since 1947 a very different Dutch code has been in active

40. See Zweigert and Kötz, *Introduction*, pp. 89ff. See also J. Gaudemet, "Les transferts de droit," *L'année sociologique* 27 (1976): 48ff; R. Piret, "Le Code Napoléon en Belgique de 1804 à 1954," *Revue internationale de droit comparé* 6 (1954): 753ff.

preparation, and parts of it are already in force. The code includes commercial law, in which regard it is in line with a current trend.

In Italy, too, with the exception of Sicily and Sardinia, Napoleon's conquest introduced the *Code civil* with a few necessary changes. French law, in fact, was influential even before the promulgation of the *Code civil.* For instance, a *Projet* was produced for the Roman Republic in 1798, and this was very much influenced by the French *Projet* of 1796.[41] The *Codice civile di Napoleone il Grande* was repealed almost everywhere in 1814. Italy was then again a land of many independent territories, which began to produce their own civil codes, all of them based on the *Code civil.* Lombardy and the Veneto, being under Austrian rule, were subject to the *ABGB.* Italy became a unified kingdom in 1861, and since the individual civil codes were based on the *Code civil,* it was no difficult matter to frame an Italian civil code, heavily indebted to the *Code civil,* which was enacted in 1865. Plans for a reformed code existed in the 1920s and 1930s, but a new approach was devised in 1939: a code was to be prepared that would comprehend not only traditional private law but all the possible personal and professional relationships of the citizen. The new *Codice civile* of six books came into force in 1942, and it also deals with commercial law, with book 4 concerning labor law.

Napoleon's conquests meant that in Germany also the *Code civil* came into operation in the Rhineland in 1804, and later in Westphalia, Baden, Frankfurt, Danzig, Hamburg, and Bremen. After Napoleon's defeat the *Code civil* remained in force in the Rhineland, and in a translation called the *Badisches Landrecht* it was the law of Baden. Likewise in Switzerland in the cantons of Geneva and the Bernese Jura the *Code civil* applied from 1804 as the result of conquest. The *Code civil* served as the model for the civil code of cantons in western Switzerland: Vaud (1819), Fribourg (1834–1850), Ticino (1837), Neuchatel (1854–1855), and Valais (1855). These codes survived until 1912.

In Europe even countries unconquered by Napoleon felt the power of the *Code civil.* The Rumanian civil code above all was simply a translation. In Spain, a commercial code based on Napoleon's *Code de commerce* was issued in 1829, and a modernized version appeared in 1885. The Spanish *Código civil* appeared only in 1889 and in substance owes much to the *Code civil,* especially with regard to obligations, though much of family law and succession is native to Spain. The structure has original features. After a preliminary title the *Código civil* divides into

41. *Projet du code civil de la république romaine,* intro. F. Ranieri (Frankfurt am Main, Klostermann, 1976).

four books. Book 1 is "Persons"; book 2 is "Things, Ownership, and its Modifications"; book 3 is "The Different Ways of Acquiring Property," namely occupation of unowned property, gift, and succession; and book 4 is "Obligations and Contract". Spanish law has had a complicated legal history, in that law in Spain, as elsewhere in western Europe, underwent a Reception of Roman law while retaining vigorous indigenous elements. Different kingdoms of Spain had their own laws, which remained important and were not all displaced by the code. In fact, of the *Código civil* only the general introductory provisions on statutes and private international law and the sections on matrimonial law applied throughout Spain. Where the fueral system, a system based on local charters and customs, prevailed, the *Código civil* had only subsidiary effects in other matters. The fueral laws are now being codified.

Portugal, too, adopted in 1833 a commercial code based on that of France, and this was replaced in 1888. The Portuguese civil code of 1867, though heavily influenced by the *Code civil,* is less dependent on it than other codes of the nineteenth century. A new Portuguese civil code of 1967 still excludes commercial law and labor law.

France was also until recently the holder of a great colonial empire, and into the colonial territories, most noticeably in sub-Saharan Africa, the *Code civil* and the *Code de commerce* were introduced, though sometimes with modifications. These codes did not apply to "French citizens of local status" who were subject to African customary law or to Islamic law if they were Muslims. The various systems of law were dealt with in separate courts. Since the former colonies have become independent, they have been remodeling their law, using French techniques and French terminology. In Algeria the two main French codes were introduced in 1834, while Tunisia in 1906 and Morocco in 1913 received a *Code des obligations et des contrats,* which was largely a modified version of the appropriate sections of the French codes.[42] French influence still dominates in these areas. For political reasons French law also dominated these fields of law in Egypt and Lebanon.

In North America Louisiana, which was ceded by France to the United States in 1803, adopted a civil code in 1808. The main direct sources for the substantive provisions and even more for the structure of this code were the French *Projet de code civil* of 1800 and the *Code civil*

42. But N. J. Coulson argues that the 1906 code "rested squarely on Islamic sources, and was designed simply to achieve uniformity and certainty in the application of the law." *History of Islamic Law* (Edinburgh, Edinburgh University Press, 1964), p. 157.

itself.[43] The Louisiana code did not include commercial law. New codes were issued in 1825 and again in 1870.

Codification in Quebec was noticeably later. France had lost Quebec to Britain in 1759, but the previously existing law of Quebec continued to be used. This law consisted of the Custom of Paris, the ordinances in force within the jurisdiction of the Parlement of Paris before 1663, the decisions of the King's Council (*Arrêts du conseil de roi*), and the ordinances published between 1663 and 1763 which were registered by the Superior Council. A statute was passed in 1857 providing for codification, and the *Civil Code of Lower Canada,* now known as the *Code civil de la province de Québec,* came into effect in 1866. The draftsmen were not instructed to modify the law but to codify the existing rules, and article 2613 provides that the old law is abrogated where the code contains provisions that have expressly or impliedly that effect or where the old law is inconsistent with any provision. Hence not all of the old law is abrogated. The first three books of this code are modeled on the *Code civil,* but a fourth book deals with commercial law. As the instructions to the draftsmen would suggest, the Custom of Paris and the writings of Pothier are more influential than the *Code civil* for the substance, and the common law also leaves its mark.

Most remarkable of all has been the success of the *Code civil* in Central and South America where the French never had much territorial control. The legal systems in force were civil law in character as a result of the domination of Spain and Portugal. The various states achieved their independence in the nineteenth century and, one after the other, adopted civil codes all heavily influenced by the French code. Thus, the Dominican Republic accepted the *Code civil* in French in 1845 and had it translated into Spanish only in 1884. The civil code of Haiti (1825) and that of Bolivia (1845) were little more than translations. The Chilean civil code of 1855 was much more original but still clearly deriving from the French model, and in its turn it was adopted by Ecuador (1860), Colombia (1871), and several Central American states. The main model of the Argentinian civil code of 1869 was still the *Code civil,* but much use was made of French writers and the Chilean code. Argentina had promulgated a commercial code a decade earlier.

Earliest of all in this context is an older Haitian code, the *Code Henry,* issued in February 1812 for King Henry of Haiti in the first year

43. There was once doubt whether the draftsmen had access to the *Code civil* and it is now disputed whether the code should be regarded as "Spanish" in substance or "French." See H. W. Baade, "Marriage Contracts in French and Spanish Louisiana: A Study in 'Notarial Jurisprudence,'" *Tulane Law Review* 53 (1978): 1ff.

of his reign and the ninth of the island's independence. The preamble to the king's edict states that the Haitian nation was ruled by laws made for a people which did not have its genius, customs, and character; that different successive governments in the island sought to remedy the lack by a large number of particular decrees; that the nation had long demanded laws appropriate to its customs and climate; and that the king's first thought on mounting the throne was to procure this benefit for his people. The *Code Henry* is very original in its conception and contains a number of individual laws, each of which is, in effect, a separate code. Thus, the first and largest is the *Loi civile,* the civil law. The code is divided not into books but into thirty-four titles, in a familiar order: publication of laws, enjoyment and loss of civil rights, acts of the civil state, domicile, persons, things, ownership, real rights less than ownership, acquisition of property (especially succession), gifts, contracts in general, quasi-contract, delict, quasi-delict, particular contracts, and prescription. Separate laws, just as is expected of separate codes, deal with commerce, civil procedure, crimes, and criminal procedure; and there are further particular laws, such as the prize law, agricultural law, military law and military legal procedure. Thus, despite its originality, the code fits squarely within the civil law tradition.

The enormous success abroad of the *Code civil* and the advent of many other codes demonstrate that civil law systems were ready for codification. One explanation for the success of the *Code civil* is that the newly liberated countries of Central and South America needed some model, and that Spanish law was out of the question since Spain had been the previous colonial power. But a better explanation is availability. Thus, after Napoleon's downfall the newly liberated Belgium, Geneva, Bernese Jura, and the Rhineland all retained the *Code civil,* and Italy and the Netherlands issued fresh codes directly descending from the *Code civil.* Since the Second World War, the dominant influence on the structure of the law in the former French colonies of sub-Saharan Africa has again been French law. The sole essential and the most important factor in any large-scale voluntary reception of foreign law is thus the accessibility of the foreign law. As Zweigert and Kötz note in the context of South and Central America, "the only available model was the French Civil Code.[44]

44. See e.g. Zweigert and Kötz, *Introduction,* pp. 106. On p. 91 they stress the seductive thesis of Paul Koschaker that "reception occurs when the law being received is in a position of power, at least intellectually and culturally, as being the law of a country which still enjoys political power or did so until so recently that its strength and culture are still clearly remembered." But cf. Watson, *Society and Legal Change,* pp. 98f.

The most systematic and logically rigorous of all civil codes is the German *Bürgerliches Gesetzbuch,* which came into force in 1900, and whose structure differs from that of previous codes.[45] The first great impulse toward a civil code for all Germany came from Anthon Thibaut's pamphlet, *Über die Notwendigkeit eines allgemeinen bürgerlichen Gesetzbuchs für Deutschland,* which was published in 1814. Thibaut, as a German patriot, claimed that the civil law needed a total and rapid alteration, and that the Germans would not be happy in their civil relations othewise than if all the German governments with their united strength attempted to create a law book for all Germany. The pamphlet called forth, in the same year, the riposte of Friedrich von Savigny, *Vom Beruf unsrer Zeit fur Gesetzgebung und Rechtswissenschaft.* For Savigny, law sprang from the consciousness of the folk, or *Volk,* a cultural concept, and every codification was inorganic and thus either unnecessary, if it merely repeated existing law, or harmful, if it interrupted the growth of the law from the *Volk.* Law, in this view, was a product of history, and all of the existing law should be carefully sifted and absorbed over a period of time. Though Savigny was well aware of the diverse elements, Germanic and Roman, in the law used in Germany, both he and his followers concentrated on Roman law, whose qualities they esteemed above all.[46]

The historical school, as it has come to be called, is usually seen as a reaction against natural law. Law was not to be regarded as the fundamentally unalterable product of reason but as the offspring of varying experienced conditions. The stress nevertheless remained on Roman law not on Germanic, for three reasons. First, according to Zweigert and Kötz, Savigny accepted the contemporary aesthetic ideas which favored classicism.[47] Second, Roman law had always remained powerful and, for reasons of legal education, still prevailed over Germanic law. Third, in its bid for acceptance in practice, natural law was inevitably tamed: existing authority had to be given for propositions of law. And although there were books setting out side by side natural law, Roman law, and Germanic law, the books on natural law itself, written by scholars like Pufendorf, Thomasius, and Wolff, cited Roman law in support and seldom mentioned Germanic law. To mount an intellectual challenge to existing

45. See Wieacker, *Privatrechtsgeschichte,* pp. 468ff; Zweigert and Kötz, *Introduction,* pp. 139ff; Schwarz, "Zur Entstehung"; Koschaker, *Europa,* pp. 278ff.

46. See Wieacker, *Privatrechtsgeschichte,* pp. 392ff.

47. *Introduction,* p. 140.

law or to compete on a footing of equality, natural lawyers had to compare and contrast their ideas with those of the legal academic giant. Hence it was to be expected that a reaction against natural law should stress Roman law.

No doubt through a combination of the opposition of the historical school and others and of unfavorable political circumstances, the codification of German law was delayed. An early outstanding work of Savigny, his *Recht des Besitzes,* came out in 1803, and his *Geschichte des römischen Rechts im Mittelalter* began to appear in 1815. In 1839 was published the first volume of his *System des heutigen römischen Rechts.* With his colleagues and followers, Savigny was thus organizing the concepts of Roman law and showing their systematic later development and even their contemporary working. Georg Friedrich Puchta (1798–1846) showed views quite similar to those of Savigny in his *Gewohnheitsrecht* —of which the first volume appeared in 1828, the second in 1837—and in his *Lehrbuch der Pandecten* and *Cursus der Institutionen.* Bernhard Windscheid (1817–1892) is remembered for his *Lehrbuch des Pandektenrechts,* which first appeared in 1862 and whose seventh edition, the last prepared by the author, came out in 1891. During this same period three great scholars devoted to the history of German law emerged: K. F. Eichhorn (1781–1854), Jacob Grimm (1785–1863), and Georg Beseler (1809–1888).

The most striking feature of the *BGB,* where it parts company with the existing tradition of codification, is its structure, above all in the existence of the *Allgemeiner Teil,* the "general part." The *BGB* is in five books. book 1, the general part, is divided into seven sections: persons, things, legal transactions, periods of time, prescription, exercise of rights (self-defense and self-help), and the giving of security. Book 2 is the law of obligations, book 3 is the law of things, book 4 is family law, and book 5 is succession. The general part does not set out general rules or basic principles but contains provisions on institutions that are common to much of private law, such as capacity, juristic persons, persons of limited capacity, classes of things, and periods of time. Nothing corresponding to the general part appears in the Roman sources, and at first sight it would seem that a general part is out of place in a system deriving from Roman law. Yet in fact it is a marked feature of the books of *Pandektenrecht* which emerged from the university teaching of Roman law. The earliest work to show the typical modern Pandect system, by G. H. Heise in 1807, is actually called *Grundriss eines Systems des gemeinen Civilrechts zum Behuf von Pandecten-Vorlesungen* ("Outline of a System of the Common Civil Law as an Aid to the Lectures on the *Pandects*").[48] The connection with teaching the course on Pandect law is expressly stated in the preface to both Anton Thibaut's *System des Pandekten-Rechts* (1803) and Bernhard Windscheid's *Lehrbuch des Pandektenrechts* (1862–1870).[49] *Pandects* is another name for Justinian's *Digest,* and the lecture courses devoted to the *Pandects* came to deal with Roman law as it was interpreted and applied in contemporary Germany.

The history of the structure of the modern Pandect system, which is the immediate foundation of that of the *BGB* as of the Saxon civil code of 1865, has been described by A. B. Schwartz.[50] This system is a combination of the influence of natural law and Roman law; in a sense, it is actually natural law ideas working upon Roman law substance. The growth of the general part can be traced through works on natural law, pure Roman law, and on the law as applied in Germany. To a considerable extent the general part is the result of the very abstract reasoning used by natural lawyers to reach the common, basic principles of law. At the same time it is the scarcely recognisable offshoot of the division into natural law proper, to which it corresponds, and natural law "by reduction." Thus, the major difference in structure between the *Code civil* and the *BGB* is explained by the greater penetration of the civil law tradition in Germany by natural law.

In 1873 a *Vorcommission,* Precommission, was established to form an expert plan, and on its recommendation the *Erste Kommission,* First Commission, was established in 1881 to prepare a draft. The First Commission was composed of eight practitioners and three professors, among whom the leading spirits were Windscheid, the professor, and Gottlieb Planck, a practitioner. The commission worked very much in isolation, remote from other practical or academic sentiment, and their draft gave rise to a flood of protest. The language was said to be wooden, the system too doctrinaire, and the draft too remote from real life. Above all Otto von Gierke objected to the neglect of living German private law.[51] The

48. The system was actually set out earlier by Gustav Hugo in his *Institutionen des heutigen römischen Rechts* (1789), but he abandoned the approach in later editions. Hugo has a claim to be considered the founder of the historical school. See e.g. Karl Marx, "The Philosophical Manifesto of the Historical School of Law," in Marx and Friedrich Engels, *Collected Works* (London, Lawrence & Wishart, 1975), I, 203ff. Hugo seems even to have invented the term *Volksgeist.* See Wieacker, *Privatrechtsgeschichte,* p. 357n38.

49. Although Thibaut's work is earlier than Heise's, the structure of the latter prevailed. In his preface Thibaut admits that his title is odd but claims that his intention is to deal with the material of lectures on the *Pandects.*

50. "Zur Entstehung."

51. *Entwurf eines Bürgerlichen Gesetzbuchs und das deutsche Recht* (1888/89).

Zweite Kommission, Second Commission, was established in 1890 with ten permanent members and twelve unestablished members, among them the Roman law professor Rudolf Sohm, and it worked much more in public. The Second Comission had little real effect on the nature of the code. They added the famous "few drops of social oil," but their main changes were to the language. Their draft, published in 1895, was scarcely altered by the Bundesrat, and it came into force in 1900. A separate commercial code, the *Handelsgesetzbuch* (*HGB*), was promulgated in 1897, but a still earlier commercial code, *Allgemeines deutsches Handelsgesetzbuch,* dates from 1861.

The *BGB* has been enormously admired, but its direct effect on foreign civil codes has been limited, partly because it was late in the field, partly because it is so abstract. But the civil codes of Japan (1898), of the Kingdom of Siam (1924–1925), and of China were drawn mainly from German law, with the exception of family law and succession. The influence of the *BGB* on foreign codes is most clearly seen in Greece.[52] From the first half of the nineteenth century German legal scholarship was the strongest influence on Greek law, and in that country German professors taught Pandectist law. The Greek civil code was long in the making but eventually came into force in 1946. Its structure is that of the *BGB,* though the influence of the codes of Switzerland, France, and Italy can also be seen. From the late nineteenth century onward German law was also influencial in Hungary and, from 1918, in Czechoslovakia and Yugoslavia.

The law of some Swiss cantons was within the sphere of influence of the *Code civil.* The first of the German-speaking cantons to adopt a civil code was Bern (1830–1831), and this code, though founded in old Bern law, followed the *ABGB* in structure and to some extent in content. The example of Bern was followed by Luzern, Solothurn, and Aargau. A rather different creation was the civil code of Zurich, the *Zürcher privatrechtliches Gesetzbuch* (1853–1855), which was the work of Johann Kaspar Bluntschli, who had studied long in Germany and was very much in the Pandectist tradition. This model was followed in various cantons of northern and eastern Switzerland, and of all the cantonal codes it had the greatest effect on the Swiss civil code.

The division of Switzerland into numerous cantons, each with its

Anton Menger, *Das bürgerliche Recht und die besitzlosen Volksklassen* ("The Civil Law and the Propertyless Classes of the People" 1891), showing that the rules of law injured the weaker classes of society and protected the stronger, had no noticeable impact, since its stance was foreign to the existing legal tradition.

52. See Zweigert and Kötz, *Introduction,* pp. 154ff.

own law, gave rise to many problems of conflict of laws, especially in commercial law, and this led to the creation in 1881 of a partial code, the *Schweizerisches Obligationenrecht,* which was based on the *Allgemeines deutsches Handelsgesetzbuch* and on what is called the *Dresdner Entwurf,* a draft of the law of obligations which had been produced in 1865 by German professors and judges. To prepare the way for unification of cantonal law, Professor Eugen Huber was asked to produce a comparative comprehensive account of the private law of all the cantons, and even before the last volume had appeared of his *System und Geschichte des schweizerischen Privatrechts* (1886–1893), Huber was asked to prepare a draft code. The draft was available for public discussion in 1900, and the *Schweizerisches Zivilgesetzbuch* was adopted in 1907, to come into force in 1912. The code of obligations was updated, and although it is a separate federal statute with its own numbering, it is in effect a fifth book of the *Schweizerisches Gesetzbuch.* The civil code itself has a preliminary title, book 1 is the law of persons, book 2 the law of the family, book 3 successions, and book 4 real rights.

The Swiss codification has been very much praised, and for a time there was a call to adopt it in Germany. It was adopted almost in its entirety in Turkey in 1926, though there is dispute whether this is because of its merits or because the then Turkish minister of justice had studied law in Switzerland.

IX
Institutes and Codes

In the history of a civil law system the adoption of a civil code is an event second to none in importance. The effects are profound, since the code marks a new beginning. Indeed, in typical modern-style civil codes, the preexisting law ceases to have even subsidiary force. To use a cliché, "The circle has been closed." The movement has gone all the way from the codification of Justinian's *Corpus juris civilis* to the new civil code. Just as in precodified civil law systems the existence of the *Corpus juris* naturally dominated the shaping of private law, so that role is now played by the civil code. Some of the effects of these civil codes are more or less universal and seem well-nigh inevitable, although great differences in substance and approach exist between individual civil law systems.

The civil law code itself and its effects are comparable with, but different from, the *Corpus juris* and its effects. Upon codification, the civil law system remains ahistorical but with quite different effects. Before codification, civil law judgments and juristic writings lay great stress on the opinion of jurists who may have lived several centuries before and who worked in other lands. For the interpretation of the appropriate text of the *Corpus juris,* the remoteness in age of the commentator is irrelevant; hence, despite multiple citation of old authority, the authorities themselves are treated ahistorically. With the advent of a civil code, the code itself becomes the historical starting point. What is wanted is the correct interpretation of the code provision, not its forerunners. The code would lose a great deal of its usefulness, for laymen and practitioners alike, if its provisions could be interpreted with the aid of earlier law.[1]

Both practically and ideologically it becomes of great importance to separate the code from what went before. As a consequence, precodification writers like Bartolus or Johann Gottlieb Heineccius are not cited in court for the elucidation of the law, nor does a professor of modern civil law refer to their views in the exegesis of provisions of the code. Yet the interpretations of postcodification writers never achieve the status of those of a Bartolus, becoming treated for centuries as meaningful for the law in force, simply because provisions of a code are subject to revision in a way not possible for the *Corpus juris.* In universities professors of private law now divide more or less completely into modern civil lawyers and legal historians. In some codified jurisdictions, notably Germany, a professor may have responsibility for modern as well as Roman law. But the courses given on either subject are sharply distinguished. The books written on the civil law may contain some preliminary historical material, but historical references are absent when the precise extent of a code provision is under discussion.

The study of Roman law itself is greatly affected. Roman law can no longer, to any extent, be of practical usefulness in shaping the law. Professors of Roman law lose, gradually or not, their dominating role in law faculties. To compensate for the loss of status of their subject and themselves, they have to find a new role while remaining true to their discipline; hence, for the first time professors of Roman law concentrate the bulk of their intellectual energies on recreating the pre-Justinianic law. Interest in Roman legal history for its own sake is not a new phenomenon, as witness the French legal humanists, but what is new is the all-consuming effort to trace the stages of Roman legal growth up to and including the codification of Justinian. This interest in its turn drives a wedge between the Roman lawyers and the professors of civil law who are ahistorical and lack patience with what they regard as historical, even antiquarian, studies. Again, students find it more difficult to appreciate Roman law, because the techniques needed to separate older law from the new in the *Corpus juris* are very specialized and do not appear directly relevant to the job of knowing the law in force. Moreover, in any attempt to trace the growth of Roman law, the *Institutes* of Justinian obviously lose in prominence. Although it takes time, eventually the very

1. The *École de l'exégèse,* the first "school" of interpreters of the *Code civil* nevertheless made extensive use of the *travaux préparatoires,* the preparatory papers, and in the early days of the *Code civil* the writings of older jurists were cited in court.

existence of Roman law in law school curricula is threatened: first it ceases to be a compulsory subject, then it may disappear altogether. Whether or not Roman law disappears from the curricula is of less significance than that Roman law becomes peripheral in any event.

The process of "alienation" of Roman law is increased by the fact that the more historical the study of Roman law becomes, the less relevant to it becomes the work of medieval, renaissance, and later commentators. Even scholars who wish to uncover the meaning of Justinianic texts scarcely find these later jurists illuminating because, from the middle ages onward, jurists were less anxious to find the historically accurate meaning for Justinian's time than a solution that could be used for contemporary practice. Thus, few modern Roman lawyers show much interest in post-Justinianic law, and the works, approaches, and developments that link Roman law to the world of codified law are neglected. Consequently, the role of Roman law in shaping contemporary codifications comes generally to be misunderstood, and the influence of Roman law is seen above all in terms of the survival of particular rules. The decisive importance of Roman law for codification itself, for legal rationality, and even for the structure of codes is easily overlooked. The net result, which has great significance for civil law systems, is to make even more marked the separation between the modern law and its forebears.

Scholars who stress the ahistorical approach of modern civil law sometimes point out that, in contrast to the Anglo-American world, legal history on the Continent is primarily not seen in terms of the growth, transformation, and decay of specific legal institutions, but in terms of schools of legal thought.[2] To make this observation in the context of an ahistorical attitude to law, however, is misleading, since to a large degree it reflects private law developments in civilian systems in post-Roman times. The continuous development of sophisticated law in Roman law and derived systems dates from at least the Twelve Tables around 450 B.C.[3] In contrast, the beginnings of the common law are usually placed around the Norman Conquest of England in 1066.[4] Roman private law developed so speedily and so skillfully that in many parts later ages have simply tinkered with the existing concepts. In many cases where modern civil law differs from Roman law, the modern law has accepted ideas already adumbrated in Roman times. The growth of a legal system from

2. Cappelletti et al., *Italian Legal System*, p. 186.

3. See e.g. A. Watson, *Rome of the XII Tables* (Princeton, Princeton University Press, 1975), pp. 3ff.

4. See e.g. R. C. van Caenegem, *Birth of the English Common Law* (Cambridge, Cambridge University Press, 1973).

the stage at which it is recognizably civilian, such as Scots law from the late sixteenth or early seventeenth century, very speedily becomes a matter of absorbing influences. The fundamental influence is Justinianic law. But when the law accepted is not that of Justinian, the rule may have arrived in Scotland in that form because of the interpretation of a particular continental civilian, or because it was already current doctrine in Holland, France, or part of Germany, or the rule may be a survival or modification of an existing Scottish practice. For Scots law at a later stage of development, the English influence is also a factor. Again, since civil law is learned, scholarly law, its history is very much a history of schools of ideas.

A civil code, where it exists, is commonly regarded as central to the whole legal system. "*Droit civil* has been regarded in France, throughout the 19th century, as the hard core, the true heart of the law," observes Rene David.[5] And Mauro Cappelletti and his colleagues remark, "The belief that this group of subjects [those contained in the *Institutes* and modern codes] is a related body of law which constitutes the fundamental content of the legal system is deeply rooted in Europe and the other parts of the world that have received the essentially Roman civil law, and is one of the principal distinguishing marks of what common lawyers call the civil law system.[6]

But a civil code is very different from the *Institutes*. Its role is much greater because it is so obviously the basic law. There is no such thing as the *Digest* behind it. However much interpretation there may be, any decision judicial or academic must rest squarely on provisions of the code. In course of time there are ever-increasing amounts of statute law, but the basic picture does not change. Moreover, any civil code is both more abstract and more systematic than the *Institutes*. In a civil code there are no cosy historical reminiscences, such as that a definition is due to Servius, or that a particular view was expressed by Pomponius, or that on a point jurists disagreed, or that a rule has a specific historical origin, or that a ruling is now being laid down because it accords with an earlier favored jurist's view, or even that a law is now obsolete.[7] A civil code does not reveal historical levels. Nor does a civil code descend in an almost chatty way to a discussion of factual details. In the *Institutes*, in contrast, there appears in place of an abstract legal proposition:

5. "The Civil Code in France Today," *Louisiana Law Review* 34 (1974): 907ff.

6. Cappelletti et al., *The Italian Legal System*, p. 215. See also Watson, *Legal Transplants*, pp. 42f.

7. See e.g. *J.*1.13.1; 2.10.5; 3.23.2; 2.11; 2.17.3; 2.17.8(7); 2.14pr; 3.29.2; 2.14pr; 4.3.7; 4.1.4.

> Again, the question is asked, if a goldsmith agree with Titius to make rings of a specified weight and shape out of his own gold and to receive, say, ten gold pieces, is the contract to be regarded as sale or as letting and hiring? Cassius indeed says that there is a sale of the material but a letting and hiring of the work. But the view prevailed that the contract is sale. If, though, Titius gave his own gold and a fee was settled for the work, there is no doubt that the contract is letting and hiring.[8]

This is very different from the use of explanatory examples found in a few civil codes, notably the Austrian *ABGB*.[9] Moreover, a civil code does not offer justification for its rules, whether from (false) etymology, from the evidence of Homer, from utility, justice, or morality, or from legal deduction.[10]

The upshot of all this is that, to a degree unparalleled in common law countries or in ancient Rome, users of a civil code are rule conscious and adopt an abstract approach to legal problems.[11] The approach of the civil law scholar is described by Cappelletti and his colleagues in the case of Italy:

> The attitude is that the law is a self-contained discipline or phenomenon that can be understood and perfected by systematic study. It is summed up in the phrase *legal science,* which carries with it the assumption that the study of law is a science, in the same way that the study of other natural phenomena—say those of biology or physics—is a science. The work of the legal scholar is like the work of other scientists, not concerned so much with the solution of practical problems as with the search for scientific truth, for ultimates and fundamentals; not concerned so much with individual cases as with generic problems, the perfection of learning and understanding, not, in a word, with engineering, but with pure science.[12]

What has happened to the institutional idea from Justinian's *Corpus juris* through to a modern civil code is indeed curious, though each step

8. *J.*3.24.4.

9. See e.g. art. 297.

10. See e.g. *J.* 1.12.5; 1.13.2; 4.1.2; 3.23.2; 4.3.1; 1.11.10; 3.2.7; 2.1.40; 2.16.1; 1.5.1; 4.3.13; 4.1.15(17); 4.2.1.

11. Later writers on Roman law frequently had to uncover the rules buried in the *Institutes* and *Digest.*

12. *Italian Legal System,* p. 170.

can be seen as a natural progression from the preceding step. Justinian's *Institutes* were a relatively well-organized, but not very abstract, introduction to law for students: the real meat of the law was to be found above all in the *Digest* and *Code*. By contrast, the civil code is the abstract authoritative statement of private law, no more detailed than the *Institutes,* yet not supported by a massive corpus of at least equally authoritative law. The place of the *Digest* and the *Code* has, in a sense, been taken by the various private commentaries on the code, which are not themselves sources of law. To carry the analogy further, the role of legislation subsequent to the civil code was performed for Justinian's time by the *Novels*.

One consequence, then, of codification is that it increases the tendency toward conceptualizing the civil law. This happens, first, because the codes themselves are more abstract, more concerned with statements of pure law, than are Justinian's *Institutes,* any commentary on them, or any institutes of local law. A second reason is more important. Decisive though Justinian's *Institutes* are for the structure of modern codes, that elementary textbook never stood in first place as a statement of the law. The *Digest* and the *Code* were both treated much more seriously. However, not only are these works remarkably badly arranged, but the substance of the law has to be found from numerous separate, ill-fitting, and often contradictory texts. Hence, any full-scale attempt to explain a point of Roman law, in treating these texts, usually had to deal in effect with case law and was related to practical decisions that often could not be explained easily on any theoretical basis.

Because a civil code does not reveal historical levels, although there is awareness of the historical elements that go into the makeup of a code, the claim is often made that a particular code represents a precise historical and ideological moment. Thus it is said that the *Allgemeines Landrecht für die Preussischen Staaten* represents not only natural law but, more especially, Prussian enlightened despotism and is "rooted in the class structure of Frederick's Prussia," or that the *Code civil* is a victory of the French bourgeoisie.[13] To some degree at least, such claims must be correct. A code does give the law as it is, and usually as the draftsmen want it to be, at a particular time and place. In order to be self-consistent, the code will contain elements of the ruling ideology. This ideology may appear more marked in a civil code than it does in common law systems simply because the code is drafted as a piece at one point of time.

13. Zweigert and Kötz, *Introduction,* p. 138; M. E. Tigar and M. R. Levy, *Law and the Rise of Capitalism* (New York and London, Monthly Review Press, 1977), pp. 250ff.

A further fundamental consequence of codification is that it brings to an end the unity of the civil law tradition. Whether a civil code is, as it may well be, an expression of national sentiment or not, it does involve the creation of a national, or at least distinctively local, law. The more original and powerful a code is, the more this is true. Certainly the precodification unity was never complete, but not only did the various civil law systems have the *Corpus juris* in common, they also shared the same tradition of international romanist jurists and even made common intellectual property of works on feudal law and criminal law, such as Julius Clarus, *Practica criminalis,* J. Harprecht, *Tractatus criminalis,* and A. Matthaeus, *Commentarius de criminibus.* After codification there is nothing but French law or Spanish law or German law.

For various reasons, however, a supranational dimension inevitably continues to be prominent in codified civil law systems. First, there are the shared traditions, of both legal rules and legal approach, existing at the moment of codification. Second, the very form of a code, its relative shortness, its abstraction, its freedom from background explanation, means that the draftsmen in any civil law country have easy access to the basic law in any other. Even commentaries on a code can be easily used by foreigners since their structure following the code is already familiar. It must become second nature for anyone involved in law reform in a codified system to take into account solutions in other codified civilian systems.

Third, individual codes with their need for precision are very difficult to draft, hence there is a natural reluctance to embark on the process afresh and an inbuilt tendency to make use of existing codes. The shared tradition makes it easy to adopt wholly or largely an existing foreign code, as witness above all the reception of the French *Code civil.* But then the whole process gets carried further. Commentaries written on the donor code become relevant for the transplanted system. The commentaries are widely used in the transplanted system and, where appropriate, translated into the local language, as shown by the numerous nineteenth and twentieth century translations into Italian and Spanish of commentaries on the French *Code civil.*[14]

14. See e.g. J. Bonnecase, *Elementos de derecho civil* (Pueblo, Mexico, 1945–1946), 3 vols.; A. Colin and H. Capitant, *Curso elemental de derecho civil,* transl. of 2nd ed. (Madrid, 1952–1958), 9 vols.; F. Laurent, *Principii di diritto civile* (Milan, 1898–1908), 33 vols.; *Principios de derecho civil,* 2nd ed. (Mexico and Havana, 1912–1918), 33 vols.; M. Planiol and G. Ripert, *Tratado elemental de derecho civil frances* (Pueblo, 1945–1948), 7 vols.; R. T. Troplong, *Commentario dei privilegi e delle ipoteche,* 2nd ed. of transl. (Naples, 1848), 2 vols.

Conversely, works written in the jurisdiction of the transplanted code affect the donor system. The outstanding example here is the nineteenth century influence of Germany on French law. Long after Napoleon's fall the *Code civil* continued to be the law in force in parts of Germany. In 1807, a chair at Heidelberg was offered to the Saxon Karl Salamon Zachariae, and as early as 1808 there appeared the first edition of his *Handbuch des französischen Civilrechts,* a work which in 1866 was described as "the most strongly conceived and the most rigorously deductive that perhaps has ever been written on the new French law. It has a concision which may be called algebraic, and has the great advantage of showing the logical development of the science of the law, and of making one think instead of providing ready-made solutions."[15] Zachariae did not directly follow the arrangement of the *Code civil* but adopted what seemed to him and many others a more systematic order. Thus there is a three-part introduction, on legal science in general, French law, and French civil law. The first major division, which occupies by far the greatest bulk of the book, is entitled "Theoretical Civil Law." In the first part of his theoretical civil law, Zachariae deals with the civil status of the French. Then the second part, on the civil rights or laws with regard to external objects, is divided into two books. The first book has three main subdivisions, on the law of things, obligations, and family law. The second book, entitled "Rights to External Objects, These Objects Treated as a Legal Whole, or Property," deals with the concept of property, things such as debts, and the law of succession. Then comes "Practical Civil Law," dealing with topics relevant to the legal process. This arrangement in itself indicates that Zachariae has his own place of honor in Pandectist tradition and was among the foremost in attempting to make law a scientific discipline. The book was translated twice into French, once by G. Massy and C. Vergé (Strasbourg, 1834–1846), who destroyed Zachariae's arrangement, and again by Charles Aubry and Charles Rau (Paris 1839–1846, 6 vols.), who retained Zachariae's synthetic order and augmented the work. By the time of the third edition in 1856–1858, Aubry and Rau's book had ceased to be termed a translation and had become *Cours de droit français d'après l'ouvrage allemand de C. S. Zachariae;* and by the fifth edition (1897) it was Aubry and Rau, *Cours de droit civil français d'après la méthode de Zachariae.* This work became the most influential doctrinal work in nineteenth century France both on judicial decisions and on university teaching. In this way, as in others, German legal thought permeated the French tradition.

15. *Nouvelle biographie générale* (Paris, Firmin Didot, 1866), XLVI, 926f.

A fourth supranational dimension to codification is that, once there is even a small number of civil codes in existence, the drafting of any new or original code inevitably involves taking stock of other codes, indeed of foreign law. An outstanding example is the Argentinian *Código civil* of 1869, which was the work of D. D. Vélez Sársfield. An edition of the code with Sársfield's notes is still in print, and the notes show the great use of foreign law made by the draftsman.[16] For instance, in the notes on the preliminary titles, he cites among others the *Code civil,* the codes of Naples, Prussia, Louisiana, Chile, Austria, and Baden, the project for a code for Brazil, Justinian's *Code* and *Digest,* the *Nueva récopilacion,* and numerous jurists including Zachariae, Savigny, and perhaps most interesting of all, Joseph Story's *Conflict of Laws.* Another instructive example of the importance attached to foreign law at the moment of codification is drawn from the debates in the German Reichstag on the future *BGB.* Of the few clauses that attracted the attention of the members or gave rise to debate, one was §817 on liability for damage caused by animals.[17] The argument was adduced in favor of one version that it would be to the same effect as the corresponding rule of French law.[18] Why on a point such as this there should be a particular practical advantage in having German law similar to French law is hard to see. The rule is not one that can affect transnational commerce or that frequently gives rise, as family law issues do, to problems of conflict of laws.

Another important distinction between civil law and common law systems which arises from the codification of the former is in the form and reporting of judicial decisions. And the final result of codification is that the revision of a code, whether of individual provisions or of the whole, is difficult for both practical and psychological reasons. The practical obstacles to partial revision are twofold. First, the revision may affect more than one clause, and a rewritten clause might have unforeseen consequences for an untouched clause situated in a remote part of the code. In the event of a conflict, there will be no guide to follow one provision rather than another. Second, a short clear provision or provisions cannot easily be passed by a legislature, which may make amendments that in their turn have consequences for other provisions. A statute is a more useful form for new provisions, but then pressure on parliamentary time and lack of interest in private law on the part of legislators may prevent the transmutation of the statute into code provisions.[19] As a result,

16. Ed. L. A. Estivill (Buenos Aires, Zavalía, 1972).
17. The clause on damage by animals is now §833.
18. See *Bericht der Reichstagskommission* (1895–1896), III, 1988.
19. See e.g. Watson, *Society and Legal Change,* pp. 115ff.

standard editions of civil codes of many countries, such as Argentina, Austria, Brazil, France, Germany, and Italy, have appendices containing statutes subsequent to the code which represent important modifications to it. The replacement of the code with a new one is such an enormous undertaking that it usually is successfully concluded only in extreme circumstances; the existing code must be felt to be quite outdated and ideologically unsuitable, or a powerful leader must feel it important for his prestige to leave a new code as a legacy. The cases of Italy and Quebec are instructive.

The social and legal values represented by the Italian civil code of 1865 were coming to be regarded as not really satisfactory for the country by the end of the century. The main reasons for the lack of rapport between the code and the society were the development of large enterprises, the formation of an industrial proletariat, the increased problems relating to work, and the progress of socialist ideas, all factors leading to a greater need for rules expressing social solidarity rather than individualism. Although calls for a reform of the code were neither numerous nor authoritative before the First World War, ideological developments following the war led to the strong demand for change.

At first the movement for reform proceeded in two different directions. On the one hand, the law of December 30, 1923, delegated to the government the power to make appropriate changes in the code, as well as to produce new codes of civil procedure, commerce, and mercantile marine. In consequence, a royal commission was appointed which between 1924 and 1937 produced preliminary projects for the first three books of the code, on persons and family, things and real rights, and succession and gift. On the other hand, a mixed Italo-French commission was established with the object of producing uniform legislation in Italy and France on obligations and contracts. The commission published a joint project in 1928, but in neither country was legislation forthcoming. That project is now generally regarded as being of disappointing quality.[20]

One cannot tell, of course, whether a government of a different complexion would have proceeded with codification, but it is certain that from 1939 on there was considerable pressure from active Fascists for the incorporation into a code of "the general principles of the fascist legal order."[21] A first result was the coming into force on July 1, 1939, of the

20. See e.g. R. Nicoló, s.v. codice civile, in *Enciclopedia del diritto* (Milan, Giuffrè, 1960), VII, 244.

21. See e.g. Cappelletti et al., *Italian Legal System,* p. 219.

first book of a new code, which was the project on persons and family. The minister of justice reported to the king that individualism was no longer to inspire the law, that the principle inspiring law was the sense of social solidarity, and that the selfish interest of each individual was to be subordinated to the preeminent interests of the state. On this basis, even the old rules that had not been altered were subjected to reinterpretation; the justification was no longer primarily the protection of the individual but the protection of the superior interests of the national community.[22] There is considerable agreement on the high quality of book 1 of the code, and it has since proved easy to expunge the racist clauses.[23] The project on succession became book 2 of the new code, which went into effect on April 21, 1940. Racial views were not made express in this book, nor did they need to be, because it was to be read in conjunction with book 1. At this stage, when what was needed was the promulgation of books on property and obligations, a sharp conflict arose between two contrasting groups. One wished to incorporate Fascist ideology into the code; the other group, which prevailed, wished to maintain the values of the existing legal tradition. This success, like that of the civil law for the French *Code civil* of 1804, demonstrates the power of survival of legal tradition.[24] There were nonetheless significant changes of structure. Thus, book 3 is on property; book 4 is on obligations, including commercial law; book 5 is on labor law; and book 6 is on protection of rights. The new Italian *Codice civile* came into force in 1942.

Quebec's civil code dates from 1866.[25] The first obligation placed on the code commissioners was to incorporate such law as they believed to be actually in force. Thus, the code was to be a consolidation of existing law. The major sources are the Custom of Paris, the laws and case law followed by the Parlement of Paris in 1663, French royal ordinances specifically promulgated for Canada until 1759, French laws registered in Canada by order of the Conseil Supérieur, English statutes enacted after the cession of the province either for Canada expressly or in which Can-

22. See e.g. A. Montel, "The First Book of the New Italian Code," *Tulane Law Review* 15 (1940): 99ff.

23. See e.g. M. Sarfatti, "The New Italian Code," *Journal of Comparative Legislation and International Law* 23 (1941): 18ff; Nicoló, *Enciclopedia,* p. 246; Cappelletti et al., *Italian Legal System,* pp. 218ff. In fact, Italian jurists were quite successful in resisting the encroachment of fascist doctrines into private law.

24. So does the failure of the attempt which will not be examined here to produce a new German civil code under the Nazis.

25. See e.g. J.-G. Castel, *Civil Law System of the Province of Quebec* (Toronto, Butterworths, 1962), pp. 5ff; J. E. C. Brierly, "Quebec's Civil Law Codification," *McGill Law Journal* 14 (1968): 521ff.

ada is mentioned, and laws passed by the Legislative Council or after 1791 by the Legislature.[26] A primary aim was to make the law intelligible to all of the inhabitants, whether French or English speaking.[27] Inevitably, therefore, the contents were not progressive even at the time that the code was introduced. Further particular difficulties arose when, eleven months later, the British colonies in North America became a federal state as a result of the British North America Act, 30 Vict. c. 3. As a consequence of that act, some matters in the code, such as those having to do with marriage and divorce, could not be amended by provincial legislation. For other matters, family law in particular, neither the federal nor the provincial legislatures could make overall reforms, and it was by no means always clear where the line of jurisdiction was to be drawn between the authorities. Reform was consequently stultified.[28]

Paul-André Crépeau, in 1974 when he was in charge of the Civil Code Revision Office, claimed that the ways of living had changed completely in Quebec since 1866. The attitudes, for instance, toward recognition of human rights, the position of the family in society, the status of members of a family, the role of ownership, the sanctity of contract, and the basis of civil responsibility, had all changed, but for a long time the changes were not reflected in the Civil Code. He ascribed this situation in part to the view held until recently by Quebec civilians, namely jurists trained in the civil law, that the Civil Code was "the incarnation of Reason and Justice in human affairs," which "came to be considered as a sacred book that no one ought to touch for fear that our precious French heritage might crumble to pieces."[29] Not until 1955 was the need for comprehensive reform given concrete expression, when the Quebec Legislature entrusted a jurist with the responsibility of producing a new draft.[30] The project of the new code was presented to the Quebec National Assembly on June 20, 1978. This elegant code is in nine books. Book 1 is on persons, book 2 on the family, book 3 on successions, book 4 on things, book 5 on obligations, book 6 on proof, book 7 on prescription, book 8 on publication of law, and book 9 on private international law.[31]

26. See Brierly, "Codification," p. 547ff.

27. See preamble to the Act to Provide for the Codification of the Laws of Lower Canada (1857) 20 Vict. c. 43; quoted in Castel, *System,* pp. 24ff.

28. See e.g. P.-A. Crépeau, "Civil Code Revision in Quebec," *Louisiana Law Review* 34 (1974): pp. 922ff.

29. "Revision," p. 928.

30. An Act Respecting the Revision of the Civil Code, S.Q. 1954–55, 3–4 Elizabeth II, c. 47 §1.

31. See P.-A. Crépeau, "La Réforme du Code civil de Québec," *Revue internationale de droit comparé* 31 (1979): 283.

A further success story for recodification, which nonetheless is instructive for the difficulties of producing a new code, relates to the Netherlands. The task of drafting a code to replace the existing civil and commercial codes of 1838 was entrusted to Eduard M. Meijers in 1947. The new code in its entirety will soon become law—more than thirty years later.[32]

The psychological obstacle to the reform or replacement of a civil code derives from its position at the center of the legal system. Crépeau's remarks on the Canadian attitude to that code as the "incarnation of Reason and Justice in human affairs" can be repeated for many other countries. The authority of the legal system at home and abroad is seen to depend on the prestige of the code. To admit grave weaknesses in the civil code is to attack the basis of the legal order.

The prime example is France. Twice there have been full-scale official attempts at producing a complete revising or a new code, and each time the attempt has ended in failure. The first began in 1904, the year of the code's centenary; the second in 1945, immediately after the Second World War. The arguments given for the *Code civil's* remaining relatively unchanged for so long before a second reform attempt at revision also explain the failure of that attempt.[33] The code was "considered a legislative model of unequaled clarity, precision and simplicity." Again, it had proved adaptable to new and unforeseeable conditions, and case law based on it was more satisfactory than legislative modifications would have been. It sanctioned great principles and rested upon a legal foundation that was well drafted, harmonious, and reasonable; changes in it would therefore involve serious risk. France and Belgium alike had a respect for the code which was sometimes called "fetishism." The movement for revision was called "premature." And on a more mundane level it was said that a total change would have involved a modification in the numbering of the provisions, which would have been irritating for practice.[34]

32. See A. S. Hartkamp, "Civil Code Revision in the Netherlands," *Louisiana Law Review* 35 (1975): 1059ff.

33. See e.g. M. Ancel, "Revision of the French civil code," *Tulane Law Review* 25 (1950–1951): 435f.

34. See e.g. A. Weill, *Droit civil, introduction générale,* 3rd ed. (Dalloz, Paris, 1973), pp. 74f; for a summary of the important changes which came out of the revision movement see G. Marty and P. Raynaud, *Droit civil,* 2nd ed. (Paris, Sirey, 1972), I, 137.

X
Divisions of the Law

Codified civil law is extremely systematic and therefore very structured and highly articulated. Divisions between one branch of the law and another are sharply marked, and the particular divisions largely derive directly from Roman law and from the long centuries of study of the *Corpus juris civilis.* The "block effect" of Roman law has resulted in the existence of easily recognizable units of law.

The dividing lines between one area of law and another are artificial and therefore, to some extent at least, arbitrary. The Roman divisions and their developments have been so successful even in common law countries that it takes a conscious effort for a trained jurist to accept that other divisions are possible or that existing divisions may be unsatisfactory—for instance, that succession might be considered part of family law, or that family law might be a separate unit distinct from the law of persons, or that contract and delict should not be classed together as the law of obligations, or that one contract, hire, should not comprise both the use for payment of another's services and the use for payment of another's inanimate property. In some countries this juristic effort is being made. The German *BGB,* for example, treats family law as a separate subject, in book 4, and this notion, which is fairly well accepted there, has also been followed elsewhere, as in the *Código civil* of Peru.

The fundamental division in civil law systems is into public law and private. The division exists on two levels, which might be called the theoretical, though it is more than that, and the processual. On the theoretical level, public law is vigorously excluded from the *Code civil* and in university teaching is the subject of separate law courses. On the processual level, cases involving public law are heard in a distinct set of courts. The fact that the *Corpus juris civilis* has been the organizing instrument of the structure of civil law systems and that legal divisions contain arbitrary elements explains why the division into public and private law was not readily apparent in medieval Europe, why it appears sharply first in the writings devoted to the *Corpus juris,* then in writings affected by the *Corpus juris* but expressly devoted to local law, and why only later are courts divided into those dealing with private law matters and those dealing with public law matters.

For the distinction in the *Corpus juris,* the scene is set at the outset of Justinian's *Institutes* in 1.1.4: "There are two aspects (*positiones*) of this study, public and private. Public law is that which pertains to the Roman state, private that which concerns the well-being of the individual." J. A. C. Thomas, the most recent English translator and commentator of the *Institutes,* insists that the nature of a legal provision does not depend on whether it is established in the interest of the community as a whole or for the benefit of the individual citizen, since all law is for the benefit of the corporate society as such, and the individual member benefits thereby. Hence, positivist jurists "deny either the existence of public law or the existence of a difference in nature between private and public law."[1] Yet the Romans drew this distinction and maintained it firmly. As early as the fifth century B.C. the earliest Roman code, the Twelve Tables, rigorously excluded administrative and constitutional law and public sacral law.[2] In Justinian's *Institutes* themselves, although the introductory texts do not say so, only private law is treated, plus the intermediate subjects of criminal law and court procedure. The same is true of the fifty books of Justinian's *Digest,* though in book 1 a few uncharacteristically short titles deal, not very systematically, with the duties of some officials, and a little more is said about public law in the final book. Justinian's *Code* is rather different; of the twelve books, the last three concern public law. But by no means do they give a full or systematic account, as witness the observation of François Hotman that Roman public law cannot really be known from the *Corpus juris.* Again, for whatever reason, these three books were treated separately from the others in the Middle Ages and later. The early printed editions of the *Corpus juris,* which follow the established tradition of the manuscripts, do not put these three books in

1. *Institutes,* p. 3.

2. The distinction between public and private law seems to have been expressly made at Rome only much later. The reason for the distinction occurring so early in Roman law requires investigation.

the same volume as the rest of the *Code* but place them separately in a different volume which also contains the *Novels* and the *Institutes*. Further, unlike the first nine books, they were not the subject matter of the ordinary lectures in the medieval law schools. The explanation often given for this treatment of the three books is that, when the *Corpus juris* came to be recovered in the eleventh century, the appropriate manuscript of the three books was found later than that of the other nine. A different explanation might be that they were always regarded as subsidiary because their subject matter does not correspond to anything in the *Digest* or *Institutes*.

In the *Corpus juris* the branch of law entitled "public law" was of little interest to the Roman jurists and was never subjected by them to the rigorous analysis reserved for private law. This in itself would inevitably cause difficulties for any later acceptance of the division. If the "seamless web" of law is to be treated as divided in two, then each part should have received at least a reasonably equal amount of attention.

The division into public and private law is not really discernible in medieval law, at least not before the rise of the Bologna law school.[3] And on the practical or processual level, the distinction remains unimportant until the eighteenth century. The social and political explanation usually given is that a seigneurial regime, with courts subject to a local magnate, was hostile to any division of jurisdiction, and that an absolutist concept of power scarcely allowed individuals to vindicate rights against the state, although the question is why eventually the distinction came to be accepted as fundamental. For the earlier part of the period, moreover, French law, like old English law, lived through practice without being studied or taught and was far from being a *Juristenrecht,* a law made and expounded by scholarly jurists.[4] Before the Reception of Roman law there was no fundamental difference between the systems operating in what are now classed as common law and civil law countries.

The distinction between public and private law inevitably appears in the works of the glossators, but in a way that stresses its lack of importance. In his *Quaestiones super institutis* Rogerius, known to be active in 1158, passes over the distinction in silence and jumps from the "precepts of the law" (1.1.3) to the distinction between natural law, the law of nations, and civil law (1.2pr.).[5] The *Gloss* on the *Institutes,* as on the *Di-*

3. See e.g. G. Chevrier, "Remarques sur l'Introduction et les Vicissitudes de la Distinction du 'jus privatum' et du 'jus publicum' dans les Oeuvres des Anciens Juristes Français," *Archives de philosophie du droit* 1, n.s. (1952): 5ff.

4. See Chevrier, "Distinction," p. 6n2.

5. See H. Kantorowicz, *Studies in the Glossators of the Roman Law* (Cambridge, Cambridge University Press, 1938), pp. 271ff.

gest, is so written as to give the impression that the main interest of the relevant text resides in determining whether there are two species or perhaps two genera of law. The *Gloss* also reports, as a result of D.1.1.2, that public law relates to religious rites, priests, and magistrates. This has little meaning for the distinction. And one looks in vain for a more meaningful discussion in the commentaries of subsequent centuries, such as those of the German Oinotomus, or Johann Schneidewin (1519–1568); of Matthew Wesenbecius (1531–1586), a native of Antwerp, student at Louvain, and professor at Jena; and of the Dutchman Johannes Voet (1647–1713).[6] Yet the distinction is, of necessity, endemic in their work. Public law is not dealt with in the *Institutes* or *Digest* and hence will be also omitted in commentaries written on these Roman works. Stress on the *Corpus juris* drives an intellectual wedge between private and public law; the great civilians were, in general, not public lawyers. The greater the prestige of Roman law, the less the status of public law, which derives and continues to derive from other sources. The institutes of local law which came to be so influential from the seventeenth century do not deal at all with public law. In the case of Scotland, for example, one of the most obvious distinctions between Stair's *Institutions of the Law of Scotland* (1681) and the earlier law books called "practicks," such as that of Lord Advocate Hope written around 1633, is that the latter, but not the former, deal with numerous aspects of public law as well as private law.

On the distinction in the works of the early French jurists, G. Chevrier suggests that "the appearance in the twelfth and thirteenth centuries of a legal mentality favorable to the learned concepts of *jus publicum* and *jus privatum* was not enough to impregnate our old law."[7] This and the evidence produced by Chevrier himself rather misstates the position.[8] Thus, Chevrier observes that for Irnerius, the earliest of the glossators, *ius publicum* is the totality of rights of a *universitas,* a "community," and relates to its common good; *ius commune,* a term destined to have a great future, designates the legal rule whose use is available to all individuals.[9] For Bulgarus, *ius commune* seems to be assimilated to *ius publicum.*[10] When such a *ius commune* tends toward *utilitas privata,* it is scarcely distinct from private law. Placentinus went beyond this point of view, interpreting *ius commune* restrictively as *ius commune omnium,*

6. *In quattuor institutionum imperialium Justiniani imp. libros commentarii; Commentarius in institutionum juris libros quattuor; Commentarius ad pandectas.*

7. "Distinction," p. 9.

8. "Distinction" pp. 26ff.

9. Gloss on *a jure communi* in D.2.14.7.16: *jus commune est id quod permittitur unicuique singulorum quod in re privata vertit, nam publicum universitatis est.*

10. Gloss on D.50.17.116.1.

"the law common to all', and thus a branch of public law whose other branch relates to public things considered individually.[11] Placentinus adopted an almost material criterion: *ius publicum* relates to publicly owned property, *ius privatum* to private property. Azo, in the appropriate place in his *Summa institutionum,* exaggerates Placentinus' opinion and claims that on this material basis there would be infinite species of law: equine law, asinine law, vineyard law, field law, a law of Peter and a law of John. Among French medieval civilians pride of place is given to Petrus de Bellapertica of the school of Orleans, who died in 1308. In the appropriate place of his *Commentary on the Institutes* he takes the word *positio,* "aspect," of Justinian's text as meaning *consideratio,* "point of view"; hence the determining factor for the classification is not the material object but the principal end in view, public utility or private interest. The distinction is then developed, and public law is declared to be triple in nature. Public law, "properly so called," is that which is publicly useful, such as relates to the *sacra* (religious observance).

All these medieval distinctions show the jurists as uninterested in public law as it was understood either by the Romans or by modern lawyers. Constitutional and administrative law are quite excluded from examination.[12] The consequence of the treatment of the distinction is either that public law is so defined that it falls within the scope of private law as understood by the Romans and as treated in the *Institutes* and *Digest,* or that public law is defined roughly in terms of its constituent elements and then ignored, as above all in the *Gloss.* There is no sign of "a legal mentality favorable to the learned concepts of *jus publicum* and *jus privatum.*"

Chevrier emphasizes that little progress is made for the distinction in the French customs of the fourteenth and fifteenth centuries, but he lays great stress for development on the *Pandectes du droit français,* first pub-

11. *Summa institutionum,* on 1.1.1.4: *In summa illud sciendum est quod jus publicum dicitur multis modis. Dicitur jus publicum scientia de rebus publicis et dictum est jus publicum jus commune omnium . . . Dicitur quoque jus publicum quod est constitutum in dominio cujuscumque rei publicae . . . Hujus studii duae sunt positiones, id est duo rerum genera in quibus posita est, id est de quibus loquitur haec scientia. Jus publicum, res publica; jus privatum, res privata. Vel aliter due sunt positiones: jus publicum, id est scientia de rebus publicis, consistentibus in sacris, in sacerdotibus, in magistratibus et haec scientia traditur in primo Codicis. Et jus privatum, id est scientia de rebus privatis.*

12. Some scholars of the time, including the Four Doctors and Bartolus, had political involvements in favor of or against the emperor. See e.g. Q. Skinner, *Foundations of Modern Political Thought* (Cambridge, Cambridge University Press, 1978), I, 8ff. But this involvement is not reflected in their disinterest in public law in general, though it may emerge for particular issues.

lished in 1593, by Charondas de Caron.[13] Caron divides civil law into two parts, public and private, and devotes the bulk of his first book to a treatment of civil public law. In his turn the abbot Claude Fleury (1640–1723) wrote in four parts his larger *Droit public de France,* which was published only in 1769 after his death. More important is *Le droit public* by Jean Domat (1625–1696), which was also published posthumously, as a continuation of his *Les loix civiles dans leur ordre naturel.*

When the institutions of local law appeared in France, they dealt only with civil law. For instance, Jerôme Mercier says of public law nothing more than: "The division of law into public and particular is retained in France, but the public actions are quite different from those practiced in Roman law. For in France they reside in the person of the King and of his Procureurs, whereas Roman law permitted them to each individual among the people. There is also this very remarkable difference that only the public avenger has this interest."[14] Even more to the point are the opening words of Argou in his *Institution au droit françois:* "French law has two parts: public law which concerns the nation in general and which covers everything that serves to protect Religion and the State; and the law of individuals which relates to them all equally, and which serves to regulate their rights and the differences they have, one with another. Private citizens concern themselves little in France with what relates to public law, knowledge of it being for them more of a curiosity than useful. That is why we will speak here only of the law of private individuals."

Chevrier observes that the contents of treatises on public law do not cease to be "floating and almost paradoxical" and claims that the works on private law are "bridled by the remembrance of the plan of Justinian's *Institutes.*"[15] But it is not a "remembrance" of Justinian's *Institutes* that accounts for the institutes of local law having in general the same contents; it is the immediate influence of Justinian's *Institutes* that specifically excludes from the institutes of French law any real treatment of public law—an exclusion that is observable in the earliest glosses and commentaries after the twelfth century renaissance, even though the jurists then were little interested in the distinction. The more the treatments of French law, including the *Code civil,* become formed in the mold of the institutes, and the less the impact of customs on form, the more marked becomes the distinction between public and private law.

13. "Distinction," pp. 44ff.

14. *Remarques nouvelles de droit françois sur les instituts de l'empereur Justinien,* book 1 on the words *Hujus studii.*

15. "Distinction," p. 58.

Chevrier brings forward a number of sociopolitical factors that may have been responsible for the growth, over some centuries, of public law.[16] But what is of importance for us is not the growth of public law, but the division of law into public law and private law. In old French law that division did not exist, and much of what was later classed as public law was in being long before any division was made. The distinction is created for later law by the commentaries and glosses on Justinian's *Institutes*. It is perpetuated because of the sophistication that permeates private civil law as a result of the concentration on it by the jurists, and because of the view that public law has very different roots since it does not derive, as French private law only partly does, from Roman law.

France stands as the example of all western continental Europe for the division of law into public and private at the theoretical level. The same history is repeated, with minor variations, in the other countries. The distinction at the processual level leads to the heart of a problem for legal history and development. In addition to a system of courts of private law, a "typical civil law nation will also have a set of administrative courts, entirely separate and exercising an independent jurisdiction."[17] A separate set of public law courts is not itself an inherent trait of Western legal systems, as witness its absence from common law systems; indeed, it is not an inevitable result of the legal doctrine that kept public law out of commentaries on the fundamental Justinian's *Institutes* and out of institutes of local law. But given that approach of legal doctrine and the power inherent in legal tradition, the separation of civil law and public law courts appears to follow easily from the legal tradition. The difficulty is to find political, social, and economic explanations that account not only for one legal system but generally for the division of public and private law courts in civil law countries and the absence of the division from common law countries. To put the problem at its crudest, Montesquieu's views on the separation of powers greatly influenced the French revolutionaries and are frequently given much of the credit for the different approaches in France to public and private law. That philosopher also had intellectual importance for the Constitution of the United States, where the influence of Montesquieu is even sometimes said to be greatest.[18] Yet the processual distinction between public law courts and private law courts has not appeared in that country. If an explanation of the differ-

16. "Distinction," pp. 39ff.

17. Merryman, *Civil Law Tradition*, p. 94.

18. See e.g. B. Russel, *History of Western Philosophy* (London, Allen & Unwin, 1946), p. 616; W. Jellinek, *Verwaltungsrecht*, 3rd ed. (Berlin, Springer, 1931), p. 7.

ence is then sought in the details of French life before the Revolution, such as the grave distrust of the judiciary, the explanation may suit France but not other civil law countries.

Marcel Waline, in explaining the processual distinction in France, stresses the importance of the historical circumstances in which the division of the tribunals occurred.[19] The existence of administrative jurisdictions goes back to the ancien régime, and before the Revolution there were specialized jurisdictions for some administrative matters. Thus, from 1309 there were *Chambres des comptes* to judge the accounts of persons publicly accountable. From at least 1413 there was a *Cour des aides* to judge the right of recourse of persons subject to tax against their indirect impositions, which also had appeal jurisdiction in some other public matters. By 1551 there was a *Cour des monnaies* for litigation on the striking of coin; and even earlier there was the *Chambre du trésor,* also called at other times *Chambre du domaine.* Furthermore, there were officials who in addition to their administrative functions had jurisdictional functions; the most important of these officials were the *intendants* of police, justice, and finance. Waline nonetheless denies a duality of orders of jurisdiction, or an order of jurisdiction of public law, largely on the ground that these courts of public law were not subjected to any supreme control, but each operated mainly on its own terms. The theoretical problem here is partly that the superior judicial bodies, namely the parlements, were not themselves subject to the jurisdiction of any supreme court which imposed uniform standards and rules. This problem for private law resulted from the fact that there was no unified law of France but only local customs. The parlements, of course, heard cases on both private and public law.[20]

Waline concludes that, although there were some courts specialized for particular parts of public law, there were not two separate orders of courts under the ancien régime. The separation is due rather to historical factors of the eighteenth and ninteenth centuries. The parlements under the ancien régime were hostile to the creation and multiplication of specialized administrative jurisdictions and above all to the granting of powers to the *intendants,* for the income of the members of the parlements depended on the number and importance of the cases they had to judge. The members of the parlements, all of whom were from the same

19. *Droit Administratif,* 9th ed. (Paris, Sirey, 1963), pp. 21ff; cf. O. Kahn-Freund, C. Lévy, and B. Rudden, *Source-Book on French Law,* 2nd ed. (Oxford, Clarendon Press, 1979), pp. 204ff.

20. See J. Brissaud, *History of French Public Law,* trans. J. W. Garner (London, Murray, 1915), pp. 432ff.

social background, showed great solidarity with one another, and they fought a determined battle against the administration. Their opposition to administrative and judicial reform made them very unpopular with the people as with the king.[21] Accordingly, one of the first acts of the Constituent Assembly was to suppress the parlements. It declared by title II article 13 of the law of August 16–24, 1790: "Judicial functions are distinct and will remain always separate from administrative functions; judges may not, under penalty of forfeiture, disturb in any way whatsoever the operations of administrative bodies."[22]

Thus at one stroke, observes Waline, the Constituent Assembly prevented the return of a particular abuse and applied the theory of Montesquieu. A law of 16 fructidor of year III (1795) set out the restriction on judges in even stronger terms: "Judges may not infringe upon administrative functions nor summon before them administrators on account of their functions. Iterative defenses are presented to the tribunals in order to recognize acts of administration of any kind." Napoleon, then, in 1799 set up administrative law tribunals and established the Conseil d'Etat. In the result, public law cases are decided by persons who are members of the executive or administration rather than of the judiciary.

The French system was enormously potent for many other civil law systems, as in Italy. Before Napoleon, Italy was made up of many states each having its own court system. Public law was not well developed and was certainly not the subject matter of a separate court system. The French structure was imposed on Italy by legislation of Napoleon, but with his fall the preceding organization was reintroduced except in the Duchy of Parma. Nonetheless the idea of public law courts had made progress, and as early as 1817 the Kingdom of Naples, succumbing to the pressure of a select company of jurists, appointed its own administrative law judges. This example was followed by the Papal States in 1835 and the Kingdom of Sardinia in 1842. Despite the unification of Italy, the various regions did not adopt a single system of public law courts until the administrative legislation of March 20, 1865.[23] Italian public law scholars, too, give much credit for modern administrative law to Montesquieu. Thus M. S. Giannini declares that from the beginning of the nineteenth century when it was born until around the middle of the twentieth century, administrative law lived, metaphorically, under the wings of the

21. See also David, *French Law,* pp. 23f.

22. Cf. Art. 3 of ch. 5 of the 1791 Constitution and Art. 203 of the 1795 Constitution.

23. See e.g. A.M. Sandulli, *Manuale di diritto amministrativo,* 12th ed. (Naples, Jovene, 1969), pp. 802ff. The Sardinian system, however, was extended to Lombardy and the Marches.

theory of the separation of power, in the specific formulation of the theory of the three parts of power as it was presented by Montesquieu and developed in the eighteenth century by successive political theorists.[24]

For such a development in Italy and elsewhere no answer can probably be given to the question of whether the result is due to the preceding tradition resulting from the study of the *Corpus juris* or to the direct influence of French law. For most countries the question probably poses a false dichotomy: both factors were influential, and they cannot be disentangled. The significant fact is that the approach adopted by the French was overwhelmingly successful, but successful only in countries with a civil law tradition. Even if the only direct *causa causans* of the acceptance of the division had been the French model—which it was not—the importance of the happening as an example of the force of the legal tradition for legal growth would not be diminished. At most there would be a switch of emphasis from the direct effect of using the *Corpus juris* as an organizing instrument at a time when France produced an instructive model to the direct effect of the French model on soil rendered fertile by study of the *Corpus juris*. In either event a massive legal transplant would be rendered possible or easy by the preceding legal transplant.

In Germany the first specialized tribunals for administrative law appeared only between the years 1863 and 1873, and they were not organized in a national framework but were for the individual states, a situation that continued until 1953 when a common appeals jurisdiction was set up for all the federal states. At the end of the eighteenth century, according to the standard view as expressed by Ernst Forsthoff, the science of public law was still at a very low point.[25] The condition of public law was against fruitful study. The decline and disappearance of the empire took from theoreticians their matter for study, and the Rhine Confederation did not replace it. The limitations of the law of the various states presented little interest for those seeking principle. Fundamentally, however, this view continues, the real reasons for the absence of any true science of public law were to be found in the structure of the state in the age of despotism: the administration of the police state (*Polizeistaat*) could not furnish material for a systematic theory of public law; for that there was needed the emergence of the law state (*Rechtsstaat*).

There nevertheless were published in the seventeenth century numerous works on the public law of the Holy Roman Empire. Some examples

24. *Diritto amministrativo* (Milan, Giuffrè, 1970), I, 33.

25. E. Forsthoff, *Lehrbuch des Verwaltungsrecht,* 10th ed. (Munich, Beck, 1973), I, 41ff.

are Daniel Otto, *De jure publico Romani imperii* (1616), on which there appeared notes and criticism in J. H. Boeclerus, *In Danielis Ottonis jus publicum notae et animadversiones* (1675); B. Schwederus, *Introductio in jus publicum imperii Romano-Germanici novissimum* (1681); N. Danckwerts, *Institutiones juris publicae selectissimae modernum imperii Romani statum* (1683); and P. R. Vitriarius, *Institutiones juris publici Romano Germanici selectae* (1686), in four books. There even appeared in 1691 a commentary on Vitriarius, the *Vitriarius illustratus* of J. F. Pffeffingerus. This grew into a two-volume work (1698, 1699), a three-volume (1725), and a four-volume (posthumously in 1731). The eighteenth century produced its own crop on public law, of which a few examples are J. E. Zschackwiz, *Einleitung zu dem teutschen jure publico oder Staats-Rechte* (1710), in question-and-answer form; Burkhard Gotthelf Struve, *Syntagma iuris publici imperii nostri Romano Germanici* (1711); and K. F. Haeberlin, *Handbuch des teutschen Staatsrecht* (1794–1797), in three volumes. Much earlier the most successful of the several collections on the subject appeared, J. J. Schmauss, *Corpus juris publici s. r. imperii academicum enthaltend das heil. röm. Reichs Grund-Gesetze.* Seven editions appeared between 1722 and 1794, and it is still made use of today.

Inevitably local conditions—political, social, and economic—play a large role in determining legal change. But these local conditions cannot, of themselves, explain why it is typical of civil law countries to have a separate set of public law tribunals or courts, and of common law countries to deal with public law and private law disputes in the same courts. Nor can the theories of Montesquieu bear the weight that is often put on them. A first problem is that Montesquieu's doctrines of separation of powers found most acceptance in practice in the framing of the Constitution of the United States, yet in that common law country the division of courts did not emerge. Clearly great reliance on Montesquieu's doctrines does not mean that the division of jurisdiction is inevitable. A second difficulty is how to take that division of jurisdiction from the theory of separation of powers; indeed, the division seems to run contrary to the thrust of the theory. The basic doctrine is that government has three parts—executive, legislative, and judicial—and that for liberty, each part should be independent of the others but able to exercise some degree of control over the others. Unfortunately Montesquieu devotes little attention to control of the executive and legislative powers by the judiciary. But prima facie it would appear obvious that there can be no liberty, at least in theory, if the executive is not subject to any independent judicial process; if, for example, when it acts contrary to enactments of the legislature, there is no means of formal restraint. An independent judiciary which has competence only for disputes among private individuals would not meet the needs of liberty. Montesquieu never claims that there should be an order of public law tribunals separate from the private law courts.[26]

None of this is meant to suggest that the views of Montesquieu were not in the minds of the speakers in the debates on the organization of the judiciary in the Constituent Assembly, though in actual fact Montesquieu was seldom mentioned. But the reports of the debates show the complexity of the arguments.[27] On the vexed question of whether there were three powers of government or only two, with that of judging being part of the executive, Montesquieu is cited on both sides. For persons who believe in the sovereignty of the people, an independent judiciary presents a genuine problem: judges, once appointed with security of tenure may, even deliberately, frustrate the will of the people. One solution widespread in the United States is to have judges popularly elected and holding office only for a limited term. Another, solution, widely canvassed in the Constituent Assembly and deriving from Montesquieu himself, is to place legal decisions in the hands of juries, where the jurymen are appointed for a relatively brief period. A difficulty here that was recognized in the Assembly is the untrained juryman's ignorance of law.

The solution accepted in France of a system of private law courts and a separate system of administrative tribunals is not obviously satisfactory since it basically does not resolve the problem, and it would have been even less obviously satisfactory at a time before it was anywhere in operation and when it had not been proposed by a political philosopher of the stature of Montesquieu. But the solution would have been both more obvious and more immediately attractive and acceptable to lawyers schooled in a legal tradition which not only made a clear distinction between private law and public law but also concentrated attention on the former, leaving the latter undeveloped. The words of Argou, whose *Insti-*

26. In ch. 6 of book 11 of *De l'esprit des lois* Montesquieu does write: "Il pourroit encore arriver que quelque citoyen, dans les affaires publiques, violeroit les droits du peuple, et feroit des crimes que les magistrats établis ne sauroient ou ne voudroient pas punir." But whatever he is thinking of here—the king?—he clearly has in view an exceptional case, for he continues: "Mais, en général, la puissance législative ne peut pas juger; et elle le peut encore moins dans ce cas particulier, où elle représente la partie intéressée, qui est le peuple."

27. See B.-J.-B. Buchez and P.-C. Roux, *Histoire parlementaire de la révolution française* (Paris, Paulin, 1836), V–VI. See also E. Thompson, *Popular Sovereignty and the French Constituent Assembly, 1789–91* (Manchester, Manchester University Press, 1952), pp. 86ff.

tution au droit français was among the many law books in Montesquieu's library, are germane: "Private citizens concern themselves little in France with what relates to public law, knowledge of it being for them more of a curiosity than useful."[28] Though the concerns of citizens had become politicized, lawyers were still trained to think of law as private law. And many of the members of the Constituent Assembly, especially those active in the debates on the judiciary—including Bergasse, Thouret, Duport, and Chabroud—were lawyers. In particular, Thouret had studied law at Paris and had been a counselor at the Parlement of Paris, and Duport had studied law at the University of Caen and had been official procurator of the provincial assembly of the subdivision of Rouen.

Thouret presented to the Assembly his report on the organization of the judiciary on December 24, 1789, though the debate on it did not begin until March 24, 1790. He claimed that while it was necessary that the judiciary be a separate power of government, its strength had to be controlled. Above all, with regard to administrative jurisdiction, he argued that when a nation elects its administrators, those ministers involved in the distribution of justice must not concern themselves with administrative duties that had not been entrusted to them. Duport had presented his project for judicial organization on December 22, 1789, and in the debate on March 29, 1790, he expressly drew a distinction between two kinds of law: the law governing relations between individual citizens was one kind, and that governing relations between a citizen and the state was another. "Judges," he announced, "should judge differences between citizens alone." Justinian's *Institutes* seem not to have been mentioned in the debate, but it would be unreasonable to deny them ultimate responsibility for the fundamentally important division of civil law jurisdiction, private law courts, and administrative law tribunals.

It is not at all clear whether Montesquieu's discussion of an independent judiciary related to public law matters as well as to private law. The topic is much disputed. Certainly, Montesquieu was aware of the traditional distinction between public law and private law. If his arguments about the independence of the judiciary relate only to judges or jurymen in suits between individuals, as can be claimed, then he seems to have expressed no opinion on how disputes relating to public law should be determined.

Local conditions are also relevant for legal change. The abuse by the

28. See L. Desgraves, *Catalogue de la bibliothèque de Montesquieu* (Geneva, Droz, 1954), p. 56. The library also included Mercier, *Remarques du droit françois sur les institutes de Justinien.*

parlements of their power in administrative matters is a case in point. And often local factors are particularly potent in determining the timing of legal change. The French Revolution, for example, forced a full questioning of the form of all aspects of government. But for the momentous reform of the judiciary, it was the existing legal tradition that determined the precise shape of the solution adopted. Local factors affected the development of the same processual division in Italy, Germany, and elsewhere, but there they were not the same. There was no abuse by parlements to be avoided, and the upheavals in those countries were not along the lines of the French Revolution. No legal development—typical of civil law countries, ignored in the common law world—better illustrates the force of legal tradition on legal growth, and in particular for civil law systems, the importance for the legal tradition of the prolonged study of the *Corpus juris* than the separation of public and private law.

The final word on the distinction between public and private law comes from Alexis de Tocqueville, *Democracy in America,* chapter 6, in the translation of Henry Reeve:

> In the year VIII of the French Republic a constitution was drawn up in which the following clause was introduced: "Art. 75. All the agents of the government below the rank of ministers can only be prosecuted for offences relating to their several functions by virtue of a decree of the Conseil d'Etat; in which case the prosecution takes place before the ordinary tribunals." This clause survived the Constitution of the year VIII and is still maintained, in spite of the just complaints of the nation. I have always found a difficulty in explaining its meaning to Englishmen or Americans, and have hardly understood it myself. They at once perceived that, the council of state in France being a great tribunal established in the center of the kingdom, it was a sort of tyranny to send all complaints before it as a preliminary step. But when I told them that the council of state was not a judicial body in the common sense of the term, but an administrative council composed of men dependent on the crown so that the king, after having ordered one of his servants, called a prefect, to commit an injustice, has the power of commanding another of his servants, called a councillor of state, to prevent the former from being punished. When I showed them that the citizen who has been injured by an order of the sovereign is obliged to ask the sovereign's permission to obtain redress, they refused to credit so flagrant an abuse and were tempted to accuse me of falsehood or ignorance.

The importance of the *Corpus juris* for divisions in the law that have practical consequences—above all of the division between private law courts and public law tribunals—is reinforced by the major division of private law in systems that regard the *Corpus juris* as authoritative. In these law systems private law typically divides into civil law—the subject matter of the civil codes—and commercial law. Of European civil law countries, only Switzerland and Italy—and Italy only from the reforms of 1942—have no separate commercial code; and most countries—with a few exceptions, such as Italy, or Holland from 1838—have separate tribunals for hearing commercial cases. Commercial law, as it is understood in civil law countries, does not appear in Justinian's *Institutes* and has mainly non-Roman historical roots. It would be an amazing coincidence if factors unconnected with this legal tradition were mainly responsible for this separation of commercial law from the rest of private law. Commentaries on the *Institutes* from the glossators onward by their very nature omit commercial law, and the same is true of writings on the *Corpus juris* generally. Even more significantly, the form and contents of institutes of local law follow the model of Justinian's *Institutes,* hence commercial law is not dealt with in them either. To this pattern the Dutch institutes are a significant exception, but even in them the treatment of commercial law is rather sparse.

The connection between this division and legal tradition is clarified by events at the time of the French Revolution. Commercial law in civil law systems is attached to the person as well as to the subject matter; it is the law used by business people in the conduct of their business affairs. Following through the abolition of noble and feudal privileges, the revolutionary leaders wished to suppress corporations and the commercial class. The Decree of May 2–17, 1791, granted liberty of commerce to all Frenchmen under the sole condition of paying the new tax for the right; and the Decree of June 14–17, 1791, suppressed the corporations and forbade their reconstitution. Logically the legislators should now have abolished commercial law, for commercial law was the law of the commercial class, and with the disappearance of the class, there was no raison d'être for commercial law.[29] Yet in 1801, within a year of setting up the commission to draft the civil code, Napoleon set up a commission of seven members to prepare the Commercial Code, which was promulgated in 1807.

The connection between the separation of commercial law from civil

29. See e.g. J. Hamel and G. Lagarde, *Traité de droit commercial* (Paris, Dalloz, 1954), I, 30; David, *French Law,* pp. 112ff.

law and the former's historical derivation from roots other than the *Corpus juris* is widely admitted, though other factors favoring the separation are often urged. Sometimes it is said that the rules of commercial law are peculiarly different from those of civil law.[30] To the extent that this statement is true, the explanation in large measure is the historical evolution; the statement also contains an exaggeration, as the trend toward unifying commercial law with the rest of civil law shows.

Sometimes the internationality of the legal rules involved and of commerce itself are stressed.[31] But there are two arguments against that explanation. First, the general rules of the law of contract and the individual contracts, such as sale, barter, loan, hire, partnership, and mandate, that derive from Roman law are equally international in character as law and are equally involved in transnational business, yet they are always treated in the civil code, though commercial sale appears in the commercial code. Second, the international character of the rules of commercial law largely follows from historical legal conditions. From the Middle Ages onward there was no legal basis to be found for them in Roman law, and the powers of legislation in the individual states were extremely limited. Hence to a considerable extent the law had to develop on the foundation of the customs of merchants trading among themselves. Franz Wieacker concludes that a requirement for the growth of this kind of international legal system is that there exists a weakness in the national, territorial, or local legislative powers.[32] Commerce is frequently across legal frontiers, but it does not follow from this that the legal rules for each jurisdiction should be set out separately from the rest of the local law or be administered by separate tribunals. Thus, Switzerland with its numerous small cantons had more than its fair share of transjurisdictional transactions, before a more or less unified Swiss law developed, yet this did not lead to commercial law being treated separately from the rest of the law of obligations. Moreover, when commercial disputes require speedier, more flexible resolution, this can be achieved by an agreement to arbitration by the contracting parties and need not involve the state setting up a separate system of courts or tribunals.

A further justification for the separation of private law and commercial law is that in the Middle Ages trade tended to be closely regulated and was usually carried on under license by members of privileged asso-

30. See e.g. W. Hefermehl's Introduction to his edition of the *Handelsgesetzbuch* (Munich, Deutscher Taschenbuch Verlag, 1967), p. 9.

31. David, *French Law,* pp. 112ff.

32. "On the History of Supranational Legal System of Commerce," in *Legal Organization of Commerce* (Aarhus University Symposium, Provinsbanken, 1979), pp. 11f, 14.

ciations. Thus, it might be urged that commercial law, not being generally applicable, was not thought to be part of private law. But the separation of treatment on this account would have been deliberate, and there is no indication in early writers that they recognized any such explanation for the separation of treatment. Another objection would be that the particular rules applying to guilds, fairs, markets, and merchants are in fact set out along with private law in such books of medieval aspect as the *Practicks* of around 1579 of the Scot, James Balfour. These topics drop out of later works with the Romanization of Scots law.

In a number of European countries a commercial code was promulgated earlier than the civil code. Here, too, the phenomenon is more easily explained in terms of legal tradition than in economic and political terms. Although in the nineteenth century industrialized Germany urgently needed its commercial law set out clearly and authoritatively to benefit its international trade, such was hardly the case for Spain or Portugal. What, however, was of general application in the countries of the civil law was a greater need to have a clear and authoritative statement of commercial law, precisely because that body of law did not have behind it, to the same extent as the rest of private law, centuries of scholarly exposition, interpretation, and development based on an accepted text such as Justinian's *Institutes.* The rules of commercial law, before codification, were just less easily knowable.

The modern trend in civil law systems is toward a unified code that includes commercial law and civil law. This was accomplished for Italy in 1942, and for Holland it will be accomplished by the new *Burgerlijk Wetboek.* It was also under consideration in France before the movement for reform of the *Code civil* came to a halt for other reasons.[33] And it is now a live issue in Germany.[34] This trend by itself shows the weakness of some of the explanations of the distinctions made between commercial law and the rest of private law. The simplest explanation of the trend is that now commercial law and civil law have the same kind of source, namely their respective codes, and the gulf that historically existed between them is less noticeable. Since otherwise they are not so very different as law or in function, the argument for treating them separately is weak.

Private law is also subdivided and one branch of law is much more highly developed in the civil law systems than in the common law. Justin-

33. See e.g. David, *French Law,* pp. 115f.

34. See e.g. W. Müller-Freienfels, "Zur 'Selbständigkeit' des Handelsrechts," *Festschrift für E. von Caemmerer* (Tübingen, Mohr, 1978), pp. 583ff.

ian's *Institutes* rather artificially forces divisions and subdivisions of obligations into groups of four. The basic division is into obligations "from contract or as if from contract or from delict or as if from delict."[35] Subsequent ages made substantives out of "as if from contract" and "as if from delict," namely quasi-contract and quasi-delict. The *Institutes* deal *inter alia* with *negotiorum gestio,* "unauthorized administration," and *indebiti solutio,*" payment of something not owed," as obligations "as if from contract".[36]

The obligation of *negotiorum gestio* came into existence when one person, without authorization, acted on behalf of another, whether the acting was to enter contractual relations with another person or not. The principal had the right to an action if the *gestor* was negligent; but if the matter had involved urgency, the *gestor* was liable only for fraud. The *gestor's* action was for useful expenses, that is, expenses which benefited the principal at the time they were incurred, even if later they proved to be in vain. The *gestor's* action was available only if he had acted to benefit the principal and if it was reasonable for him so to act. If he had intended to benefit himself even partially, he lost his right to bring an action. Since *negotiorum gestio* was equiparated to the contract of mandate which was essentially gratuitous, the *gestor* had no claim to receive fees or payment for his services.[37]

Indebiti solutio gave rise to an action called the *condictio,* which was available in a range of situations though only *indebiti solutio* is dealt with in the *Institutes.* The *condictio* was in form an abstract action in which the grounds of the claim were not set out in the pleadings. In general the action could be brought only if there had been a previous transfer of ownership from the plaintiff to the defendant and if there was no reason for the defendant's retaining the thing. In addition, the object of the action had either to be a fixed sum of money or a particular thing, though the condemnation in a Roman action was always for a sum of money, not for delivery of a thing. Although the form of the *condictio* was always the same, the Roman jurists, according to the *Digest,* often wrote of the action in terms of the legal situation involved. Thus, there was a *condictio* for *mutuum,* loan of a fungible for consumption, and a *condictio indebiti,* where payment had been made of a debt that was not owed or

35. *J*.3.13.2. In other texts *maleficium* appears as *delictum.*

36. *J*.3.27.

37. For *negotiorum gestio* see Thomas, *Textbook,* pp. 321ff. For particular modern civilian developments in the criminal law and in the law of compensation which arise from the acceptance of *negotiorum gestio* see Watson, *Society and Legal Change,* pp. 144f.

due. Again, there was a *condictio causa data causa non secuta,* where something had been given for a cause or consideration and the anticipated result had not transpired. The *condictio ob turpem causam* lay when something had been given for an immoral purpose and the recipient's immorality was greater than that of the donor. Finally, there was the *condictio furtiva,* an action by the victim against the thief which was quite exceptional since the plaintiff, not the defendant, was the owner of the object of the action.[38] The *condictio* is therefore basically an action for unjustified enrichment.

Negotiorum gestio and the general action for unjustified enrichment have become integral and prominent parts of modern civil law. French law on the former is typical, as are German and French law on the latter.

The French *gestion d'affaires,* unauthorized administration, is governed by the *Code civil:*

> Art. 1372. When one voluntarily manages the affairs of another, whether the owner knows of the management or whether he does not know, he who manages contracts the tacit engagement to continue the management which he has commenced, and to complete it until the owner is in a position to be able to do it himself; he must also take responsibility for all the incidentals of these affairs. He is subject to all the obligations which would have resulted had the owner given him an express agency.
>
> 1373. He is obligated to continue his management when the owner dies before the affairs are consummated, until the heir is able to take over control.
>
> 1374. He is required to bring to the management of affairs all the care of a good father of a family. Nevertheless, the circumstances which led him to undertake the matter may authorize the judge to moderate the damages which resulted from the faults or negligence of the manager.
>
> 1375. The owner whose affairs have been well administered must fulfill the engagements which the manager contracted in his name, indemnify him for all personal engagements into which he entered, and reimburse him for all the proper and necessary expenses which he incurred.[39]

38. There may also have been a *condictio* on the contract of *stipulatio.* For the *condictio* see Thomas, *Textbook,* pp. 326ff.

39. *French Civil Code,* trans. J. H. Crabb (Rothman, South Hackensack, 1977), p. 252. See also R. Bout, *La gestion d'affaires en droit français contemporain* (Paris, Pichon & Durand-Auzias, 1972).

In addition, *gestion d'affaires* is equiparated to the contract of *mandat* (mandate). Since mandate in French law is gratuitous by nature but not in essence and hence the mandatory may contract for payment, the unauthorized agent may also in certain circumstances be entitled to claim payment.

Title 24 of book 2 of the German *BGB*, §§812–822, is dedicated to unjustified enrichment, and the treatment there derives ultimately, but clearly, from Justinian's *Digest*. Thus, the first sentence of the basic section, 812, reads: "Whoever, through the performance of another or in any other way acquires something at that person's expense, without legal justification, is duty bound to return it to him." In addition to the three very Roman requirements in the section—an acquisition by the defendant, made without legal justification, at the expense of the plaintiff—the German courts have added a fourth requirement, which is frequently attacked, namely that the movement of benefit from plaintiff to defendant must have been direct and so must not have passed through the estate of a third party.

The *BGB* then proceeds in various articles to set out specific circumstances for the action which German scholars call *Kondiktion* instead of *condictio*.[40] Indeed, they talk in terms of a plurality of actions, *Kondiktionen*, conceived of in Roman terms whether or not they use the Latin words.[41] Sections 813-814 deal with the *condictio indebiti*. Section 815 relates, thus, to the *condictio causa data causa non secuta*, *condictio* where something has been given without the intended return: "The right to demand return on account of the nonoccurrence of the result intended by a performance is excluded if the production of the result was impossible from the beginning and the person who performed knew this or if the person who performed had obstructed the production of the result in bad faith." This section, like others, is constructed on the basis that it can be assumed, presumably on account of §812, that normally return can be demanded. Section 817 deals with the *condictio ob turpem causam*, *condictio* for an immoral cause. As in Roman law, the action is available only if the immorality of the defendant is greater than that of the plaintiff. Though this last stated rule is extended to all cases of unjustified en-

40. See e.g. K. Larenz, *Lehrbuch des Schuldrechts*, vol. 2, *besonderer Teil*, 10th ed. (Beck, Munich, 1972), pp. 401ff.

41. Thus Larenz, *Schuldrecht*, II, 419, talks of the *condictio indebiti*. For a scholar of German origin writing in English see E. J. Cohen, *Manual of German Law*, 2nd ed. (London, British Institute of International and Comparative Law, 1968), I, 304ff, who talks of *condictio indebiti, condictio causa data causa non secuta, condictio ob causam finitam, condictio ob iniustam vel turpem causam*.

richment in German law, it applies only within that sphere. A post-Roman, particularly German, *condictio* is that known as the *condictio post finitam causam, condictio* where the legal ground falls away after a performance by the plaintiff but before performance by the debtor.[42]

Previously, the French *Code civil* had taken the other Roman approach, that of Justinian's *Institutes,* and dealt in §§1376–1381 only with *indebiti solutio.* At first the Cour de Cassation was unwilling to admit the existence of a general action, but this attitude changed notably in a famous decision in 1892.[43] This general action, known as the action *de in rem verso,* "for property turned to account"—a Roman term, though the action does not greatly correspond to the *actio de peculio et de in rem verso,* "action on a son or slave's fund and property turned to account—is now judged in terms of a formula of Charles Aubry and Charles Rau: "the action *de in rem verso* based on the principle of equity that prohibits enrichment at the expense of another" should be admitted "in all cases in which the patrimony of one person is, without legitimate cause, enriched at the expense of that of another, and that latter person would not enjoy, to receive what was due him, any action arising from a contract, quasi-contract, delict or quasi-delict."[44] According to Gabriel Marty and Pierre Raynaud, this formulation has acquired a quasi-legislative authority.[45]

Thus, quasi-contract has in civilian systems a substantive importance quite foreign to its equivalents in the common law.[46] This remains true even for codes such as the *BGB,* which does not treat quasi-contract as a separate classification of obligation, or the Colombian *Código civil,* which at article 2304 treats *negotiorum gestio* as a contract.

One further example where a difference between civilian and common law systems is explicable only on the basis of established legal tradition is that commercial partnerships in civil law systems are endowed with legal personality on the basis of the so-called "entity theory," whereas those of common law systems have not on the premise of the so-called "aggregate theory." To the basic common law position, Ghana

42. See e.g. Larenz, *Schuldrecht,* II, 422f. This *condictio* is important largely because of *BGB* §323.

43. See e.g. G. Marty and P. Raynaud, *Droit civil* II.i (Paris, Sirey, 1962), pp. 309ff.

44. *Cours de droit civil français,* 4th ed. (Paris, Marchal et Billard, 1869–1883), VI, 246, §578. A rather different approach appears in the most recent edition of Aubry and Rau, the 6th: *Droit civil français* (Paris, Librairies techniques, 1975), VI, 473ff.

45. *Droit civil* II.i, p. 311.

46. See e.g. A. Coleman, "The Concept of Unjust Enrichment in English Law," *Cambrian Law Review* 10 (1979): 8ff.

is a recent exception. Of the mixed systems, Scotland, Quebec, and Louisiana follow the civil law model, and South Africa retains the common law model.

Differences between the structure of law in France and in Germany are explained by the fact that the penetration of the legal tradition by natural law was much greater in Germany than it was in France at the time of the promulgation of the *Code civil.* France and Germany are both civil law systems, but they can be thought of as members of different legal families within the civil law. The legal tradition not only dominates the structure of the law, but it has profound effects on the substance of the law. This impact of the tradition on substance is obvious not just in the contrast between common law and civil law but also in important differences between civilian families as represented by France and Germany. One illustration is the requirement of equality of contractual prestations.

In Roman law generally, the validity of a contract was not affected if, in the absence of fraud or duress, one party had made a very bad bargain. But in Justinian's *Code* two rescripts attributed to the Emperor Diocletian at the end of the third century A.D. declare that a sale can be set aside if the seller agreed on a price that was less than half of the true value. The scope of the rule in the rescripts is not easily determined since they, like many others, are issued in reply to a petitioner concerned with a very concrete case. In both rescripts the question had to do with the sale of land when the price was too low. Scholars have usually, but by no means universally, held that the doctrine of *laesio enormis* (enorm lesion), as it is called, did not apply to the sale of movables or in cases where the price offered was more than twice the value of the land.

The reasonableness of setting aside a contract which was freely entered into, simply on the ground that one party made a bad bargain, raises questions. But if that issue is ignored, the Roman rule, as usually understood, is still hard to justify. Why should it apply only to sale and not also to other contracts? Why should it not equally apply where the land was worth less than one half of the agreed on price? With the Reception of Roman law the glossators considered the rescripts and from the outset treated *laesio enormis* as applying to sales of movables as well as of land. By the mid-twelfth century, the application of the benefit of the rule to the buyer was being considered, and that doctrine eventually prevailed.[47] Medieval canon lawyers and theologians, such as Aquinas, were interested in the whole question of equality of prestation because of the

47. See J. W. Baldwin, *Medieval Theories of the Just Price, Transactions of the American Philosophical Society* n.s. vol. 49, pt. 4 (Philadelphia, 1959), pp. 21ff.

prohibition of usury, and their discussions were to prove influential for the natural lawyers of the seventeenth and eighteenth centuries. Thus Grotius declares that natural law demands there be equality of obligation in bilateral contracts of all kinds and that the party who receives less has a right of action based on the inequality. He also observes that the Romans established this rule not for trivial differences but only for important differences, and he gives as one example the case "which exceeds half the just price."[48] Grotius obviously approves the view that law, unlike philosophers, should deal with injustices only insofar as it can lay hold of them, but he does not seem necessarilly to restrict the law's intervention to instances where one party's obligation is worth less than half of the other's. Grotius' approach is refined by other natural lawyers, such as Christian Wolff.

Now natural law had not much penetrated French law when the *Code civil* was promulgated. Article 1118 says that lesion vitiates only certain contracts; and article 1674 sets out the rule where the injured party has full legal capacity:

> If the seller has been injured by more than seven-twelfths in the price of an immovable, he has the right to demand rescission of the sale even if in the contract he had expressly renounced the right to demand this rescission and stated he was making a gift of the excess value.

This is very much the Roman rule. Lesion is actionable only in the sale of land, only where the seller is the party injured, and only when the discrepancy in the value of the prestations can be expressed by fractions.[49]

In Germany the natural law tradition was much stronger. Section 138 of the *BGB* reads in its original form:

> (1) A legal transaction which is contrary to good morals is void.
> (2) In addition a legal transaction is void whereby a person exploiting the situation of need, indiscretion, or inexperience of another, causes to be promised or granted in return for a performance, financial advantages which so far exceed the value of the performance that in the circumstances the financial advantages are in obvious disproportion to the performance.

48. *De jure belli ac pacis* 2.12.8–12.

49. Northern France before codification was never so civilian as, for instance, Germany was. Hence the influence of the *Glossa magna* was not so great. See e.g. Pothier, *Traité des obligations,* sections 33–39.

This time any kind of contract may be set aside for lesion, and no necessary fraction of disproportion is established.

In the drafting of the codes, opposition was raised both in France and Germany to the rules adopted. Yet in both countries the rules actually adopted harmonize with the respective strengths of the varying strands of the legal tradition.

XI
Sources of Modern Civil Law

CODIFICATION profoundly affects the civil law tradition. For example, the sources of law undergo change, and they may now reasonably be categorized as primary, subordinate, and derivative. The previous tradition, though, where the *Corpus juris* was the organizing instrument, remains obliquely important.

With codification, law becomes basically and primarily statute law, and the code is the private law statute *par excellence.*[1] The term "statute" is here used to include governmental and ministerial decrees. No other independent source of law need be recognized; if one is, it will be custom and custom alone and will be subordinate to statute, having only a minor role to play.

The systematic and comprehensive nature of the code with supporting legislation makes law statute-oriented to an extent that is otherwise impossible; and the code and supporting legislation provide the skeleton of the whole of private law. Lawmaking then, insofar as it is permitted, by interpretation whether of the code, other statute, contract, or will, or by filling gaps in the law, is in codified systems a making of derivative law, which raises the question of who has the authority to make this derivative law. The authority to interpret or to fill the gap may be attributed to legislators, to scholars, to judges, or to a combination, and the authority may be to settle the law for the instant case or also for the future.

No fixed pattern has emerged in the civil codes for the treatment of sources. Some, notably the German *BGB,* say nothing about sources at

1. David, *French Law,* pp. 155ff.

all. The French *Code civil* does not treat the sources except in a negative way: article 5 states that it is forbidden for judges to pronounce by way of general and regular disposition on the cases submitted to them. Articles 1-3 deal with statute in a way that shows, without any express statement to that effect, that it is at least the most important source of law. A valid law is not defined in the French code, but it is in some other codes, such as the *Código civil* of Chile, article 1. The Austrian *ABGB* also does not define statute, but it does explain the nature of "civil law" in §1. The 1942 Italian *Codice civile* goes so far as to list in §1 "regulations" (*regolamenti*) as a source of law and elaborates on these in §3. Again, some but by no means all codes, such as the Austrian *ABGB* §§6–8 and the Chilean *Código civil* articles 19–26, set out principles and rules of interpretation. Many codes spell out the precise status of custom, which varies from place to place, and some, such as article 5 of the French *Code civil* and §12 of the Austrian *ABGB,* deal with judicial decisions. Article 1 of the Swiss civil code has always been regarded as particularly noteworthy:

> The law regulates all matters to which the letter or the spirit of any of its provisions relates.
>
> In the absence of an applicable legal provision, the judge pronounces in accordance with customary law and, in the absence of a custom, according to the rules that he would establish if he had to act as legislator.
>
> He is guided by the solutions consecrated by juristic opinion and case law.[2]

Custom may or may not be recognized as a source of law, and if it is, the scope given to it may be restricted.[3] Thus, the *herrschende Lehre,* or dominant opinion, accepts only two sources of private law in Germany, statute and custom, and regards them as being of equal value.[4] In fact, custom has a far smaller role than statute to play in legal growth. The extended treatment of custom as a source of law in commentaries such as those of Karl Larenz is itself most easily explained as the result of legal tradition: in old Germanic law and even in the nineteenth century, custom was of great importance, as witness Friedrich von Savigny. According to §10 of the Austrian *ABGB,* attention can be paid to custom only in

2. See I. Williams, *The Sources of Law in the Swiss Civil Code* (Oxford, Oxford University Press, 1923).

3. See e.g. David, *French Law,* pp. 170ff.

4. See e.g. K. Larenz, *Allgemeiner Teil des deutschen bürgerlichen Rechts,* 3rd ed. (Munich, Beck, 1975), pp. 5ff.

situations in which a law refers to it. For the Chilean *Código civil* it is only in such situations that custom constitutes law. Article 17 of the Argentinian *Código civil,* as it now is, goes a little further, declaring that usages and customs cannot create rights except when laws refer to them or in situations which are not regulated by law. Custom, as a source of law, is thus subordinate in the sense either that it is relevant only if there is no applicable statute or that it is relevant only if mentioned in a statute.

But the particular nature of the modern civil law systems is to be seen in the treatment of the derivative sources relating to interpretation and the filling of gaps in the law.[5] One approach taken from time to time, which seems to have in it nothing peculiar to the civil law tradition, is to hold that the legislator or even only the legislator is entitled to give an authoritative interpretation of general application or sometimes even for the instant case. There is nothing theoretically strange in this approach; since the legislator is alone capable of issuing statutes whose scope he has also determined, he and he alone can on this view give the correct or authoritative interpretation. Moreover, there are political advantages to this approach, in that it is not restricted to matters of interpretation but can even deal with important legal innovations. In one version of it that was current in the Roman Empire, a litigant or other private person might petition the emperor, or a judge or official might ask the emperor for guidance on a legal point, and the emperor's written reply was conclusive as to the law. Many such rescripts, as they are generally called, are preserved in Justinian's *Code.* More recently, under §47 of the Introduction to the Prussian *Allgemeines Landrecht für die Preussischen Staaten,* a judge faced with a difficulty of interpretation has to remit the problem, without naming the parties, to the Law Commission; only on receipt of this answer is the judge to decide the case.[6] When no legal rule covers the case, the judge by §49 has to proceed to judgment, but by §50 he has immediately to inform the minister of justice of the gap in the law.[7] The first paragraph of article 3 of Chile's *Código civil* declares that it is the task of the legislator alone to explain or to interpret the law in a generally binding way. And article 5 states that the Supreme Court of Justice and the appeal courts will in March of every year give an account of the doubts and difficulties they encountered in understanding and applying the laws, and of the gaps they noticed in them.

5. See e.g. David, *French Law,* pp. 179ff; Y. Loussouarn, "Relative Importance of Legislation, Custom, Doctrine and Precedent in French Law," *Louisiana Law Review* 18 (1957–1958): 235ff.

6. This was changed by Appendix 2 of §48.

7. For a similar modern proposal see A. Watson, "Two-Tier Law—A New Approach to Law-Making," *ICLQ,* 1978, pp. 552ff.

The real contrast between common law and civil law systems, where the force of the old civil law tradition asserts itself, is in the weight to be attributed for lawmaking to judicial decision and to academic juristic opinion, in the judicial career structure and in the form of law reports. On the face of it there seems to be no compelling reason for all civil law systems to have a broadly similar approach which, however, differs strongly from the usual common law attitudes. A code is a statute, and although it is comprehensive in a way that other statutes are not, the comprehensiveness is not a factor that is usually of importance for interpretation. Practical legal issues facing a court or scholar normally concern only a few provisions, and in this regard nothing distinguishes problems arising from a code or statute in civil law countries and those arising from a statute in common law countries. Whether judicial precedent is or is not binding, whether the dominant academic opinion has or has not great weight, are questions to which the answer does not appear to flow from the nature of the system as codified civil law or uncodified common law. The distinguishing features of codified civil law systems, which are lessening, were historically determined by the nature of civil law systems before codification.

In case law before codification, technically the opinions of the great doctors and other jurists were never binding; precedent might be, if it was from the Supreme Court of the state in question and formed a series establishing a judicial custom. But the weight of citation tended very much to be on the jurists. Although no individual jurist or group of jurists or even the majority cited was decisive, the prestige attributed to juristic opinion was enormous. The more the rules were Roman in descent and the more the *Corpus juris civilis* was used as the organizing instrument, the more highly was academic juristic opinion rated, however varied it might be, as the true interpreter of the law. Likewise the more Roman, the more international, and hence the greater the possibility of celebrity and influence. No civil law judge *qua* judge could ever hope to have the fame and influence of a Bartolus or Molinaeus. Juristic opinion was cited because of its supposed merit in a way significantly denied to judicial decisions from unrelated jurisdictions. Juristic opinion was treated as valuable in itself as an interpretation of the law and was timeless, whereas judicial decision was strictly tied to time and place. Whereas judges did not ignore jurists, jurists in their writings ignored the judges.

Further, in practice, precedent suffered from two other drawbacks. First, it was often, as in France and Italy, very local in character. In a jurisdiction which had no large population it would not be common to have a line of decisions long enough to establish a judicial custom on a precise point. Moreover, a great deal of doubt could exist as to what constituted a judicial custom. How many cases need there be with the same decision? How precisely on the issue need they be? How was one to find the determining factors? Were judicial statements made obiter to be relevant? Was one recent opposing decision fatal to the creation of the custom? And so on. In the absence of a statute on the matter there was no authoritative answer to these questions. And, of course, the jurists with their academic approach to law were little interested in suggesting answers. Second, even when there was such a line, it would not necessarily be easy to uncover. Juristic writers, with the exception of Lord Stair, do not in their accounts of local law set out the judicial precedents.[8] Though Stair does, he does not cite more than one or two cases, and one has to take it on trust that the citations represent a line of decisions. At least from the perspective of the twentieth century it is usually not possible to know whether Stair's citation is of the final and decisive case. Then not every jurisdiction had accessible or, above all, printed reports; and the reports that were available were at times inadequately indexed, if at all.

Thus on the eve of codification the heroes of civil law systems were academic jurists, not judges.[9] Logically this result of the emphasis on the *Corpus juris* need not have carried over to codified systems. A code is not usually a legal source remote in time, place, and language from the courts that enforce it. Codes are local, not supranational, in character, even though codified civil law systems retain some degree of internationality. Abstract and systematic legal reasoning may seem less valuable, and social and economic awareness more valuable, for the understanding of the law. Timeless exegesis for its own sake is not obviously relevant. Defects in a code can be remedied by revision in a way not possible for the *Corpus juris*. There is no longer such a premium on sophistical reasoning. Again, the law students at any national university, who intend to practice law, are for the most part natives of the country, and what they want to know is the law of that geographical entity, for which they want to know how the courts of that jurisdiction will decide.[10] If there is a difference between the interpretation of judges and of academics, then what the stu-

8. Stair's is a unique situation in that he was the first Scot to write a comprehensive account of the law and was also Lord President of the Court of Session, i.e. the supreme judge. His account of the local law might therefore be more readily accepted.

9. See e.g. Cappelletti et al., *Italian Legal System*, pp. 170ff.

10. Cf. major contemporary American law schools, which draw students from all over the United States and which may not teach at all the law of the state in which they are situated, teaching instead a generalized law of the United States. They are reminiscent of much civil law practice before codification.

dent needs for his subsequent career is an appreciation of the former. Moreover, with the advent of an adequate civil code there is not even a great need for dedicated and outstandingly able theoreticians and scholars. This claim may seem prima facie perverse in view of the centuries of civilian scholarship and the continuing academic tradition, in Germany above all. But codification makes law much more accessible on a day-to-day level, if not necessarily at the most abstruse level, to law student and practicing lawyer alike. Confirmation for this can be found in the numerous civil law countries, particularly in Latin America, where in some states virtually all law teaching is conducted by part-time professors who are above all engaged in practice. In such countries the writing of law books or articles of any kind may be an exceptional activity; students may not be expected to read books or articles, or cases, apart from the code and some statutes but to concentrate for examinations on the lectures they have attended; and university law libraries may contain only a few hundred volumes, of which the vast majority concern foreign jurisdictions, international law, Roman law, and legal philosophy. Even among the foreign law books relatively few may be on private law. It is one of the great glories of codified law that it makes possible, if not exactly desirable, adequate law teaching at a very low level of competence.

Academic jurists nevertheless continue to have great influence in the civil law systems, though this influence seems to be waning.[11] Unless some jurists are officially "licensed" to give particularly authoritative opinions, as seems to have happened in the early Roman Empire, no opinion of an individual jurist *qua* jurist can be binding.[12] Nor can an unofficial system be devised that can technically give preference to the opinion of selected jurists. Of course, it can happen that in particular fields the reputation of one scholar is so high that his opinion is regularly given preference over others, but a less formal approach is usually adopted. A jurist's authority depends not on any specific position that he holds but on his persuasiveness both in general and on the particular point. This persuasiveness, to be effective, must be communicated to the judges, and this is most readily done if the jurist enjoys a generally high reputation among his fellows and if on the particular point his opinion is shared by his colleagues. Thus arises the doctrine in Germany and else-

11. See e.g. David, *French Law*, pp. 188ff.

12. The scope of the *ius respondendi*, whether at the time of its introduction by Augustus or subsequently, is unclear. See e.g. H. F. Jolowicz and B. Nicholas, *Historical Introduction to the Study of Roman Law* (Cambridge, Cambridge University Press, 1972), pp. 359ff; Thomas, *Textbook*, pp. 43ff.

where of the "dominating opinion," the *herrschende Meinung* or *herrschende Lehre.* The prevailing opinion among the professors and also in precedent is usually followed by the courts. This approach is so accepted that authors of legal treatises usually give the *herrschende Lehre* as well as their own opinion. The importance of juristic doctrine in one country, Germany, is shown in four examples.

The first example is the doctrine known as *venire contra factum proprium,* or to act contrary to one's own past behavior. A person in whom a right is vested may not exercise that right if he has not done so in the past and if another person could and did fairly rely on his continued non-exercise of the right. This doctrine has come to be an accepted part of German law mainly as a result of a monograph, *Venire contra factum proprium, Studien im römischen, englischen und deutschen Civilrecht,* by Erwin Riezler, who at the time was an extraordinary professor at the University of Freiburg.[13] Riezler's main aim in this comparative work is to demonstrate the usefulness of the English doctrine of estoppel for contemporary German law. He expressly states that the work will offer a modest contribution to the problem of legal decision *praeter legem,* namely filling gaps in the law by going beyond the existing statute.[14]

In the second example, the German *BGB* deals with only two kinds of breach of contract: delay due to fault by §286 and impossibility due to fault by §280. But a third kind of breach of contract is accepted in German law, namely *positive Vertragsverletzungen,* or positive breaches of contractual duty. This gap in the *BGB,* which was uncovered by Herman Staub, has come to be filled thanks to the approval given to his *Die positiven Vertragsverletzungen,*[15] despite considerable opposition expressed to his first version.

In the third example, by §278 with regard to contract a person is liable for acts of persons in his service to the same extent as for his own acts, and by §831 with regard to delict he is liable for the acts of persons in his service unless he exercised reasonable care in selecting his servants. By the doctrine of *culpa in contrahendo,* or fault in contracting, which in German law is due to Rudolph von Jhering, contractual liability now applies to cases where no contract was concluded, though the parties took preliminary steps toward entering a contract, and hence an employer cannot escape liability for a servant's act at that stage on the ground that

13. (Leipzig, Duncker & Humblot, 1912).

14. See K. Larenz, *Methodenlehre der Rechtswissenschaft,* 3rd ed. (Berlin, Springer, 1975), pp. 354ff.

15. (Berlin, Guttentag, 1904). See also Larenz, *Methodenlehre,* p. 357.

he exercised due diligence in choosing his servant.[16] The article of Jhering which was so influential was published almost forty years before the *BGB* came into force.[17]

And fourth, in 1921 Paul Oertmann of Göttingen published his *Die Geschäftsgrundlage, ein neuer Begriff,* in which he argues that frequently a transaction has foundations which are vitally important but are not written into the contract because the parties mistakenly believe the foundations exist or will not cease to exist and further mistakenly believe that they have no reason to think the foundations do not exist or will cease to exist.[18] The courts, following Oertmann, have held that in such circumstances either party to the agreement may terminate the contract, provided it would be very unfair for that person to be bound by the original agreement. This so-called *Geschäftsgrundlage,* or foundations of the transaction, doctrine proved extremely valuable during the period of hyperinflation in Germany.

In these and other instances of the development by juristic doctrine, the jurists were expressly putting forward new ideas with the deliberate aim of influencing the growth of the law. In such instances the acceptance of the doctrine may take years, and the author is not primarily interested in the immediate response of the courts. When the issue is not so much the filling of gaps in the law as interpretation, matters are a little different. The scholars cannot go too far away from the practice of the courts. Whatever the effect of judicial precedent may be, academic interpretation that is consistently at variance with the decisions of judges has little practical value: the judicial decisions settle the instant issue. The position of the civilian professor in this regard is worse after codification than before. Before codification his interpretations were not directed to the attention of judges in any particular jurisdiction; hence the failure of any local court to respond did not mean the academic's view was everywhere rejected. Consequently, in codified civil law systems judicial decisions are an important source of law for the future, provided at least that the courts consistently take the same line. This is true for France despite article 5 of the *Code civil;* hence a standard edition of the code contains not only the text but numerous references to decided cases.[19]

16. "*Culpa in contrahendo* oder Schadenersatz bei nichtigen oder nicht zur Perfection gelangten Vertragen" *Jahrbücher fur die Dogmatik des heutigen römischen und deutschen Privatrechts* 4 (1861): 1ff.

17. See *Jherings Erbe,* ed. F. Wieacker and C. Wollschläger (Göttingen, Vandenhoeck & Ruprecht, 1970).

18. (Leipzig, Deichert).

19. The annual publication by Dalloz.

In Germany a line of cases makes binding law and is treated as custom.[20] Section 12 of the Austrian *ABGB* states:

> The decisions issued in individual cases and the judgments handed down in particular legal suits have never the force of a law; they cannot be extended to other cases or to other persons.[21]

Thus the code; yet since 1853 there has been kept at the Supreme Court (Oberster Gerichtshof) a *Judikatenbuch,* or book of judgments, and also since 1872 a *Spruchrepertorium,* or collection of opinions. The following rule is applied through an instruction of July 8, 1872. At the order of a Senat, or bench of judges, the decisions on the legal issues of civil law and civil procedure which were the object of discussion are entered in the *Spruchrepertorium.* If a Senat wishes to depart from such a decision, the question is brought before a Senat of fifteen members. The decisions of this strengthened Senat are entered into the *Judikatenbuch* and are then binding on all the Senate of the Supreme Court. A legal rule set out in the *Judikatenbuch* can be departed from only on the decision of a Senat of twenty-one members, and the new decision is then inserted in the *Judikatenbuch* and published.

Thus, legal precedents have considerable force in civil law countries, a force that typically is greater than that enjoyed by precedent before codification and which, to generalize, continually strengthens relatively to academic opinion. Yet the old tradition asserts itself, and professors enjoy greater prestige and pay than do judges, except for those of supreme courts who themselves are frequently academics. Cause and effect here intertwine to account for two standard features of civil law systems. First there is usually a career judiciary.[22] Judges are not chosen from among highly successful practitioners or professors. Instead, normally a young law graduate opts for a career as a judge. He starts in the lowest court and by a series of regular promotions rises to judgeships in more important courts. Second, the opinion of the court is issued as a combined judgment. The decision does not normally record any dissent among the judges, even if there should be only a bare majority, nor does

20. See e.g. Larenz, *Allgemeiner Teil,* pp. 8f. There are statutory exceptions to the rule that precedents are not binding. See E. J. Cohn, *Manual of German Law,* 2nd ed. (London, British Institute of Comparative Law, 1968), I, 5f.

21. Cf. Art. 3 of Chile's *Código civil:* "Solo toca al legislador explicar o interpretar la ley de un modo generalmente obligatorio. Las sentencias judiciales no tienen fuerza obligatoria sino respecto de las causas en que actualmente se pronunciaren."

22. See e.g. David, *French Law,* pp. 53ff.

the record reveal which points were made by which judge or the arguments that swayed individual judges.

The strong academic tradition, based on analyzing the *Corpus juris,* that existed before codification and the statutory basis of the law upon codification combine to make the law reports of civil law countries very different productions from those usual in common law countries. Naturally the reports vary greatly from system to system, but they have distinctive features. Thus, the facts of the case are generalized and are not set out in the detail usual in common law systems. An attempt is made to base the decision firmly on code or statutory provisions or on accepted rules of law. Above all, the decision is set out as expressing a legal rule or principle.[23]

Thus, a reported Italian decision usually does not occupy more than two printed pages.[24] The report begins with the name of the court, the date of the decision, and the members of the court. Then comes a bare list of the topics treated and the relevant statutory provisions, such as "Contract in general—formation of contract—presumption of knowledge of declaration that arrived at address of the person to whom sent—failure to observe postal rules in despatch of registered letter (*Codice civile,* art. 1335)." This is followed by a statement in a very few lines of the rules that are evinced by the decision. Then under the heading of "The Court" comes first the *Svolgimento del processo,* an extremely brief statement of the facts, plus the steps of the process in the lower court; then the *Motivi della decisione,* an examination and evaluation of the arguments produced on either side and of the reasons given in the lower court, and hence the higher court's own motivation and decision. To the statement of the legal rules evinced by the decision is attached a footnote which is usually much longer than the statement and which is written and usually signed by a jurist. This sets out the precedents with which the decision is or is not in harmony and the scholarly books and articles on which the decision is based or with which the decision agrees or disagrees.

French reports are very similar, although the members of the court are not named, and the jurist's note is written in a much more individual style, with the author freely expressing his own opinion on the adequacy or otherwise of the decision, of the court's reasoning, and even of the state of the law.[25] German reports do not give juristic opinions and are

23. See e.g. David, *French Law,* pp. 76ff, 80ff.

24. See e.g., *Il foro italiano, raccolta generale di giurisprudenza* (Rome, Società editrice de "foro italiano").

25. See e.g. *Recueil Dalloz Sirey de doctrine de jurisprudence et de législation* (Paris, Dalloz); David, *French Law,* pp. 45f.

written in an even more abstract form. First comes a statement of the legal rules that emerge from the case, then a list of relevant statutory provisions, and next the court that decided the case and the day of judgment. Then comes an account of the facts and of the proceedings in the lower court and finally of the grounds for the appellate decision.[26]

These modern reports show that the legal tradition continues through them. They are very much the descendants of the reports for the civil law before codification.

26. See e.g. *Entscheidungen des Bundesgerichtshofes* (Cologne, Heymann).

XII
Civil Law, Society, and Legal Growth

That Roman law was important for the development of the rules of modern civil law systems has always been admitted. What has been consistently underestimated is the fact that the Roman law influence on the structure of the legal system as a whole, on lawyers' approaches to law as well as on the rules of private law, played the decisive role in determining the features that distinguish these systems from those of the common law. Before codification, those scholars who alone could give an accurate estimation of Roman influence were too deeply involved in determining the scope and interpretation of rules of positive law to notice how pervasive the influence was on structures and general approaches. These same scholars were either Romanists or "localists," and there was typically a conflict between their interests. For the profession of Roman law, codification was a defeat; for the profession of local law, codification was a victory. Codification enlarged the gap between those interested in Roman law or the *ius commune* and the specialists in local law—Romanists were no longer also modernists—and it suited neither side to trace the relationship between Roman and living law. The Romanists, ousted from their preeminent position, wished to emphasize their intellectual purity; the localists, rejoicing in their new status, wished to stress the new beginning.

A law student of the age of Justinian, confronted with a modern civil code such as the Austrian *ABGB* and its surrounding statutes, would not be greatly astonished by the substance of the law, though he might well be taken aback by the abstract way in which the rules are set out. Differences in the substance of the law there certainly are, but scarcely what might be termed major developments. The major differences are the insistence on a public ceremony for the creation of a marriage and a formal procedure for the granting of divorce, specific requirements for the transfer of immovable property, and greater development of general rules of contract, though the individual types of contract retain much of their significance.[1] A further important change, particularly for some other countries, is the institution of matrimonial property regimes. The biggest surprise for the ancient law student would be the disappearance of a law of slavery in the Austrian code. Yet private law has not stood still. Even two hundred years ago the law of the present Austrian territories, as of France, was greatly different. What has occurred is a giant step toward Roman law, not a step beyond Roman law. Germanic custom, feudal law, and canon law alike have retreated, leaving relatively little trace. To some extent this overwhelming influence of Roman law on private law is overlooked, because in other areas Roman law influence is slight, as in commercial law, public law, and social welfare law. Areas of law in which the Romans, especially the Roman jurists, were little interested have expanded.

Modern civil codes are themselves the direct descendant of Justinian's *Institutes* in structure and range of contents alike. To give the credit to natural law or to revolutionary ideology is to miss the mark.[2] Certainly both natural law and revolutionary ideology had a role to play, but the immediate ancestors of most codes were the institutes of local law which were themselves products of the overwhelming emphasis on Justinian's *Institutes.* Codification was in the air before the law of reason became a powerful doctrinal weapon, and it occurred only within the territories of the civil law and not in the common law lands, which should also have been open to natural law influence. The relationship of citizen to state is fundamental to natural law thinking but is largely absent from modern western codes. Of the modern codes only the Prussian *Allgemeines Landrecht* is primarily a natural law code. To stress revolutionary ideology is to ignore first the movement toward codification that existed in France long before the Revolution and second the existence of early codes in Bavaria, Prussia, and Austria.

1. Until the time of Justinian particular types of property, known as *res mancipi,* among which was included Italic land, could be transferred only with the performance of prescribed formalities. Justinian abolished the distinction between *res mancipi* and *res nec mancipi.* Thereafter new specific requirements for the transfer of land became desirable. Actually the ceremony of taking sasine, which was necessary for land transfer in various countries such as Scotland until recently, has much in common with *mancipatio.*

2. See e.g. Merryman, *Civil Law Tradition,* pp. 15ff.

The major divisions of civil law systems—where public law is dealt with in public law tribunals or courts and not in the ordinary courts, where commercial law has traditionally its own code and usually its own courts—are again explicable overall only in terms of the use of the *Corpus juris civilis* as an organizing instrument. No other single explanation fits the facts with regard to public law since the same division exists in so many countries with different political and social histories. The distinction between private law and public law was sharply made by French and other jurists long before the Revolution; and Montesquieu's doctrine of separation of powers does not favor the creation of administrative tribunals that are not independent of the executive.

The logically formal rationality of law that Max Weber and others emphasize as a mark of the civil law is a further direct consequence of the stress placed on the *Corpus juris.* The same long-term stress is also the explanation for the greater abstraction to be found in civilian law reports.

On one level of analysis, civil law systems as they are today and as they have developed over the centuries represent an outstanding example, one of great complexity, of the common legal phenomenon of borrowing, of legal transplants.[3] Some Roman law is borrowed, each country or often each scholar taking according to their own individual principles or wishes; particular Roman sources come to operate as the organizing instrument of the law; a common but incomplete stock of European law then emerges, itself subject to continual development; the participating states, closely linked in law, borrow and adapt from Roman law, from the common stock, and increasingly from one to another; whole codes are at times transplanted or, more frequently, modified and adopted. The law of each territory is only in relatively small part a native growth. At the same time, partly as a result of the acceptance of foreign law because of its authority irrespective of its quality, partly because of inertia, and partly because of other factors, legal rules to a considerable extent are out of step with the needs and desires of the society in which they operate, and also with the needs of that society's ruling elite. Knowledge of the divergence of law from society and of the role of transplants

3. See e.g. Watson, *Legal Transplants;* O. Kahn-Freund, "On Uses and Misuses of Comparative Law," *MLR* 37 (1974): 1ff; A. Watson, "Legal Transplants and Law Reform," *LQR* 92 (1976): 79ff; E. Stein, "Uses, Misuses—and Nonuses of Comparative Law," *Northwestern Law Review* 72 (1977): 198ff; Watson, *Society and Legal Change,* pp. 98ff; Watson, *Nature of Law,* pp. 99ff; J. Gaudemet, "Les transferts de droit," *L'Année Sociologique* 27 (1976): 29ff; Twekiat Menakavist, article in Thai, *Thammaset Law Journal* 4 (1978).

in legal development makes it possible to draw up an abstract scheme of the factors that cause or inhibit changes in the law. The scheme, which applies equally to substantive rules and to structures, enables one, at least with regard to civil law systems, to attempt to evaluate the force of these factors.

The conditions relevant for legal change may be isolated and reduced to nine factors.[4] They are termed source of law, pressure force, opposition force, transplant bias, law-shaping lawyers, discretion factor, generality factor, inertia, and felt needs. On the first factor, the development of law within one system may be affected to a considerable extent by the sources available for making law, and each source has its own characteristics. Thus, when law develops by precedent, the law always waits upon events, that is, on litigated events, and it always is retrospective. The scope for development of legal principle is very limited, especially in the short term, and there is no organized, systematic development. Important questions remain unanswered. Economic factors especially determine who is able to litigate, hence there is a bias in the shape of the law. In the particular case, the morality of the parties may be so mingled with the facts that the binding precedent may reflect individual circumstances more than general social awareness. Generally the judges have no opportunity for a wide-ranging discussion with other lawyers of the ramifications and implications of their decisions, which may therefore be founded on limited experience. The law based on precedent is difficult to find, and only when there is a line of decisions does it become possible to isolate the *ratio decidendi.* Above all perhaps, law based on precedent is slow to change. Legislation is very different: it can and usually does provide primarily for the future; it can be very systematic, general in purpose, and removed from particular issues, and it can make drastic reforms speedily. Development by legislation, although not everywhere the same, can have a very satisfactory theoretical base and in consequence point the way for further reform.

The source of law available for the lawmaker was not normally made today. English law can develop by precedent because precedent was accepted as a source of law at some time in the past; it cannot take a code as the starting point of a reform since no English code was made in the past. Hence to the extent that legal change is conditioned by the source of law available, the change is dependent on the *past.*

The term "pressure force" indicates the organized person or persons, recognizable group or groups, who believe that a benefit results

4. See A. Watson, "Comparative Law and Legal Change," *CLJ* 37 (1978): 321ff.

from a practicable change in the law. The power to change the law that a particular pressure force has varies in accordance with the political, social, and economic position of its members and its capacity to work on an existing source of law. The various sources of law are responsive to pressure forces in differing degrees; thus legislation is particularly open to pressure, development by precedent is much less so, and juristic doctrine is largely immune. The reason for the last is that the rating of a jurist's opinion depends on his intellectual standing with his fellows, and this is diminished if he seems subject to a pressure force. Again it is often not for any considerable time that a jurist's doctrine is accepted; hence there is often little point for a pressure force to try to influence legal doctrine. As for precedent, a judge is not usually supposed to be making law; he is not usually elected and thus has nothing to fear from voters; his role is not seen as primarily political; and in every law suit there is an opposition force as well as a pressure force.

The opposition force is the organized person or persons, recognizable group or groups, who believe that harm results from a suggested change. There is no opposition force unless it is organized. It may easily happen that more persons suffer harm than benefit from a proposed change in the law, but the only opposition force is that which is organized.

Law develops mainly by borrowing, which may well be the best way for a particular system to grow in terms of both economizing resources and getting the best rules. The transplant bias, however, is not the extent of borrowing but the receptivity of a system to a particular outside law, which is distinct from an acceptance based on a thorough examination of alternatives. Thus, it denotes a system's readiness to accept Roman law rules because they are Roman law rules, or French rules because they are French rules. The transplant bias varies from system to system and depends on such factors as a linguistic tradition shared with a possible donor, the general prestige of the donor system, and its accessibility through writings.

Lawyers are very well placed to act as pressure forces or opposition forces. This alone would not justify their being regarded as a separate factor, but in addition, a legal elite exists that shapes the law; legislation is usually drafted by lawyers; judicial precedent is the work of judges; and juristic doctrine is the opinion of lawyers. Nonetheless, law-shaping lawyers should not properly be considered a separate factor in legal development because their role is adequately covered by the notions of source of law—the drafting or shaping of a law, for instance, is inseparable from legislation—and by transplant bias. At the same time, however, law-shaping lawyers give the law such a particular flavor that their role must be set out, though in parenthesis, in the main equation that follows.

Some degree of discretion seems to be inherent in all legal systems, and the discretion may be vested in the individual parties, the judge, or the executive, or it may actually be built into the legal rules. The discretion factor, by providing a choice, limits the impact of the legal rule on the person or group making the choice, and it may increase the impact of the rule on the person or group against whom the choice is exercised. In general the discretion factor widens the acceptability of a legal rule, but there are at least two exceptions. First, where discretion is abused, especially by the executive, it may cause a violent reaction, and second, in restricted circumstances the possibility of discretion existing for others, as in the case of divorce, may cause some people to feel moral outrage and to seek to impose their views on the law.

Typically legal rules regulate several very different and recognizable groups of people or apply to different types of transaction or situation. For instance, in most Western countries the law of marriage and divorce is the same for atheists, Catholics, Moslems, and Hindus. The rules relating to immovable property in any one country are basically the same, whether the property is in a city, island, fertile valley, or remote inhospitable mountain. Of concern is not the number of persons or actual situations involved but the number of types and range of persons and situations. The greater the generality and the wider the range of situations, the more difficult it is to find a rule that is recognizably fitting. Thus, the greater what may be called the generality factor, the less concordance a rule has with what seems precisely needed. And the greater the generality factor in a proposed change, the greater the difficulty of finding agreement in the appropriate rule and hence the greater the difficulty of effecting change.

The impulse to change law must overcome the inertia or general absence of a sustained interest on the part of society and its ruling elite to struggle for the most "satisfactory" rule. Society's essential stake in law is order, and if order is maintained, there may be no consuming interest on the part of society or of its ruling elite in the precise legal rules. Society and above all the ruling elite have a generalized interest in no change. Most legal rules and structures have no direct impact at any given time on the lives of most of the inhabitants of a territory; this is true of such diverse matters as divorce, conveyancing, and defamation. A mystique surrounds law and makes an approach to it difficult for nonlawyers, and the basic stock-in-trade of lawyers is their knowledge of existing law. There is a cost to all reform, and resources are required, such as the legislature's time and academics' intellectual energy. The role of inertia in inhibiting law reform has been grossly underestimated; society is often willing and able to tolerate a great deal of disfunctional law.[5]

Legal rules and structures should also fulfill various purposes in society, some of which may be nearer, others distant. Felt needs are the purposes known to and felt appropriate by the pressure force, not by the ruling elite or by society as a whole. Whatever needs may be recognized for a society, they are not felt needs unless they are supported by an active pressure force.

With the use of these nine factors it is possible to present models for legal development and the relationship between legal rules or structures and society. Thus, a legal rule or structure is stable when felt needs, weakened by the discretion factor, activating the pressure force as affected by the generality factor to work on the relevant source of law, are less than inertia plus opposition force. Some legal change occurs when felt needs, weakened by the discretion factor, activating the pressure force as affected by the generality factor to work on the source of law, are greater than inertia plus opposition force.

The factors placed on either side of each model all interact with their peers, but the models try to indicate the main thrust of the interaction. Thus the discretion factor diminishes the extent to which needs are felt; in turn, these felt needs rouse the pressure force to work on altering the law, a result that can be achieved only through a source of law; and so on.

The precise relationship between legal rules or structures, both particular and in general, and the society in which they operate can be expressed as the balance between two opposing sets of factors, the first inhibiting change, the second determining the change that is proposed. For example, on the one hand may be inertia plus opposition force; on the other hand may be felt needs, weakened by the discretion factor, activating the pressure force as affected by the generality factor, to work on the source of law, all as modified by the transplant bias (and law-shaping lawyers). A legal change occurs when the force of the second set of factors increases so as to become greater than the force of the first set of factors, but the balance and the relative weight of the factors determine the nature of the change.

Nowhere in these models does society at large or its ruling elite appear as factors. This accords with reality. Legal change is triggered by pressure forces, not by the society at large or its ruling elite. This remains

5. See Watson, *Society and Legal Change.*

true even though at times the pressure force and society at large may be coextensive, and even though in nondemocratic states especially the pressure force and the ruling elite may be the same.

The models would be virtually meaningless if it were not that recognizable patterns are to be found among modern Western legal systems. Aside from Scandinavia, all Western systems of law can be distinctly and primarily categorized as civil law systems, common law systems, or mixed systems. The fact that legal systems can be so categorized means that supranational forces are at work shaping the destinies of the legal systems, at least to a considerable extent, and that these forces directly relate to the legal system. This proposition would fail if it were the case that local political, economic, or social conditions, independent of any shared tradition of law, determined whether a system was civil law or common law. That is to say, the proposition would fail if in important political, social, or economic conditions Germany resembled Paraguay or the Ivory Coast but did not so resemble the United Kingdom or the United States; or if Quebec resembled South Africa or Puerto Rico but not Ontario or Nova Scotia. No one would argue for this proposition. Not only are the suggested correlations between political, social, and economic conditions obviously not present, but also the shared legal tradition of Germany, Paraguay, and the Ivory Coast is easily demonstrated and documented.

At this stage it is appropriate to make express use of "Ockam's razor," whether in the form "Plurality is not to be assumed without necessity," or "What can be done with fewer is done in vain with more," or in the more famous form, probably not used by Ockham, "Entities are not to be multiplied without necessity." The use of "Ockham's razor" indicates that if territories subject to one legal tradition undergo the same or a relatively similar legal development at different times and in different political, social, and economic circumstances, and if territories subject to a different legal tradition undergo their own development which is common to them but not to those of the first legal tradition, and if this happens at various times and in various political, social, and economic circumstances, then credit for the common aspects of the tradition and for the development of relevant law must be given above all to the tradition itself.

Further, the existence of recognizable patterns of law suggests *a priori* that there is an organic connection, at least in general, between a society and the legal system operating within it. Yet, law does not by any means always change because the social, economic, or political conditions of the society have changed, nor do legal rules by any means always develop to the stage where they are most beneficial to the society or the ruling elite. Law in the West at any rate is disfunctional to a considerable extent. But if there is an organic connection between a society and its law, as seems plausible, then this must be seen in terms of a correlation between society and the legal tradition; and the role of the latter must on no account be minimized. Thus, felt needs activating the pressure force are often not enough to result in legal change, even in the absence of an opposition force. Then the extra that is needed for change relates to the legal tradition, and the changes that do occur are shaped in accordance with the legal tradition.[6] Conversely, as a result of transplant bias, societies may accept a major legal change even when needs are scarcely felt. Examples are the acceptance in seventeenth century Scotland of the progressive civilian contract system and the acceptance in less developed countries of a code primarily based on that of France.

A more extreme proposition might be argued for from the fact that legal systems can be primarily categorized as civil law, common law, or mixed, namely, that the supranational forces which shape the destinies of Western legal systems and which directly relate to the legal system are the most important forces in legal development. This more extreme proposition would fail if the civil law and common law systems are much alike, if this similarity is the result of basically similar political, social, and economic conditions and not of a general unitary legal tradition, and if the distinctions between the civil law systems on the one hand and the common law systems on the other are of minor importance and do not impinge on matters of political, social, and economic consequence.

It seems impossible to put a percentage figure on the accuracy of this extreme proposition. What can be said is, first, that in the industrialized West, political, social, and economic conditions have had relatively much in common, and that much of legal development has been broadly similar from one country to another. Second, the differences of civil law systems with common law systems are not slight, and these differences can greatly impinge on matters of public consequence, as witness above all the fact that public law issues are tried before special public law tribunals or courts. Third, the major differences between civil law systems and common law systems in the industrialized West primarily arise from the different legal traditions. The legal tradition also profoundly affects the growth of rules of substantive private law, and here too important differences exist between civil law and common law systems. But the differences actually understate the impact on law of differing legal traditions because

6. See Alexis de Tocqueville, *De la Démocratie en Amérique* (1835), pt. 2, ch. 8.

the same legal historical elements have gone into both traditions, which are in fact basically unitary; the decisive difference has only been the use by the civil law systems of the *Corpus juris* as the organizing instrument. The use of this organizing instrument affects primarily only the factors of development that are called source of law and transplant bias. Yet for civil law systems and common law systems there is a considerable overlap with regard to both source of law and transplant bias.

Among civil law systems lesser differences exist that are in part the product of varying political, social, and economic conditions, but also in part the result of divergences within the legal tradition. There is a split into families of the civil law, into the Romanistic and the Germanistic family, and the systems belonging to one family or the other are to be found in countries of differing political, economic, and social backgrounds.[7] This fact again stresses the importance of source of law and transplant bias. Moreover, civil law countries of very different political, social, and economic background may have the same or a very similar code. A foreign code may be borrowed in its entirety. This likewise emphasizes the importance of the transplant bias for the formal structure of a system and for legal rules.

Though the importance of source of law and transplant bias cannot be quantified as factors for legal change, and though their force as independently existing factors must vary from time to time and from place to place, it is beyond question that source of law and transplant bias are extremely important factors for legal change. The existence of the two main traditions of Western law means at the least that insofar as Western law responds to political, social, and economic factors, it does so in terms that are, in considerable measure, dictated by the legal system. In extreme cases the transplant bias itself above all determines the nature of the legal system. The legal tradition itself is not independent of the society, and the law-shaping lawyers are members of the society and are open to the same nonlegal influences, pressures, and culture as are other citizens.

In the development of civil law systems as distinct from common law systems, a legal elite, the academic jurists, played and to a lesser extent still plays a central role in shaping the law. To characterize civil law systems in terms of their historical dependence on a particular legal tradition, without invoking societal conditions, is not to deny that the conditions in society play an important role in legal change. The legal history of a particular country is bound up with the societal pressures for legal change and the forces that opposed change. But an exclusive focus on the

7. See e.g. Zweigert and Kötz, *Introduction,* pp. 57ff, 68ff, 133ff.

history of one civil law system fails to give due weight to what that system has in common with other civilian systems and what separates these from common law systems. Only by widening the focus can one see how important is the role played by the legal tradition itself in legal change.

Again, among the characteristics that make civil law systems markedly different from common law systems, it has proved possible to avoid almost any reference to the elements of Germanic customs, feudal law, and canon law that have gone into the two groups of systems. The importance of these laws in determining modern rules should not be denied, though the passage of time has had the overall effect in civil law and common law systems alike of bringing modern private law nearer to that of the Roman law world. Rather, these laws can be left aside because they were common to both civil law and common law traditions and hence could offer no explanation of the differences between civil law and common law systems. Although Roman law was also an element common to civil law and common law systems alike, the essential difference is that in the former systems the *Corpus juris* came to be the organizing instrument of the law. This development likewise focuses attention on the importance of a legal elite for legal change.

If this conclusion is accurate, it should be possible to test it with regard to other legal systems. It should be the case that the source of law, however that came into existence, through the guise of law-shaping lawyers plays a basic role in determining legal change. A general pattern of legal change within a system or group of systems, whether it is for speed of growth or for systematization, should be explicable in terms of the law-shaping lawyers. The conclusions are indeed consistent with what is known about law in the last two centuries of the Roman Republic, the time and place in the West when law developed most mightily.

In the later Roman Republic statute was not a major factor in the making of private law. The real power for change resided in the praetor, ably assisted and encouraged by the jurists. The elective office of praetor was the second highest in the Roman Republic, ranking below only that of consul, was held only for one year, and could not be held more than once. Although the number of praetors elected annually varied from time to time, the urban praetor and the peregrine praetor between them controlled the most important private law courts at Rome.

Technically the praetor could not change the law, but he did have control over the law courts: he could decide to allow an action in circumstances where previously none was possible, and he could likewise refuse an action where previously one had been given. In this way the praetor was responsible, for example, for the creation of the all-important consensual contracts, those for whose valid formation no formalities were required but simply the agreement of the parties, namely sale, hire, partnership, and mandate. For each of these contracts the praetor set out model forms of action, which are striking in their starkness and brevity. The forms of action reveal very little about the scope of the contract or the obligations of the parties. All the substantive law is created by the permissions from praetors for a plaintiff to proceed against a defendant on particular facts, by the decisions of judges, and by the activity of free-lance jurists writing more or less systematically on the state of the law.

The collaboration here between the praetors and the jurists is fundamental. The jurists were wealthy men from powerful families, for whom a reputation as a legal expert, along with a career in politics and military service, was the route to social importance.[8] For instance, the most famous of the republican jurists, as a jurist, was Quintus Mucius Scaevola, who is said to have been the first to set out the civil law in its *genera*.[9] Yet he was consul of 95 B.C. and also held the position of chief priest, *pontifex maximus*. The jurists were from the same social stratum as the praetors, and relations between praetors and jurists must frequently have been close. The jurists gave legal advice not only to individuals with legal problems but also to praetors and judges. Neither praetors nor judges needed to have had any particular legal training. Praetors especially, simply as members of their class, may have had. But in general there would have been considerable reliance by both praetor and judge alike on the scholarly, unpaid jurist. The praetor overall had great opportunities to affect the growth of the law; and the judge, following the advice of jurists, had considerable freedom with the individual decision.

From early days the praetor could issue edicts, clauses setting out how he would operate the law in his court. The practice resulted in an annual Edict, consisting of various edicts, and by the beginning of the first century B.C. at the latest the praetor's annual Edict contained individual edicts that were in fact changing the substantive law. A praetor was not bound by his predecessor's Edict but always issued his own, which nonetheless tended to take over much of his predecessors' work. In practice, new edicts were made only when new ideas occurred; and changes to earlier edictal clauses were made only when jurists, including possibly the praetor himself, had envisaged what appeared to be im-

8. See e.g. W. Kunkel, *Herkunft und soziale Stellung der römischen Juristen*, 2nd ed. (Weimar, Böhlau, 1967), pp. 50ff.

9. *D*.1.2.2.41; cf. A. Watson, *Law Making in the Later Roman Republic* (Oxford, Clarendon Press, 1974), pp. 143ff.

provements. The evidence suggests that modifications were frequent in the late Republic.

The period, then, is one of extraordinarily rapid development of law, occurring at a time when the main source of law, the praetor's Edict, permitted of rapid change and was very open to the influence of personally disinterested law specialists. Family law, however, was scarcely affected by the Edict, since such a politically sensitive area would be handled gingerly by an elected official who has his eye on the highest office of all, the consulship.[10]

In large measure the famed Roman genius for law comes down to their having found a method of lawmaking where there could be continual easy innovation at the desire of the best legal brains, coupled with equally easy and frequent amendment of the innovations. This development of the Roman Republic contrasts with that of civil law systems after the Reception of Roman law. For centuries the main legal development was in the hands of legal scholars working on the written sources of the *Corpus juris* and having no hand directly on the levers of legal change. In these circumstances legal change was in general slow, but marked above all by ever growing systematization and abstraction. The available sources of law have a tremendous impact, but one easily underestimated, on the speed of legal change and on the shape and nature of the rules and of the legal system itself.[11] These findings on the making of the civil law suggest that, for an understanding of how and why law changes and how law is related to society, it would be instructive to make a comparison with non-Western systems of law, particularly with those like Islamic law where the legal tradition itself is opposed to legal change.

10. See Watson, *Law Making*, pp. 97ff.

11. See F. H. Lawson, "Legal Orthodoxy," in *Many Laws* (Amsterdam, North-Holland, 1977), I, 51ff.

INDEX

Accarisius, J., 47n2
actio de dolo, 17
action *de in rem verso,* 164
actions, law of, 27
Aediles, 40
Africa, 125
Africanus, 73f
Alciatus, 26
Alexander Tartagna de Imola, 42, 50
Algeria, 123
Allgemeine Gerichtsordnung Josephs II, 108
Allgemeines Bürgerliches Gesetzbuch, 109, 116, 122, 135, 169, 176, 179f *Ur-Entwurf,* 109f
Allgemeines deutsches Handelsgesetzbuch 129f
Allgemeines Gesetz über Verbrechen, 108,
Allgemeines Landrecht für die preussischen Staaten, 3, 89, 98, 101, 106f, 136, 139, 170, 180
Altdorf, 76
Althusius, J., 90
Alvarez, J. M., 82
Alvarottus, 46
America: Central, 124f, 173; South, 124f, 173
Ancel, M., 143n33
Anglo-India, 100
Aquinas, T., 88, 116, 165
Argentina, 124, 139
Argou, G., 67f, 71, 111f, 149, 155f
Aristotle, 84n2
Arnaud, A.-J., 111n22, 112, 112n23
Ataturk, 103n11
Aubry, C., 138, 164
Australia, 37f, 100
Austria, 70, 107ff, 120, 176, 179f
Authenticum, 60
Azo, 26, 148

Baade, H. W., 124n43
Bacon, F., 84
Baden, 122, 139
Badisches Landrecht, 122
Balduinus, F., 76
Baldus, 42, 46, 49, 54, 57
Baldwin, J. W., 165n47
Balfour, J., 160
Bamford, B. R., 41n6
Barbeyrac, J., 92, 116
Bardet, P., 44
Bartolus, 43, 51, 54, 57, 73, 132, 148, 171
Barton, J. L., 88n9
Basta, J., 7f
Bavaria, 78, 102ff, 180
Bayitch, S. A., 100n3
Bechmann, J.-V., 55n3
Beinart, B., 5n8, 6n9
Belgium, 44, 55n3, 121, 125
Bellapertica, 148
Bentham, J., 84
Bergasse, 156
Bern, 129
Bernese Jura, 122, 125

Beseler, G., 127
Beyer, G., 67n11, 77, 79
Beyma, J. van, 59
Bigot du Préameneux, 114
Blackstone, W., 28, 101
Blois, 113
Bluntschli, J. K., 129
Boeclerus, J. H., 154
Böhmer, I. H., 43
Bohemia, 60, 108
Boherius, P., 49
Bolivia, 124
Bologna, 25, 62
Bonnecase, J., 137n14
Bourges, 26, 73
Bourjon, F., 111f, 112n24
Bout, R., 162n39
Boutaric, F. de, 67n12
Brandenburg, 79, 105
Brazil, 114
Bremen, 122
Brierly, J. E. C., 28n6, 141n25
Brissaud, J., 7n12, 8n13, 115n31, 118, 151
Brissonius, 113
Bronchorst, E., 59, 59n11
Brünn, 108
Brunneman, 45
Buchez, B.-J.-B., 155n27
Bürgerliches Gesetzbuch, 3, 21, 56n4, 102, 114, 116, 126ff, 139f, 144, 163ff, 168, 174f
Bürgerliches Gesetzbuch für das Königreich Sachsen, 114, 128
Bugnet, J.-J., 117, 119
Bulgarus, 147
Burgerlijk Wetboek, 121
Busius, P., 55n3
Bynkershoek, C. van, 71

Caecilius, 74
Caen, 156
Caenegem, R. C. van, 8n13, 133n4
Cahors, 73
Cajetan, 89
California, 3, 100
Cambacérès, 113
Cambolas, J. de, 44
Cambridge, 28, 52
Canada, 37f, 90, 141ff
canon law, 28, 77, 88, 180, 189
Capitant, H., 114, 115n31, 137n14
Cappelletti, M., 133n2, 134f, 134n6, 140n21, 141n23, 172n9
Caracalla, 74
Carmer, C. von, 106
Caron, Ch. de, 149
Carpzovius, B., 44, 77, 77n26
Carty, T., 96n24
case law, 39ff, 170ff
Castel, J.-G., 141n25
Castro, F. de, 28n9
Castro, P. de, 57
Cato, 74
Chabroud, 156
chambre des comptes, 151
chamber du domaine, 151
chambre du trésor, 151
Charles II (England), 31
Charles VII (France), 112
Chartarius, F., 47ff
Chevrier, G., 146nn3-4, 147ff
Chile, 104, 120, 176n21
Chilfettius, 71
China, 129
Christinaeus, P., 44
Cicero, 18n5, 84
Clarus, Iulius, 45, 137
Clyde, J. A., 46n18, 56n10
Cocceji, S., 104f
Code (Justinian), 10ff, 18f, 25, 27, 44, 62, 77, 165, 170
Code civil (France), 3, 8, 68, 103, 107, 111ff, 112n24, 124ff, 128, 136ff, 140f, 143, 160, 162f, 166, 169, 175
code, civil: Aargau, 129; Argentina, 124, 139f; Baden, 139; Bern, 129; Bolivia, 124; Brazil, 114, 140; Chile, 104, 120, 124, 139, 169f, 176; Colombia, 164; Ecuador, 124; Haiti, 124; Italy, 122, 140f, 160, 169, 177; Louisiana, 123f, 139; Lower Canada, 124; Luzern, 129; Naples, 139; Peru, 144; Portugal, 123; Quebec, 124, 140ff; Rumania, 122; Solothurn, 129; Spain, 122f
Code de commerce (France), 115, 118, 123, 158
Code de procédure civile (France), 118
Code de procédure pénale (France), 118
Code des obligations et des contrats (Morocco, Tunisia), 123
Code du roi Henri III, 113
Code Henry (Haiti), 124f
code reform, 140ff
Codex Euricianus, 4
Codex Ferdinandeo-Leopoldino-Josephino-Carolinus, 104n12
Codex iuris Bavarici criminalis, 102

Codex iuris Bavarici judicialis, 102
Codex Maximilianeus Bavaricus civilis, 102, 104
Codex Theresianus juris civilis, 108
Codice civile di Napoleone il Grande, 117f, 122
codification, 3, 40, 99ff, 131ff, 168ff, 179f
Coetzee, J., 40
Cohn, E. J., 163n41, 176n20
Coing, H., 57n8
Colbert, 113, 115
Coleman, A., 164n46
Colin, A., 114, 115n31, 137n14
Colombia, 124, 164
commercial law, 158ff
Commodus, 74
common law systems, 1, 4
condictio, 161ff
Conrad, H., 8n16, 104n12, 105n13, 108nn18-19, 111n22, 115n31
Conring, H., 9, 79
Conseil d'Etat, 152
Constantinaeus, 71
Constituent Assembly (France), 113, 152, 155f
Constitutio criminalis Theresiana, 108
Consultatio, 73
contract, 15f, 22, 27, 51ff, 88, 94ff, 161, 165ff
Convention (France), 113
Coquille, G., 7f, 65ff, 65n6
Corasius, J., 49
Corpus juris canonici, 99
Corpus juris civilis, 4f, 9ff, 15, 19, 24, 27, 29, 31f, 35f, 41, 53, 58, 75ff, 79, 83, 95, 99, 103, 131ff, 135, 144ff, 152, 157f, 171f, 177, 188, 191
Corpus juris Fredericiani, 106
Corvinus, J. A., 63
Coulson, N. J., 123n42
cour de cassation, 164
cour des monnaies, 151
Covarruvias, 89
Craig, J., 56
Craig, T., 5f, 46f, 46nn14,18; 56ff, 57nn8-9, 66
Cravetta, A., 49f
Crépeau, A., 142, 142nn28,31
criminal law, 108
Cromwell, O., 31
Cujas, J., 45f, 57, 61, 71, 73
culpa in contrahendo, 174f
Cunningham, A., 33
Curzon, A. de, 28n7
Custom (Paris), 8, 112, 124, 140f
Customs (France), 7, 28, 66, 115, 117
Czechoslovakia, 129

D'Aguessau, H.-F., 113, 116
Dainow, J., 41n5
Damhouder, J. van, 45f
Danckwerts, N., 154
Danzig, 122
Daube, D., 119
David, R., 28n6, 134, 152n21, 158n29, 159n31, 160n33, 169n3, 170n5, 173n11, 176n22, 177nn23,25
Dawson, J. P. 8n15, 43n8, 44n11, 66n8
Decius, P. 59
Declaration of the Rights of Man, 114f
Dekkers, R., 54nn1,2
delict, 17, 27, 161
Desgraves, L., 156n28
Des-Maisons, M.F., 44
Diermanse, P.J.J., 92n20
Digest, 11f, 18f, 25, 27, 33, 36, 43f, 55f, 59f, 62, 76, 85f, 120, 134, 161ff
Diocletian, 74, 165
Directory (France), 113
discretion factor, 182, 184f
divorce, 22
Doctores, 42, 49, 51, 148n12
Domat, J., 116
Dominican Republic, 124
Donellus, H., 75f
Dorotheus, 63
Dovring, F., 30n12
dowry, 48ff
Dresdner Entwurf, 130
Duarenus, 57
Dumoulin, F., 8, 43, 59, 66, 66n9, 113, 115, 171
Duport, 156
Dutch East India Company, 92
Dyemenus, G., 59

Eck, C. van, 56
école de l'exégèse, 132n1
Ecuador, 124
Edict, 2, 16, 36, 189f
Edinburgh, 33, 59, 93
Egypt, 123
Eichhorn, K. F., 127
Engels, F., 128n48
England, 4, 23, 26, 28, 37f, 51f, 56, 58, 63, 100, 124, 186

enorm lesion, 95, 165ff
equity, 18
Erskine, J., 70
Erste Kommission (Germany), 128
Esmein, A., 7n12, 8n14
Everardi, N., 53ff, 66, 71
exceptio doli, 17, 40

Faber, A., 27n5
Faber, P., 60
family law, 17
Farinacius, 45
fascism, 140f
Feenstra, R., 7n10, 59n11, 75n19
felt needs, 182, 184ff
Fenet, P., 113n26
feudal law, 1, 46, 56ff, 77, 79, 105, 180, 189
Field, D. D., 103
Fischer, H. F. W. D., 30n12
Fleury, C., 149
Florence, 47n20
Florentinus, 86
Forsthoff, E., 153, 153n25
Fortescue, J., 28
France, 1, 3, 6ff, 20, 29, 33, 44, 55n3, 56, 58, 65ff, 73, 102f, 111ff, 124, 129, 134, 137f, 143, 155f, 160ff, 165f, 171, 177, 187
Franeker, 59
Frankfurt-am-Oder, 55
Franz I (Austria), 101n7
Franz, J. B., 70n15
fraud, 17f, 40ff
Frederick the Great, 27n5, 104f, 136
Frederick William I (Prussia), 105
Freiburg, 76
Fribourg, 122
Friesland, 45, 53, 69

Gabrielius, A., 49f
Gabrielius, H., 49f
Gaill, A., 43, 43n9
Gaius, 15, 19, 36, 64
Galgut, A. J. A., 40
Galicia, 109
Gandilhon, R., 112n25
Gaudemet, J., 121n40, 181n3
general part, 107, 114, 127
generality factor, 182, 184f
Genestal, R., 7n12
Geneva, 122, 125
Genoa, 47ff
Gentili, A., 26
Germanic customs, 1, 69, 72, 79, 126, 169, 180, 187
Germany, 3, 8, 14, 23, 42, 55n3, 58, 75ff, 93, 97, 120, 126f, 134, 137f, 140, 144, 152f, 157, 160, 163f, 165f, 173, 176f, 186
Giannini, M. S., 152
Gierke, O. von, 128
Ghana, 164f
Glasgow, 72
Gloss, 9, 20, 27, 42ff, 46, 50, 54, 60, 76f, 146ff, 165, 166n49
Glück, 45
Goeddaeus, J., 20
Gordley, J. R., 3n4, 102n10
Gorla, G., 42n7
Gothofredus, D., 72, 76
Göttingen, 175
Grant, A., 33n22, 34n34
Greece, 3, 129
Grimm, J., 127
Groenewegen, S. van, 6
Grondwet (South Africa), 70
Grotius, H., 27, 30, 30n12, 40, 65n6, 68, 70ff, 89ff, 93ff, 98, 104f, 116, 166
Grotius, W., 30
Guatemala, 82
Güntzelius, C., 59

Hadrian, 11
Haeberlin, K.F., 154
Haiti, 1, 124
Halle, 77, 105
Hamburg, 122
Hamel, J., 115n32, 158n29
Handelsgesetzbuch, 129
Harprecht, J., 137
Hartkamp, A. S., 143n32
Hasselt, van, 45
Hefermehl, W., 159n30
Hegel, 83
Heidelberg, 76, 183
Heineccius, J. G., 7, 80, 82f, 132
Heise, G. H., 127, 128n49
Helagabalus, 74
Hermesdorf, B. H. D., 7n10
Hermogenianus, 11
herrschende Lehre, 169, 174
hire, 17f, 190
historical school, 126
Hobbes, T., 84
Hofacker, B. C. C., 78
Hoffman, C. G., 80
Holland, 10, 14, 53, 69, 91, 134

Holtermann, A. M., 59
Homer, 135
Honoré, T., 10n20
Hope, T., 6, 38n25, 147
Hostiensis, 46
Hotman, F., 46, 57, 71, 72n18, 73ff, 145
Huber, E., 130
Huber, U., 45, 69
Hugo, G., 83, 128n48
humanism, 72ff, 79, 83, 89, 132
Hungary, 60, 129
Hunt, P. M. S., 54n13

Ihering, R. von, 26, 174f
Imbert, J., 65n7
inertia, 182, 184
Innocent IV, 42
Inns of Court, 25, 52
Institutes (Gaius), 15, 64
Institutes (Justinian), 12, 15, 19, 25, 27, 32, 60, 62ff, 71, 76ff, 83, 85, 91, 103, 111, 114, 116, 121, 132, 134, 145ff, 150, 156, 161, 179ff
Intendants, 151
international law, 78, 97
Ireland, 100
Irnerius, 62, 147
Irvine Smith, J., 45n12
Islam, 123, 191
Italy, 58, 70, 122, 125, 129, 140, 152f, 157f, 160, 171, 177
ius commune, 60, 104, 106, 108, 179
ius gentium, 1, 91
ius respondendi, 173
Ivory Coast, 186

Japan, 129
Javolenus, 74
Jellinek, W., 150n18
Jena, 55, 147
Jolowicz, F. H., 10n20, 11n23, 13n24, 35, 35n27, 173n12
Joseph II (Austria), 108
Josephinisches Gesetzbuch, 108
judges, 29, 154ff, 176ff
Judikatenbuch (Austria), 176
Julian, 10
Juliot de la Morandière, L., 114n28
Julius Caesar, 101
justice, 20f, 142
Justin, 10
Justinian, 4, 10f, 36, 63, 74, 101, 132ff

Kahn, E., 41n5
Kahn-Freund, O., 32, 33n19, 38, 181n3
Kantorowicz, H., 62, 63n2, 87nn5-6, 146n5
Kaser, M., 40
Kees, J. G., 70n15
Kelsey, F. W., 94n22
Kemmerich, D. H., 97
Khraisser, S., 78
Klein, E. F., 106
Klenckius, J., 92
Koschaker, P., 8n16, 9n18, 19n7, 29n11, 76n22, 98n25
Kötz, H., 115nn30-31, 121n40, 125, 125n44, 126, 129n52, 136n13, 188n7
Kunkel, W., 107f, 190n8

Lagarde, G., 115n32, 158n29
Lamoignon, 113
Larenz, K., 163nn40-41, 164n42, 169, 169n4, 174nn14-15, 176n20
Laurent, F., 137n14
Law of Citations, 36
law-shaping lawyers, 182f, 185
Lawson, F. H., 3, 3nn3,5; 15n2, 36n30, 100nn3-4, 102, 191n11
Lebanon, 123
Lee, R. W., 91n15
Leeuwen, S. van, 40, 45f, 69f
Legislative Assembly (France), 113
Leibnitz, 83, 89
Leiden, 26, 59
Leipzig, 55, 59
Lestang, A. de, 44
Lessius, 89
Le Trosne, 120
Levy, E., 4
Levy, M. R., 136n13
lex Aquilia, 56
libri feudorum, 46, 60
Liebs, D., 11n21
Linden, J. van der, 69f
Livonia, 59
Lizet, P., 7
loan for consumption, 17
loan for use, 17
loci, 54f
Lombardi, L., 42n7
Lombardy, 71, 122
'Lotharian Legend,' 9, 79
Louis (Netherlands), 121
Louis XI, 112
Louis XIV, 28, 67
Louisiana, 5, 123f, 139, 165
Loussouarn, Y., 170n5
Louvain, 53, 58, 149

Lovet, G., 44
Lübeck, 77f
Luig, K., 8n16, 65n5, 66n9, 70n16, 77n24, 78n28, 79n30, 80n33
Lukács, G., 36f
Luzac, E., 98

McCall Smith, A., 96n24
McKechnie, H., 57n6
Mackenzie, G., 5, 27, 31n17, 65n6, 70
McKerron, 41n6
Mackintosh, J., 92
McNair, A. D., 36n30
Magirus, D., 59
Maino, J. de, 50
Malleville, 114
mancipatio, 180n1
mandate, 17, 190
Manilius, 74
Marcellus, 73
Maria Theresa, 108
Marongiu, A., 49n21
marriage, 22, 88
Marta, O., 50n23
Martinage-Baranger, R., 112n23
Martini, 108f
Marty, G., 143n34, 164, 164n43
Marx, K., 128n48
Massuerus, 49
Massy, G., 138
matrimonial property regimes, 2
Matthaeus, A., 137
Mechelen, 53
Meijers, E. M., 130n12, 143
Menakavist, T., 181n3
Menger, A., 129n51
Mercier, J., 67, 149, 156n28
Merryman, J. H., 3n3, 150n17, 180n2
Merula, P., 30
Mevius, D., 44, 77, 77n26
Mexico, 102
Milan, 60
Minos, 84n2, 87
Modestinus, 36, 74
Molina, 89
Mommsen, T., 45
monks, 54f
Montel, A., 141n22
Montesquieu, 106, 114, 150, 152, 154ff, 155n27, 181
Montil-les-Tours, 112
Montpellier, 26, 67
Moravia, 108
Morocco, 123
mos gallicus, 73
mos italicus, 71, 73
Moyle, J. B., 41, 45
Mucius, 74
Muhlenbruch, 45
Müller-Freienfels, W., 160n34
Mynsinger, J., 42f, 43n9, 47

Naples, 70ff, 139, 152
Napoleon, 8, 68, 102, 107, 111ff, 121f, 125, 138, 152, 158
natural law, 69ff, 78, 83ff, 103ff, 109f, 115ff, 127f, 165f, 180
negotiorum gestio, 161ff
Neldelius, J., 59
Neratius, 73
Netherlands, 6, 8, 33, 44, 65ff, 75, 121, 125, 143, 158. *See also Friesland; Holland; Zeeland*
Neuchatel, 122
Nevers, 66
New Zealand, 100
Nicholas, B., 10n20, 11n23, 13n24, 35, 35n27, 173n12
Nicoló, R., 140n20
Nieuw Burgerlijk Wetboek, 21, 121f, 143, 160
Noodt, G., 71
Norman Conquest, 133
Nova Scotia, 186
Novels (Justinian), 12f, 19, 25, 60
Novissima Recopilacion, 82
Nueva Recopilacion, 82, 139
Nussbaum, A., 92nn17-18

oath, 48ff, 96
obligations, 116f, 120
Ockam's razor, 186
O'Donovan, B., 41n6
Oertmann, P., 175
Oldendorp, J., 89f
Ontario, 186
Oosterga, C. R. ab, 55n3
opposition force, 182f, 185
ordinances (France), 113
Orleans, 148
Otto, D., 154
Oven, J. C. van, 40
ownership, 88, 90f
Oxford, 26, 28, 52

Panama, 14
Pandects, 127ff
Papa, G., 49
Papal States, 152
Papinian, 36, 73

Paraguay, 146
Paris, 44, 56, 156
Paris de Puteo, 50
Parlement, 44, 124, 151, 156
Parma, 152
partnership, 164f, 190
Paul, 11, 17, 36, 73, 95
pays de droit coutumier, 7, 120
pays de droit écrit, 7f, 67
Perez, A., 63
persons, law of, 27
Pfeffingerus, J. F., 154
Philip V (Castille), 28
Philippus, J., 78
Pinckerton, J. M., 33n21
Piret, R., 121n40
Placentinus, 26, 147f
Planck, G., 128
Planiol, M., 137
Plato, 84n2
Polac, J. F., 80
Poland, 31
Polizeistaat, 153
Pomponius, 85f, 134
Portugal, 20, 123f, 160
positive Vertragsverletzungen, 174
Pothier, R., 27n5, 41, 45, 68n13, 116f, 120, 120n39, 124, 166n49
power, paternal, 22, 88
practicks, 147, 160
precedent, 171ff
pressure force, 182f, 185
Pringsheim, F., 36n30
procedure, 15f, 29, 31f, 77, 108, 150ff, 154
Proculian school, 35
Project (Brazil), 139
Projet (France), 122ff
Projet (Roman Republic), 122
promise, 48ff, 95f
property, 27
Provence, 26
Prussia, 3, 14, 105ff, 136, 139, 180
public law, 144ff
Puchta, G. F., 45, 126
Puerto Rico, 5
Pufendorf, S., 93, 97f, 106, 116, 126
Pütter, J. S., 81

quasi-contract, 27, 161ff
quasi-delict, 27, 161
Quebec, 14, 124, 165, 186

Ranieri, F., 122n41
Rau, C., 138, 164
Raynaud, P., 143n34, 164, 164n43
Rechtsstaat, 153
Recopilacion de Indias, 82
Regiam majestatem, 65
Reichskammergericht, 8,42
Renner, K., 32n18
rescripts, 36
Rhetius, J. F., 78
Rhineland, 3, 106, 122, 125, 153
Riccobono, S., 40
Riezler, E., 174
Rintelen, M., 70n14
Ripa, J. F. de, 49
Ripert, G., 137n14
Robespierre, 113
Rogerius, 87, 146f
Roman-Dutch law, 40, 45
Rostock, 55, 59
Rota, 49
Rouen, 156
Roux, P.-C., 155n27
Rudden, B., 151
Rumania, 122
Runde, J. F., 81
Russel, B., 150n18
Rutherford, J., 56

Sabinian school, 35
St. Andrews, 56
sale, 16ff, 95, 165ff, 190
Sande, J. à, 44
Sandulli, A. M., 152n23
Sardinia, 122, 152
Sarfatti, M., 141n23
Savigny, F. von, 14, 103, 107, 126f, 139, 169
Saxony, 55n3, 77, 79, 97, 114
Scaevola, C., 73
Scaevola, Q. M., 190
Scandinavia, 4, 70, 186
Schaumburg, G., 81
Schilter, J., 9, 78f
Schlesinger, R. B., 2n2
Schmauss, J. J., 154
Schneidewin, J., 147
Schoeffer, P., 63
Schoepffer, J. J., 55f, 58, 66
Scholasticism, 89
Schotanus, B., 63
Schulz, F., 19n8
Schwartz, A. B., 107n14, 114, 126, 128
Schweizerisches Obligationenrecht, 130
Schweizerisches Zivilgesetzbuch, 130, 169
Scotland, 5f, 29n10, 33ff, 44ff, 51f, 56ff, 65, 70, 100, 134, 147, 165, 180n1, 187
Scott, J. B., 92nn17,19

Selchow, J. H. C. von, 81
Sens, 112
Seraphinus, 50
Serres, C., 67n12
servitudes, praedial, 17, 22
Servius, 74, 134
Shuman, S. J., 4n6
Siam, 129
Sicily, 122
Siete Partidas, 82
Sigismund III (Poland), 59
Silemannus, 46
Silesia, 77n27, 108
Simpson, A. W. B., 51n25
Skinner, Q., 148n12
slavery, 20, 54f, 82, 87
Smith, D. B., 33n20, 56n5, 57n8
Smith, T. B., 33n22
Sohm, R., 45, 129
Sójka-Zielińska, K., 115n31
Söllner, A., 77n25
Soto, 89
South Africa, 5, 10, 14, 40ff, 45f, 47n19, 52, 70, 100, 165
Southern, R. W., 63n3
Spain, 10, 14, 20, 28, 82, 99, 122ff, 137, 160
Speculum Saxonicum, 46
Spruchrepertorium (Austria), 176
Stair, Lord, 30f, 31nn14,17; 34, 34n24, 65n6, 70, 72, 147, 172, 172n8
States-General (France), 113
Staub, H., 174
Stein, E., 181n3
Stein, P., 63n3
stipulatio, 15, 17, 95
Story, J., 139
Strassburg, 76f
Struve, B. G., 154
Struve, G. A., 78, 81
Stryck, S., 44, 60, 78
Sturckius, C., 59
Styria, 108
Suárez, F., 88
Suarez, G., 106
succession, 22, 27
Suetonius, 101
Suidas, 74
Suttinger, B., 70
Switzerland, 10, 58, 76, 102, 120, 122, 129f, 158f

Taglioni, O., 117
Tarello, G., 93n21, 98nn25-26, 105n13, 107n14, 108n18
Ten Commandments, 90
ter Meulen, J., 92n20
Theodosius II, 36
Theophilus, 63
Thibaut, A., 126, 128, 128n49
Thieme, H., 76n20
things, law of, 27
Thomas, J. A. C., 36n29, 64n4, 86n4, 91n16, 145, 161n37, 162n38
Thomasius, C., 72, 77, 105f, 126
Thompson, E., 155n27
Thou, C. de, 7
Thouret, 156
Ticino, 122
Tigar, M. E., 136
Tocqueville, A. de, 157, 189n6
Torrance, T. F., 96
Toulouse, 44, 60
transplant bias, 182f, 185, 187f
transplants, 181ff
Tribonian, 63, 74f
Tribunate (France), 114
Trigland, T., 63
Tronchet, 114
Troplong, R. T., 137n14
Trubeck, D. M., 23
Tryphoninus, 73, 85
Tunisia, 123
Turkey, 10, 103n11, 130
Twelve Tables, 90, 99, 133, 145
Tyrol, 108

Ulpian, 11, 36, 73f, 86
unauthorized administration, 161ff
universities, 25ff, 53ff, 76f, 80, 82, 93, 105, 127f, 132f, 144f, 177
United States, 37f, 100, 123, 150, 154, 172n10, 186
unjust enrichment, 161ff
usus modernus, 9, 76, 78, 81
utility, 18

Vacarius, 26, 63
Valais, 122
Valentinian, 36
Vanderlinden, J., 100n3, 112n25
Varga, C. S., 36f
Vaud, 122
Vélez Sársfield, D. D., 139
Veneto, 122
venire contra factum proprium, 174
Vergé, C., 138
Victoria, F. de, 88
Vienna, 108
Vinnius, A., 59n11, 71, 82

Visigoths, 4
Vitriarius, P. R., 154
Voet, J., 20, 40, 55n3, 59n11
Volk, 126
Von Mehren, A. T., 3n4, 102n10
Vorderoesterreich, 108
Vorkommission (Germany), 128

Waal, C. J. D, 59n11, 75n19
Waline, M., 151f
Walther, B., 70
Watson, A., 10n20, 13n25, 15n2, 18nn5-6, 24n2, 35n26, 39n1, 51n24, 99nn1-2, 102n9, 125n44, 133n3, 134n6, 139n19, 161n37, 170n7, 181n3, 182n4, 185n5, 190n9, 191n10
Weber, M., 22f, 32, 36f, 38n35, 187
Weill, A., 143n34
Weingarten, J. J., 104n12
Weingärtler, J., 70
Wesembeckius, M., 147
West Indies, 20
Westgalizisches Gesetzbuch, 108f
Westphalia, 106, 122
Wieacker, F., 8n16, 9, 9nn18-19, 75n19, 76, 77n23, 79, 81n35, 89, 90n12, 104n12, 105n13, 107n15, 108nn17-18, 111n22, 115n31, 126nn45-46, 159, 175n17
Williams, I., 169
Wittenberg, 59, 77, 80
Wolff, C., 98, 106, 126, 166
Wollschläger, C., 175n17

Yiannopoulos, A. N., 100n3
Yugoslavia, 129

Zachariae, K. S. von, 81, 138f
Zasius, U., 46, 57, 76
Zeeland, 53
Zeiller, F. von, 109
Zschackwiz, J. E., 154
Zulueta, F. de, 63n3
Zurich, 129
Zweigert, K., 115nn30-31, 121n40, 125f, 125n44, 129n52, 136n13, 188n7
Zweite Kommission (Germany), 129